Children's Learning From Educational Television

Sesame Street and Beyond

LEA's Communication Series
Jennings Bryant / Dolf Zillmann, General Editors

For a complete list of titles in LEA's Communication Series, please contact Lawrence Erlbaum Associates, Publishers, at www.erlbaum.com

Children's Learning From Educational Television
Sesame Street and Beyond

Shalom M. Fisch
MediaKidz Research & Consulting,
Teaneck, New Jersey

2004

LAWRENCE ERLBAUM ASSOCIATES, PUBLISHERS
Mahwah, New Jersey   London

Lawrence Erlbaum Associates, Inc., Publishers
10 Industrial Avenue
Mahwah, New Jersey 07430

Cover design by James W. Fry

Library of Congress Cataloging-in-Publication Data

Fisch, Shalom M.
Children's learning from educational television : *Sesame Street*
and beyond / Shalom M. Fisch
    p. cm. — (LEA's communication series)
Includes bibliographical references and index.
ISBN 0-8058-3935-6 (cloth : alk. paper)
ISBN 0-8058-3936-4 (pbk. : alk. paper)
1. Television in education—United States. 2. *Sesame Street*
(Television program) I. Title. II. Series.
LC6576.F57 2003
371.33'58--dc21   2003044895
                                                            CIP

Books published by Lawrence Erlbaum Associates are printed
on acid-free paper, and their bindings are chosen for strength
and durability.

Printed in the United States of America
10 9 8 7 6 5 4 3 2 1

This one is for
~
My parents, who never threw out
my comic books;

My sister Mindy, who never complained
when I woke her to watch cartoons;

My wife Susan, who understands
why I still watch them; and

My children Nachum, Chana, and Miriam,
who have given me whole new reasons
to create educational media.

Contents

Part II: Theoretical Approaches

Part III: The Future

Preface

In the interest of full disclosure...

Before devoting several hundred pages to children's learning from educational television, I should acknowledge the fact that I am not an impartial observer. After spending the better part of two decades researching and helping to produce educational television, I have no doubt that well-crafted educational television programs have a significant impact on their audience. (Note, however, the phrase "well-crafted." Not all educational television is equally well conceived or equally well produced.)

Fortunately, the evidence is with me. As we shall see, more than 30 years' worth of empirical research has documented the power of television to educate.

ACKNOWLEDGMENTS

In writing this book, I have drawn on a disparate literature that spans several disciplines and a wide variety of sources. Although my name is the only one that appears on the cover, this book would not have been possible without the support of assorted friends, family, and colleagues. Thus, apart from saying the traditional *Baruch Hashem,* I would like to express my gratitude to the following:

The writing of this volume was supported by a generous grant from the Carnegie Corporation of New York. My thanks to the Carnegie staff, and to program officer Andrés Henriquez in particular.

As always, I am grateful for the encouragement, patience, and good sense of LEA editor Linda Bathgate and series editor Jennings Bryant. I especially appreciate their not laughing too hard when I estimated the time it would take to write the book, and their not saying "I told you so" when I was wrong.

All of my work in this area would be impossible without the experience of working with so many talented researchers, producers, and educators over the years. They have helped to shape my thinking and to bridge the gap between theory and practice. Special thanks are due to the past and present research staff of Sesame Workshop (née Children's Television Workshop) for their knowledge, support, and friendship. I hesitate to single out any colleague individually, but I must acknowledge a few whose contributions are most relevant to this volume. Rosemarie Truglio and

Charlotte Cole were co-authors on the paper that evolved into Chapter 2. I also owe a particular debt of gratitude to Bill Yotive for his many years of poking holes in my theories, suggesting additions that I hadn't considered, and forcing me to think.

Equal thanks are due to my academic mentor, the late Martin Braine. Marty provided me with an understanding of cognitive development that has served me well, both in the theoretical chapters in this volume and in my ongoing work.

Because so much of the literature on educational television is scattered across obscure sources (if published at all), one of the greatest challenges in writing this book was simply finding the relevant literature. I thank the following for supplying me with their papers, suggestions, materials, and ideas: Amy Aidman, Catherine Alcoran, Daniel Anderson, the Australian Children's Television Foundation, Patty Bailenson, Denielle Bertirelli Fran Blumberg, Sandra Calvert, Chris Cerf, Michael Cohen, Valerie Crane, Alisha Crawley, Mary Ann Dudko, Ellen Lewis Gideon, Cheryl Gotthelf, Bradley Greenberg, Betsy Groban, Robyn Smith Jacobvitz, Pat Jones, Amy Jordan, Sachiko Kodaira, Dale Kunkel, Annie Lang, Geoff Lealand, Dafna Lemish, Gerald Lesser, Twila Liggett, Deborah Linebarger, Elizabeth Lorch, Mary Maxwell, David Newell, Tashna Newman, Kathy Pezdek, Christine Ricci, Mabel Rice, Everett Rogers, Bill Schmitt, Kelly Schmitt, Michelle Sergent, Sandra Sheppard, Dorothy Singer, Arvid Singhal, Barbara Stewart, Chava Tidhar, Joseph Turow, Juliette Walma van der Molen, Ellen Wartella, Sherrie Rollins Westin, Alice Wilder, Marsha Williams, Barbara Wilson, and John Wright, Aletha Huston, and the staff of CRITC. With so many people offering support, the possibility of my inadvertently omitting someone seems almost inevitable. My sincerest apologies if that is the case.

Anna Akerman and Roxanne Thomas saved me countless hours by locating and copying source material. Their contributions are very much appreciated.

Finally, I have countless reasons to be grateful to my family, and this book is far from the most important one. Nevertheless, I thank my lovely wife, Susan, and brilliantly talented children, Nachum, Chana, and Miriam, for the love and support they have shown throughout this process. I also thank Susan for reviewing the entire manuscript, to ensure that it would be comprehensible to someone other than myself.

Feedback, suggestions, and other thoughts on this book are welcome. Correspondence may be sent via e-mail to *mediakidz@lycos.com*.

—*Shalom Fisch*

1

Introduction

Mom! Arthur's not letting me watch educational television!

—D. W. Read, *Arthur*

One day, while writing this book, my 4-year-old daughter was home with a cold. As I worked, she sat beside me, watching *Mister Rogers' Neighborhood* on television. When Mister Rogers held up a photo of musician Yo Yo Ma, I sensed an opportunity to introduce my daughter to an aspect of classical music. But as I began to explain who Yo Yo Ma was, she interrupted me: "I know. I saw him before," she said.

"He was on *Arthur.*"

I had to chuckle, not only at my precocious daughter, but also at what the incident said about the reach and power of educational television. My dutiful effort to use television as a springboard for expanding my preschooler's cultural knowledge had been foiled ... because she had already been introduced to the information via another educational program. And so, my daughter and I simply watched along with Mister Rogers as Yo Yo Ma played a duet with his own son.

At its best, educational television can provide children with enormous opportunities. Educational television can serve as a window to new experiences, enrich academic knowledge, enhance attitudes and motivation, and nurture social skills. This volume documents the impact of educational television in a variety of subject areas and proposes mechanisms to explain its effects.

TELEVISION IN CHILDREN'S LIVES

In the time since television first became widely available, nearly half a century ago, the medium has grown to play a major role in the lives of children. Early studies of communities recently introduced to television found that, among families that had television sets, the average amount of time children spent watching television ranged between 1 hour, 36 minutes and 2 hours, 54 minutes per day—the equivalent of approximately

1

11 to 21 hours per week (Schramm, Lyle, & Parker, 1961). Estimates were even higher immediately after television appeared, probably due to the novelty of the medium. Maccoby (1951) found that, when television was first introduced to a community, children watched television for 3.5 hours on weekdays and 4.5 on Sundays (a total of more than 25 hours per week); after the first few months, viewing settled down to approximately 19 hours per week.

The picture has not changed considerably over the years. In the 1980s, several researchers reported average viewing time to be between 11 and 28 hours per week; although the exact figure varied across studies, all of the studies found that American children spend more time watching television than in any other activity except sleeping (Anderson, Field, Collins, Lorch, & Nathan, 1985; Huston, Watkins, & Kunkel, 1989; Huston, Wright, Rice, Kerkman, & St. Peters, 1987). In fact, despite the recent growth of new media such as computers, video games, and the Internet, television continues to be children's medium of choice. A 1999 study by the Kaiser Family Foundation found that American children spent nearly 20 hours per week watching television, far more time than they spent with any other medium (Roberts, Foehr, Rideout, & Brodie, 1999). According to parent reports, even children as young as 2 to 3 years old spend more than 18 hours per week watching television (Jordan & Woodard, 2001).

Nor is this phenomenon unique to the United States. Children in Japan spend more than 17 hours per week watching television (primarily commercial television), an average that has remained stable over a period of 10 years (Kodaira, 2001). A multinational comparison of data from 23 countries found that children spent an average of 18 hours per week watching television. Although individual children varied greatly in their viewing, the mean of 18 hours was 50% higher than the time spent in any other activity (Groebel, 1999). Similarly, a second multinational study revealed that the amount of time children spent with television varied across countries (e.g., a mean of slightly over 10 hours per week in France, Switzerland, and Germany, versus more than 17 in Denmark and the U.K.), but the overall range was consistent with viewing in the United States (Livingstone, Holden, & Bovill, 1999). Indeed, after reviewing 45 studies, Larson (2001) concluded that the time spent by adolescents in the United States, Europe, and Asia was essentially identical.

Given the ubiquity of television in children's lives, it is not surprising that researchers and laypeople alike have devoted a significant amount of attention to the effects of television on young viewers. Often, these discussions of the effects of television on children focus solely on the negative. Some critics have argued that exposure to television—even educational television—can lead to outcomes such as reduced attention spans, lack of interest in school (because teachers do not sing and dance like characters on television), or children's becoming passive "zombie viewers" (e.g., Healy, 1990; Mander, 1978; Medved & Medved, 1998; Postman, 1985; Winn, 1977). Concerns over television's potential contribution to a broad range of problem behaviors (e.g., aggressive behavior, substance abuse, obesity, sexual activity, decreased school performance) led the American Academy of Pediatrics to recommend that children's total time with television and other media should be limited to no more than 1 to 2 hours per day (i.e., 7 to 14 hours per week), and that television should be eliminated entirely for children under the age of 2 (American Academy of Pediatrics, 1997, 2001).

Yet, as Wartella (1995) has observed, many of these claims have been put forth with little, if any, basis in empirical data. Instead of growing out of experiments with children, some claims have been based entirely on content analyses of material shown in television programs or correlational research that cannot establish causal relationships. Other claims have been based on not much more than personal opinion, and have been directly refuted by research with children. For example, observational studies of children's viewing of television have shown that children watch television actively, not passively (e.g., Anderson, Lorch, Field, & Sanders, 1981; Lorch, Anderson, & Levin, 1979). Moreover, numerous studies have found that educational series such as *Sesame Street* produce long-term benefits in school rather than boredom and reduced attention spans (see chap. 2, this volume).

This is not to say that television is completely without negative effects. Hundreds of studies have confirmed the finding that violent television programs contribute to aggressive behavior among viewers (see Wilson et al., 1997 for a review). The persuasive effects of advertising on children have also been documented (Kunkel, 2001), as has the influence of stereotyped portrayals on television in shaping children's attitudes (Graves, 1993; Signorelli, 1993).

Nevertheless, even those negative effects that are supported by data do not present the entire picture. Often, far less attention has been devoted to the positive effects that carefully crafted, developmentally appropriate television programs can hold. If we believe that children can learn negative lessons from television, then it stands to reason that they can learn positive lessons, too. The same medium that leads children to learn product information from a commercial should also be able to help them learn science concepts from an educational program. And the same medium that influences children to act aggressively after exposure to violent programming should also be able to influence them toward cooperative behavior after watching prosocial programming. Research indicates that all of these propositions are true.

Why, then, has the literature on educational effects received so little attention? Part of the reason lies in the fact that a great deal of the research is not easily accessible. Because the literature covers such a wide variety of issues and academic subjects, published research in this area has been scattered across numerous disparate sources, ranging from the *Journal of Educational Psychology* to *Educational Technology Research and Development* to the *Journal of Mathematical Behavior.* Moreover, a significant percentage of the literature has never been published in scholarly circles, appearing only in conference papers, technical reports, or research reports to producers and funders.

These issues provide a central motivation for the creation of this book. It is intended to serve two main purposes. The first is to make the disparate literature on the impact of educational television more accessible by gathering it into a centralized resource. To that end, the volume draws together empirical data on the impact of educational television programs (both academic and prosocial) on children's knowledge, skills, attitudes, and behavior.

The second is to address an equally important gap in the existing research literature. Although, as we will see, numerous studies have shown that children learn from exposure to educational television, there has been very little theoretical work to explain *why* or *how* these effects occur. The last several chapters in this volume take a first step toward correcting that situation by proposing theoretical models to explore aspects of the mental processing that underlies children's learning from educational television.

TELEVISION VIEWING
AND ACADEMIC ACHIEVEMENT

As Neuman (1991) noted, television is a common target for those seeking to lay blame for educational dilemmas such as poor national test scores, academic skills, and levels of literacy. Often, the assumption underlying such arguments is what has come to be known as the *displacement hypothesis*, that is, the notion that television viewing takes time away from homework and more productive leisure-time activities, such as reading. However, research has shown that, in truth, the relationship between television and academic achievement is not nearly so simple and direct.

Comparison Studies

When television was first introduced on a broad scale, early research compared thousands of children who lived in American or British towns where television was available to children living in nearby towns where it was not (e.g., Himmelweit, Oppenheim, & Vince, 1958; Schramm et al., 1961). These studies suggested that the presence of television did lead to significant changes in children's use of their time, but that it made little difference in the amount of time that children devoted to homework. In addition, Schramm et al. found no change in the time children spent reading books, and whereas Himmelweit et al. initially found a decline in book reading (particularly among children who had shown only a marginal interest in reading in the first place), reading returned to pretelevision levels a few years after television was introduced. Where, then, did the time spent with television come from? Primarily, television took time away from activities that served similar functions, such as listening to the radio, going to movies, and reading comic books.

A similar study was conducted some years later by Williams and her colleagues (Williams, 1986; cf. MacBeth, 1996). They compared children in three Canadian towns: one in which television was unavailable (code-named *Notel*), one that received only one television station (*Unitel*), and one that received several stations (*Multitel*). As in the earlier studies, the researchers found that children who had access to television used their time differently from those who did not. However, they also found that second-grade children in Notel scored higher on tests of reading fluency and creative thinking than children in the other two towns. The differences disappeared 2 years after television was introduced in Notel, suggesting that the presence of television had been responsible for the effect (Corteen & Williams, 1986; Harrison & Williams, 1986).

Correlational Studies

A number of studies used correlational data to investigate relationships between children's television viewing and their achievement in school. Williams, Haertel, Walberg, and Haertel (1982) conducted a meta-analysis using data from 23 large-scale studies, and concluded that there was a small inverse relationship between amount of viewing and achievement $r = -.05$). However, part of the reason why the correlation was so low was that the relationship between television viewing and achievement was not linear. Rather, it was curvilinear; children who watched 10 hours of television per week performed slightly better (not worse) than those who watched less, but as viewing increased beyond 10 hours per week, achievement declined dramatically.

Comstock and Paik's (1991) analysis of data from the California Assessment Study argued for a more linear relationship, but further support for curvilinearity came from Neuman's (1988, 1991) analysis of several large-scale studies. Neuman found that there was little relation between viewing and reading performance among children who watched

2 to 4 hours of television per day (i.e., 14 to 28 hours per week), but that performance was considerably lower for children who watched more than that. Similarly, some studies have suggested that there may be thresholds of viewing, beyond which excessive television viewing is associated with poorer academic achievement. Fetler (1984) found that viewing for more than 6 hours per day (i.e., 42 hours per week) was associated with lower performance in literacy and mathematics, and Potter (1987) found that television viewing was negatively related to achievement for eighth to twelfth graders who watched more than 30 hours per week.

The complexity of the relationship between television and school achievement can be attributed to several factors. One is the fact that school achievement is predicted much more strongly by variables such as IQ and socioeconomic status (both of which predict television viewing as well). Another is that the relationship between viewing and achievement differs somewhat by age (e.g., Huston & Wright, 1997; Neuman, 1991). In addition, Comstock (1989) suggested that television viewing is inversely related to achievement when it displaces intellectually richer experiences, but positively related when it supplies such experiences.

Along similar lines, I would argue for one more factor that complicates the picture and may have reduced the strength of the relationship observed in these studies. Each of the studies mentioned above looked only at *how much* television was viewed, and not at the *nature* of the television programs that children watched. Not all television programs are the same, and they do not all produce the same effects among viewers. For example, longitudinal research by Wright, Huston, and their colleagues found that preschool viewing of *Sesame Street* and other educational television programs predicted higher performance in subsequent tests of academic skills. By contrast, however, preschool viewing of entertainment programs predicted poorer performance (Wright, Huston, Murphy, et al., 2001; Wright, Huston, Scantlin, & Kotler, 2001; see chap. 2, this volume). As the late John Wright was fond of saying, "Marshall McLuhan appears to have been wrong. The medium is not the message. The *message* is the message!" (Anderson, Huston, Schmitt, Linebarger, & Wright, 2001, p. 134).

In keeping with this idea, the bulk of the research discussed in this volume focuses not on the impact of television in general, but on the impact of one kind of television in particular—namely, educational television.

BUT WHAT *IS* "EDUCATIONAL TELEVISION"?

Over the years, numerous terms have been used to refer to television programs that are intended to educate or benefit children: *educational television, instructional television, curriculum-based programming, educational/*

informational programming, infotainment, edutainment, entertainment-educa-tion, and so on. Often, the terms refer to somewhat different classes of television programming; for example, *instructional television* often has been used in relation to television programs produced for use in classrooms, whereas *infotainment* has carried the connotation of "lite" educational content for consumption on broadcast television.

Definitional issues came to the fore during the debates surrounding the passage of the Children's Television Act of 1990 and the Federal Communications Commission's (FCC) strengthening of its regulations several years later (FCC, 1991, 1993, 1995). Because the intent of the Act was to encourage broadcasters to air more programming that would serve the needs of children—and because broadcasters worried that they would be forced to air didactic "spinach television" that no one would watch—the programming required by the Act had to be clearly defined. As one might expect, these definitions were subject to extensive debate.

One central issue concerned the breadth of the definition. Some argued for limiting the definition to programs with academic goals and excluding programming that was primarily prosocial in nature, for fear that broadcasters would simply label family sitcoms as "prosocial." Others felt that prosocial programs hold value for children as well, so that prosocial programming, too, should "count" under the Act. In fact, both positions proved to hold some merit. Empirical research has indeed shown that exposure to prosocial programs can result in beneficial effects on children's attitudes and behavior in areas such as cooperation and the reduction of stereotypes (see chap. 9, this volume). At the same time, though, some broadcasters did respond to the Act by labeling existing—and, in some cases, violent—cartoons or teen situation comedies (e.g., *Saved by the Bell*, *The Flintstones*, *G.I. Joe*) as educational/informational (E/I) because they included prosocial messages (e.g., Kunkel & Canepa, 1995). In one extreme instance, a broadcaster claimed that *Yogi Bear* met the provisions of the Act because, "despite the fact that the program is entertaining, it nevertheless does teach certain moral and ethical values such as not to do stupid things or you will have trouble; don't take what doesn't belong to you or be prepared to face the music" (quoted in Kunkel, 1998, p. 45).[1]

Apart from the definition itself, a second issue concerned the standard by which programs should be judged. Some argued that, for a television series to qualify under the Act, empirical research should demonstrate its positive impact on children. However, broadcasters countered that it

---

[1] Not that this phenomenon was limited to prosocial programming; Kunkel and Canepa (1995) also cite an extreme claim that *The Jetsons* was educational because it presented life in the 21st century.

would be unfair to require them to run the risk that, after investing millions of dollars to produce an educational television series, it might not be counted if subsequent research failed to find a significant effect on its audience. Thus, they argued for using the intent behind the program as a standard instead.[2]

In the end, the Children's Television Act of 1990 broadly defined "educational/informational programming" as carrying content that will "further the positive development of the child in any respect, including the child's cognitive/intellectual or emotional/social needs" (FCC, 1991). And although the FCC subsequently strengthened the Act by requiring broadcasters to air a specified quota of 3 hours per week of E/I programming, they decided against narrowing the definition of E/I programs. Yet, contrast the definition used in the Act with, for example, the stricter definition that Condry, Scheibe, Bahrts, and Potts (1993) used in a content analysis of children's television:

> A significant portion of the program is devoted to teaching information that the children in the audience are not likely to already know (e.g., the alphabet, vocabulary, historical or scientific information, applied information for everyday life) or demonstrating skills or crafts. (p. 5)

The history and policy implications of the Act have been discussed at length elsewhere, along with the impact of the Act on broadcasting in the United States (e.g., J. Bryant, J. A. Bryant, Mulliken, McCollum, & Love, 2001; Jordan, 2000; Kunkel, 1998; Kunkel & Wilcox, 2001; Schmitt, 1999; Steyer, 2002). For the purposes of this discussion, it is sufficient to note that educational television has been conceptualized and defined in many different ways.

In light of the diverse definitions that have been used in the past, it is useful to clarify the parameters of the educational television series included in this volume. With rare exception, the television series discussed here were produced with the intent of serving specific educational objectives. Those objectives may correspond to any of a number of academic subjects (e.g., science, literacy, mathematics), or they may be prosocial in nature. The degree to which each series succeeded in meeting its educational objectives has been evaluated through empirical research with children. Typically, this research took the form of summative research, that is, substantive assessments of educational impact after a given series was produced. In some cases, relevant data are also included from formative research that was conducted during production to inform and guide the development of the final product. (For more extended discussions regarding the distinction between formative and summative research and

---

[2]I am indebted to Dale Kunkel for bringing this point to my attention.

their application to the production of educational television, see, e.g., Mielke, 1990; Palmer & Fisch, 2001.)

The focus of this volume is on television programs designed for children rather than adults, although I occasionally draw on the adult literature when useful. (For information on the impact of educational programs aimed at adult viewers, see, e.g., Greenberg & Gantz, 1976; Singhal & Rogers, 1999; Winsten, 1994.) In addition, the bulk of the discussion concerns the effects of unaided viewing by children, rather than viewing in the context of adult-led follow-up activities. Chapter 9 examines the role of parent–child coviewing and issues relevant to the use of television in school or child care.

TELEVISION AS INFORMAL EDUCATION

In considering children's learning from educational television (particularly in the case of at-home viewing), it is important to remember that much educational television serves as an example of *informal education*, much like educational activities that children find in magazines, museums, or after-school programs. In contrast to formal (i.e., classroom) education, informal education takes place outside of school, involves experiences that are not part of a school curriculum, and often must compete with other activities to gain children's attention and engagement (e.g., Katz, 2001; Tressel, 1988; Trotta, 1998).

Because educational television series are informal education experiences, their production is subject to considerations that are less critical in the classroom. Perhaps most critical is the need for the television program to be highly appealing to children. After all, if children do not enjoy the program, they simply will not turn it on.

In addition, the series' educational approach must be designed to fit the constraints of informal education. For example, unlike classroom instruction, the educational content of a television series typically cannot depend on being presented in a particular sequence over a period of days, weeks, or months. Although there is great educational value to structuring classroom instruction to begin with simple concepts and subsequently build on previous lessons as more complex concepts are introduced, this typically is not feasible in educational television because there is no guarantee that the episodes will be broadcast in order or that children will see every episode (e.g., Fisch & Truglio, 2001b; Lesser, 1974).

One of the consequences of this point is that, when versions of existing broadcast television programs have been created for school use, they often have had to be adapted to fit the constraints of the classroom. For example, when the mathematics series *Square One TV* was adapted into its school version, *Square One Math Talk*, material was re-edited to shorten the videos to an appropriate length for classroom use, and to organize tapes thematically by mathematical content (e.g., probability, statistics) so that it would be simpler for teachers to use the videos when they reached the relevant topic in their own lessons (Yotive, 1995).

Educational television is not intended to replace formal education in school. Rather, it is intended to supplement formal education in several ways:

- By exposing children to topics that they might not encounter otherwise (or that might only be introduced formally in later grades),
- By providing compelling experiences that coax children into spending additional time exploring concepts that they are learning about in school,
- By encouraging positive attitudes toward academic subjects (particularly among populations that are typically less likely to pursue these subjects on their own), and
- By motivating children to engage actively in learning both in and outside the classroom.

OVERVIEW OF CONTENTS

The bulk of this volume is divided into two sections. The first section reviews research that assesses the impact of educational television in a variety of subject areas. Because of its pioneering role and prominence in the literature, chapter 2 is devoted to *Sesame Street*, both the domestic version seen in the United States and international co-productions that were created in other countries. Chapter 3 turns to other television series aimed at preschool children (e.g., *Barney & Friends, Mister Rogers' Neighborhood, Blue's Clues*) and their impact on school readiness. Subsequent chapters review research on the educational effectiveness of school-age programs in the areas of literacy (e.g., *The Electric Company, Ghostwriter, Reading Rainbow*), mathematics and problem solving (e.g., *Square One TV, Cyberchase*), science and technology (e.g., *3-2-1 Contact, Bill Nye the Science Guy*), and civics and social studies (e.g., news programs, *Schoolhouse Rock, Channel One*). These reviews include significant effects on children's academic knowledge, skills, and attitudes. Each chapter ends with a discussion of lessons learned and implications for the future production of educational television.

Chapter 8 takes a slightly different focus, to examine the impact of prosocial television programs on aspects of children's socioemotional development. The section then concludes with chapter 9, which steps beyond direct effects to examine the role of adult mediation. This includes research on parent–child coviewing of educational programs at home and the integration of educational television programs into school and child-care settings.

Having documented the impact of educational television, the second section of the book proposes theoretical models to explain how such learning occurs. Chapter 10 discusses the *capacity model*, which uses children's allocation of working memory resources to help explain how children extract and comprehend the educational content embedded in television programs. Chapter 11 explores transfer of learning from educational television (i.e., children's application of the knowledge and/or skills acquired from educational television beyond the contexts and problems shown on the screen) and the factors that can determine whether transfer will occur. Finally, chapter 12 attempts to bridge the gap between academic and social influences of television by showing how social aspects of educational television influence learning of academic content.

The concluding chapter (chap. 13) turns to the future of educational television. At the time of this writing, new technologies are emerging to change the face of television. This chapter draws on the lessons of the past to chart out directions for maximizing the power of educational television in the future.

I

EMPIRICAL DATA

2

Sesame Street and School Readiness

You've never seen a street like Sesame Street. Everything happens here.
You're gonna love it!

—Gordon, first episode of *Sesame Street*

More than 30 years after its premiere, no educational television series has had a greater impact—either on the research literature, on the production of educational television, or on children—than *Sesame Street* (Fig. 2.1). More than 1,000 studies have examined *Sesame Street* and its power in areas such as literacy, number skills, and promoting prosocial behavior, as well as formal features pertaining to issues such as children's attention (Children's Television Workshop Research Division, 1989). This body of literature has not only contributed to our understanding of children's interaction with *Sesame Street* itself, but also constitutes a significant portion of the literature on the educational impact of television in general.

Several books have already chronicled the history of *Sesame Street* and research surrounding it (Fisch & Truglio, 2001a; Land, 1972; Lesser, 1974; Polsky, 1977), so there is no need to rehash the same material at great length. However, in light of the prominence of *Sesame Street* in the study of children's learning from educational television, several key studies regarding *Sesame Street* are reviewed here. The focus in this chapter is on *Sesame Street*'s effects on academic knowledge and skills. Research on *Sesame Street*'s contribution to children's social development is incorporated into the discussion of prosocial television programs in chapter 8.

HISTORICAL CONTEXT AND NEED

It is difficult to recognize today what a revolutionary departure *Sesame Street* represented from the existing state of children's television in the late 1960s. Although television series for children had been produced and broadcast almost since the medium was created, no series prior to

FIG. 2.1. *Sesame Street*. (Photo © 2003 Sesame Workshop. All rights reserved. *Sesame Street* and all related titles, logos, and characters are
trademarks of Sesame Workshop.)

Sesame Street had attempted to address a set of specified educational
goals. Moreover, at the time, virtually nothing was known about the
potential of television to serve as an educational tool. There were no
studies on the impact of educational television; no empirical data were
available. Indeed, so little was known that, before Joan Ganz Cooney
set out to create *Sesame Street*, she spent 4 months interviewing cognitive psychologists, educators, producers, and filmmakers to see
whether such an idea might be feasible in the first place. Their consen-
sus was that the need was clear, and that television could play a potent
role (Cooney, 1966).

In many ways, the *Sesame Street* that debuted in 1969 was very much a
product of its time. The Civil Rights movement of the 1960s had drawn
national attention to the needs of inner-city children, and provided an
atmosphere of activism toward positive social change. Educational researchers had recently published data that both established the importance of early education and documented gaps in school readiness
between low-income, minority children and their more privileged White
counterparts—findings that gave rise not only to *Sesame Street*, but to
Head Start as well (Bereiter & Engelman, 1966; Bloom, 1964; Deutsch,
1965). President Lyndon Johnson's push to create the Great Society re-

sulted in high levels of funding for education. Finally, the growth of public broadcasting provided a platform from which a broad audience of children could be reached.

The original mission of *Sesame Street* was to help prepare all children for school, including those children who might otherwise be considered at risk. Despite the misconception of some critics (e.g., Cook et al. 1975), the goal was not necessarily to narrow existing gaps in school achievement; because television is a mass medium, it was likely that a wide range of children—including affluent White children—would watch and benefit from the series. Rather, the intent was to provide educational experiences for all viewers, but to pay special attention to the needs of underprivileged children. In this way, it was hoped, *Sesame Street* would help ensure that as many children as possible would enter school with the necessary tools to reach their potential (Lesser, 1974; Palmer & Fisch, 2001).

To that end, the educational curriculum for the first season of *Sesame Street* laid out goals in five areas: social, moral, and affective development; language and reading; mathematics and numerical skills; reasoning and problem solving; and perception. In the decades that followed, the curriculum would expand to cover topics ranging from science to health to race relations.

THE ROLE OF RESEARCH

One of the things that has made *Sesame Street* stand out among children's programs is the process under which it is produced. In developing *Sesame Street*, the Children's Television Workshop (CTW, later renamed "Sesame Workshop") created what would eventually come to be called the *CTW Model* or *Sesame Workshop Model* (e.g., Mielke, 1990), an interdisciplinary approach to television production that brings together content experts, television producers, and educational researchers, who collaborate throughout the life of the project (Fig. 2.2). This collaboration is neither trivial nor limited to the occasional involvement of educational consultants. Rather, producers and researchers work hand-in-hand at every stage of production. As *Sesame Street*'s first executive producer, David Connell, and research director, Edward Palmer, observed, "If *Sesame Street* was an experiment—and it very definitely continues to be one—this notion of broadcaster/researcher cooperation was the most bold experiment within it" (Connell & Palmer, 1971, p. 67). By all accounts, the experiment has succeeded, and similar production models have been employed in many subsequent educational television series, both at Sesame Workshop and elsewhere.

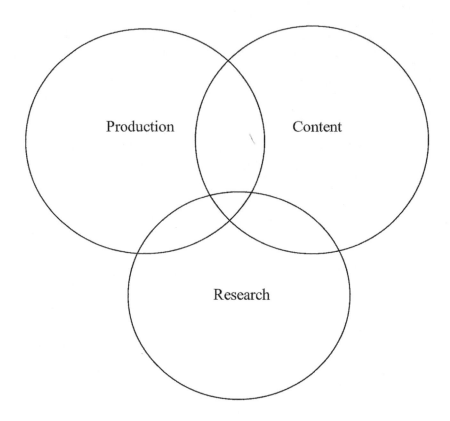

FIG. 2.2. The CTW (or "Sesame Workshop") model.

Research on *Sesame Street* has fallen into two broad categories: *formative* and *summative*. Formative research is conducted before and during production to provide information that can guide the production of new material; such research can address issues ranging from identifying the most appealing design for a new character to finding the most effective production technique to convey a specific type of educational content. For example, consider a study that was conducted on the very first piece of animation produced for *Sesame Street*, which concerned the letter *J*. Tests of an early version of the segment were encouraging, but showed that children attended more to the animated characters in the segment than to the stationary letter itself, thus interfering with comprehension. To draw viewers' attention back to the letter, the production team subsequently re-designed the segment so that the *J* itself would move via animation (Lesser, 1974). This technique was also incorporated into later segments and is still used today.

Summative research is conducted after production to assess whether the material met its goals and to examine its impact on the series' audience. Typically conducted by outside evaluators rather than in-house research staff (both to avoid accusations of bias and because of the intensive time and resources that are required), this type of research provides the acid test by which the educational success of the series is measured. Summative research forms the basis for the discussion of the educational impact of *Sesame Street* that will be presented shortly.

Criticism of the Research Model

Generally, the prominent role of research in the CTW Model has been seen as one of its greatest strengths, helping to tailor programming directly to the needs and developmental level of its target audience and providing objective standards of accountability in gauging success. Recently, however, Hendershot (1998, 1999) questioned this approach, claiming that "CTW's child-testing procedures … objectify children and narrowly define knowledge and learning" (1998, p. 162). Although Hendershot acknowledged that formative research for *Sesame Street* is directed toward altruistic ends, her concerns were fourfold: (a) specific questions regarding the validity of measures used in formative testing, (b) formative research is typically conducted in child-care settings rather than in homes, (c) the issues investigated in research are dictated by researchers, rather than shaped by the children's own interests and concerns, and (d) formative data are used to improve the series' ability to hold children's attention and, in her words, "strive to control the child in the service of a greater good" (1998, p. 163).

The first two concerns, regarding research methods, are not discussed here, both because they have been addressed at length elsewhere and because the continual evolution of research methods for *Sesame Street* has already moved past most of the techniques that Hendershot criticized (e.g., Fisch & Bernstein, 2001). Her third point is an interesting one but, in my opinion, somewhat impractical. Applied broadly, the same could be said of virtually all research in education, developmental psychology, or related fields; it is difficult to see how advances in our knowledge of many aspects of child development—or their resulting benefits for children—could have been achieved under such a constraint. Certainly, research with children must adhere to ethical practices, and child-driven approaches to educational technology hold great value (e.g., Druin et al., 1999), but child-driven approaches are not always applicable to every research issue.

With regard to Hendershot's fourth concern, it is true that one of the roles of formative research for *Sesame Street* has been to help make the series as attractive to children as possible. As noted in chapter 1, broadcast television serves as a vehicle for informal (rather than formal) education, and so educational television programs must be appealing to children or children will neither watch nor learn from them. In the words of David Connell, the first executive producer for *Sesame Street*, "You've got to get them into the church before you can preach to them" (quoted in Fisch & Truglio, 2001b). However, I believe it is an overstatement to refer to this an attempt to "control" children. Contrary to claims of television producing "zombie viewers" (Winn, 1977), television viewing is not only voluntary, but also requires active cognitive processing on the part of the viewer (Anderson, 1999; Anderson & Burns, 1991). Engaging presentations may initially succeed in drawing viewers' attention to a program, but they do not force the viewer to continue to watch.

Finally, of course, in judging the propriety of research with children, we must consider a given research study within the context of its ultimate goals. There is a vast difference between using research with children to enhance the value of an educational television program and using it to find the best way to sell them junk food. As Hendershot agreed, *Sesame Street* research is directed toward a noble purpose. Experiences in the production of many educational television series have shown such research to be essential in maximizing the educational benefits that they hold for their target audiences. The true test lies in their impact on viewers, as determined through summative research.

IMPACT AMONG VIEWERS
IN THE UNITED STATES

Research on the impact of *Sesame Street* on academic skills necessary for school readiness has been conducted both in the United States, using the domestic version of the series, and in other countries, using coproductions of *Sesame Street* created in partnership with local producers. This section of the chapter reviews research conducted in the United States. Research on coproductions is discussed in the next section.

Summative research on the domestic version of *Sesame Street* has taken two forms. Several major studies in the 1970s and 1990s assessed the short- and long-term impact of *sustained viewing* of the series over a period of several months. Other, smaller scale research focused on immediate effects of *limited exposure* to one or more brief segments taken from *Sesame Street*. Each will be considered in turn.

Effects of Sustained Viewing

Early Research on Impact. The educational impact of *Sesame Street* was first documented in a pair of studies conducted by the Educational Testing Service (ETS; Ball & Bogatz, 1970; Bogatz & Ball, 1971). The first of these studies, conducted after the first season of production was completed, assessed *Sesame Street*'s impact on a variety of cognitive skills. The participants were a geographically and ethnically diverse sample of nearly 1,000 children aged 3 to 5 (most of whom were considered to be from disadvantaged backgrounds). The children were either encouraged or not encouraged to watch *Sesame Street* (at home or at school) during a 26-week period; across the sample, exposure ranged from zero times per week to more than five. Before and after this 26-week exposure, the children were tested via an extensive battery of measures that covered several dimensions: knowledge of the alphabet and numbers, names of body parts, recognition of forms, knowledge of relational terms, and sorting and classification skills.

The results of the study indicated that exposure to *Sesame Street* produced the desired educational effects. Those children who watched the most showed the greatest pretest–posttest gains, and the areas that showed the strongest effects were those that had been emphasized the most in *Sesame Street* (e.g., letters). These effects held across age (although 3-year-olds showed the greatest gains, presumably because they knew the least when they came to the series), sex, geographic location, socioeconomic status (SES; with low-SES children showing greater gains than middle-SES children), native language (English or Spanish), and whether the children watched at home or in school.

The second ETS study (Bogatz & Ball, 1971) consisted of two components. One was a replication of the earlier study, using Season 2 shows that had been produced under a revised and expanded educational curriculum. This study confirmed the earlier results, finding significant gains in many of the same areas and in new areas that had been added in the second season (e.g., roles of community members, counting to 20 rather than 10).

The second component was a follow-up study that reexamined 283 of the children from the Season 1 study (Ball & Bogatz, 1970), about one half of whom had begun school in the interim. Teachers were asked to rate all of the children in their classes on several dimensions (e.g., verbal readiness, quantitative readiness, attitude toward school, relationship with peers), without knowing which ones had been *Sesame Street* viewers or were participating in the study. Results showed that, contrary to the claims of critics of *Sesame Street*, viewers were not bored, restless, or passive when they entered a formal classroom experience. Rather, frequent

Sesame Street viewers were rated as better prepared for school than their non- or low-viewing classmates.

These findings were challenged by critics of *Sesame Street*, most notably by Thomas Cook and his colleagues (1975). They argued that the effects observed in the ETS studies did not reflect merely the effect of watching *Sesame Street*; instead, these researchers felt that the effects reflected a combination of viewing and parents' involvement in the viewing experience. In fact, Cook's point was not without merit, as subsequent research has shown that young children's learning from television can be affected by parental coviewing and commentary (e.g., Reiser, Tessmer, & Phelps, 1984; Reiser, Williamson, & Suzuki, 1988; see chap. 9, this volume). Yet, parental involvement was not solely responsible for the ETS findings. Even when Cook et al. conducted a reanalysis of the ETS data, controlling for other potentially contributing factors such as mothers' discussing *Sesame Street* with their children, the ETS effects were reduced but many remained statistically significant. Such effects could not simply be explained through parental involvement; *Sesame Street* itself made a significant contribution.

Subsequent Studies.   The results described above are echoed and extended by several more recent studies on the effects of viewing *Sesame Street*. A 3-year longitudinal study, conducted at the University of Kansas, examined the impact of educational television (primarily *Sesame Street*) on school readiness by tracking approximately 250 low-SES children from either age 2 to age 5 or from age 4 to age 7 (Wright, Huston, Murphy, et al., 2001; Wright, Huston, Scantlin, & Kotler, 2001). The study took into account not only viewing of *Sesame Street* and other educational series, but viewing of all television, as well as nontelevision activities (e.g., reading, music, use of video games) and numerous contextual variables that have been found to affect academic achievement (e.g., parents' own level of education, native language, preschool attendance). At regular intervals over the 3 years, children were tested with a broad range of measures, including standard tests such as the Peabody Picture Vocabulary Test and Woodcock-Johnson Letter–Word Recognition Test.

The results of the study indicated that preschool children who watched educational programs—and *Sesame Street* in particular—spent more time reading and engaged in educational activities. In addition, these children performed significantly better than their peers on tests of letter–word knowledge, mathematics skills, vocabulary size, and school readiness on age-appropriate standardized achievement tests. These differences were consistent with earlier findings on the long-term impact of *Sesame Street* on children's learning of vocabulary (Rice, Huston, Truglio, & Wright, 1990), and remained significant even after the effects of various mediating variables (e.g., parents' educational level, primary language spoken at home) were removed statistically. In addition, long-term effects were found when children subsequently entered school; for example, consistent with the earlier Bogatz and Ball (1971) data, teachers more often rated *Sesame Street* viewers as well-adjusted to school.

A second study (Zill, 2001) was a correlational analysis of data from a national survey of the parents of approximately 10,000 children, originally collected for the U.S. Department of Education's National Household Education Survey in 1993. This analysis found that preschoolers who viewed *Sesame Street* were more likely to be able to recognize letters of the alphabet and tell connected stories when pretending to read. These effects were strongest among children from low-income families, and held true even after the effects of other contributing factors (e.g., parental reading, preschool attendance, parental education) were removed statistically. In addition, when they subsequently entered first and second grade, children who had viewed *Sesame Street* as preschoolers were also more likely to be reading storybooks on their own and less likely to require remedial reading instruction.

It is important to note that, because Zill's (2001) data are correlational, they do not conclusively indicate a causal relationship between *Sesame Street* viewing and these various educational outcomes. Nevertheless, they are highly suggestive and consistent with data from the University of Kansas study.

Finally, the longest-ranging evidence for the impact of *Sesame Street* is a "recontact" study conducted at the University of Massachusetts at Amherst and the University of Kansas (Anderson et al., 2001; Anderson, Huston, Wright, & Collins, 1998; Huston, Anderson, Wright, Linebarger, & Schmitt, 2001). This study examined 570 high school students who either had or had not watched *Sesame Street* as preschoolers. Results indicated that preschool viewing of educational television programs such as *Sesame Street* was significantly related to higher grades in English, mathematics, and science in high school. For boys, the effect of watching *Sesame Street* 5 days per week translated into a grade point average difference of .35 (the difference, for example, between a B+ and an A-); for girls, it translated into a difference of .10.[1]

In addition, those teenagers who had viewed *Sesame Street* as preschoolers also used books more often, showed higher academic self-esteem, and placed a higher value on academic performance. These differences held true even after the students' early language skills as preschoolers and fam-

---

[1]Conversely, high levels of viewing violent television as a preschooler were significantly related not only to higher aggression as a teenager, but also to lower grades in high school.

ily background variables were factored out. Possible reasons for the long-term effects of *Sesame Street* are presented in the "Issues Raised and Lessons Learned" section at the end of this chapter.

Effects of Limited Exposure

The studies just reviewed demonstrate significant educational benefits that resulted from sustained viewing of *Sesame Street* over a period of months or years. But what of more limited viewing of a single episode, or even a single segment taken from one episode?

Formative research for *Sesame Street* has often examined children's comprehension of the educational content in individual segments or complete episodes, with an eye toward identifying educational approaches and production techniques that can be applied to maximize children's comprehension. These studies also provide some informal indication of the effectiveness of the particular segments tested, although it is by no means as rigorous a test as that provided by summative research. Examples of such research can be found in Truglio, Lovelace, Seguí, & Scheiner's (2001) case studies of formative research, which assessed children's comprehension of several segments concerning science and literacy.

A similar, but more tightly controlled, study was conducted by Hodapp (1977) to examine children's acquisition of problem-solving strategies from a single, 100-second *Sesame Street* segment. Five- and 6-year-old children viewed either the problem-solving segment or an unrelated *Sesame Street* segment, and were then presented with two problem-solving tasks. One task was identical to that shown in the problem-solving segment, and the other was an isomorphic task that could be solved in the same way but was embedded in a context different from the one shown in the segment. As one might expect from the brevity of children's exposure to the *Sesame Street* segment, the results were consistent with those reported earlier for sustained viewing, but the effects were far narrower in scope. When presented with the identical task that had been demonstrated in the problem-solving segment, those children who had viewed the segment applied the same strategy they had seen and solved the problem correctly. However, they tended not to abstract the strategy and apply it to a isomorphic problem that was different on its surface. Thus, it appeared that even a single exposure to less than 2 minutes of *Sesame Street* could result in short-term educational benefits, although these benefits were understandably limited.

Others have examined the impact of repeat viewing of the same *Sesame Street* material over time. Sell, Ray, and Lovelace (1995) found that after watching the same 19-minute *Sesame Street* videotape three times over a period of three weeks, 4-year-olds were better able to recount the plot of the video and recalled more information that was central (rather than incidental) to the plot. (Unfortunately, Sell et al. did not also assess comprehension of the video's educational content.) Rice and Sell (1990; cf. Mielke, 2001) found that repeat viewing of four *Sesame Street* videos (a total of 2.5 to 3 hours of viewing per video, over a period of 11 weeks) led to gains in children's vocabulary, letter recognition, number recognition, and printed word identification. Lesser (1974) reported an interesting pattern of data in children's repeat viewing of a segment featuring actor James Earl Jones; in this segment, Jones recited the alphabet with lengthy pauses between each letter, and each letter appeared on screen for a moment before he said its name. On first viewing, children generally said the name of each letter along with Jones. In later repetitions of the segment, children began to name the on-screen letter before Jones. With still further repetition, children named each letter as soon as the previous one disappeared (i.e., before the new letter appeared on screen). This anticipatory effect, nicknamed the "James Earl Jones Effect" by *Sesame Street* staff, was subsequently built into other segments that employed similar approaches.

Taken together, these studies suggest that even very brief exposure to *Sesame Street* can produce limited, immediate effects among preschool viewers. These effects appear to evolve with repeat viewing, as viewers isolate central from incidental content and their comprehension improves; indeed, children may begin to anticipate the characters' presentation of educational content and respond accordingly. It seems likely that, over time, such micro-level effects contribute to the larger scale impact that has been observed for sustained viewing.

INTERNATIONAL IMPACT OF *SESAME STREET*

The globalization of *Sesame Street* began shortly after *Sesame Street*'s initial broadcast in the United States. Producers from Mexico, Brazil, and Germany independently approached CTW because they saw the value of *Sesame Street*, but wanted programs that would specifically address the educational needs of children in their own countries. To create the series the producers imagined, in partnership with CTW, they devised a flexible production plan that was subsequently used to create all international productions of *Sesame Street*. As in the United States, the various series were produced under the CTW Model, with indigenous producers, educational content specialists, and researchers. To date, 20 different adaptations of the series have been created in countries such as Brazil, China, Germany, Norway, Mexico, Poland, Russia, and Spain.

In working outside the United States, the Workshop's design is not to impose American culture or approaches, but instead, to provide a framework for a series created in-country by a local production team. Sets reflective of a given culture are created and inhabited by characters developed specifically for each adaptation, giving the local viewers a cast that participates in activities and situations that meaningfully reflect the lives of the programs' viewers. The production in Germany, for example, features a German bear who wears sneakers; in Mexico, the studio segments take place in a colorful plaza populated by Abelardo, a bright green parrot, a grouch character called Poncho the Contrarian, and others. Fifty percent or less of the program content is material dubbed from CTW's international library of segments. These segments are selected by the local production team for their pertinence to a given program's educational goals. The result is that when children view *Sesame Street*, they view a program that has the same essence as the domestic series, in a context that reflects local values and educational priorities of a specific country (Cole, Richman, & McCann Brown, 2001; Gettas, 1990).

This localization has led international coproductions of *Sesame Street* to reflect a range of educational priorities. Although the curricula contain elements in common (e.g., numeracy, literacy, perceptual skills), each has unique aspects that educators have identified as of critical importance to children in their countries. For example, the Chinese curriculum contained a section devoted to aesthetics because specialists felt it is an area that has sometimes been deemphasized in school curricula but is important to children living in their culture. In Israel and the Palestinian territories, a primary focus was teaching children mutual respect and understanding. A critical element of the production in Russia was preparing children for life in their new open society. In this way, each series has provided educational messages on some of the broad curricular areas that are common to preschoolers around the globe, as well as educational content that more specifically addresses local children's needs.

Thanks to this broad range of subject matter, research on the various *Sesame Street* coproductions has provided opportunities both to assess the impact of *Sesame Street* across cultures and to gauge the potential of television to convey educational content not addressed in the curriculum of the domestic *Sesame Street*. Like the research conducted in support of the U.S. version of *Sesame Street*, research on the coproductions includes both formative and summative work. Formative research has examined a wide range of issues, such as the development of studio sets (Gemark, 1993; Kirwil, 1996a; *Plaza Sésamo* IV Department of Research & Content, 1993) and characters (Kirwil, 1996b; *Ulitsa Sezam* Department of Research & Content, 1996), as well as the appeal and comprehensibility of specific segments or episodes.

One of the earliest studies of *Sesame Street* coproductions was also one of the most comprehensive. Researchers in Mexico conducted a controlled experimental study of children's learning from *Plaza Sésamo* (Diaz-Guerrero & Holtzman, 1974). A sample of 221 3-, 4-, and 5-year-olds were randomly assigned to either an experimental group that regularly viewed the program for 6 months, or a control group that viewed alternative children's programming. Researchers evaluated children's pre- and postviewing performance on a battery of tests representing various skills in the *Plaza Sésamo* curriculum. Children who had regularly viewed the program performed better than their nonviewing peers on tests of general knowledge, numbers, letters, and word skills. The researchers also noted differences in performance on cognitive tests (e.g., classification, relational skills) and oral comprehension. Gains differed by age, with 4-year-olds benefitting most from watching and 3-year-olds, the least.

Years later, a study in Turkey (Sahin, 1992) noted similar effects of *Susam Sokagi*, the Turkish adaptation of *Sesame Street*. The study evaluated pre- and postbroadcast performance on a range of curricular skills among 1,166 children between the ages of three and six. Comparing same-age peers before and after exposure to the broadcast, children who watched the program performed better on a range of curricular skills (e.g., literacy, numeracy), even when factors such as maturation and mother's education were taken into consideration.

A smaller scale study was used to evaluate *Rua Sésamo*, the Portugese adaptation of *Sesame Street*. The researcher (Brederode-Santos, 1993) devised a multicomponent study that brought together a compendium of information including ratings data, surveys of parents and teachers, and pre–post viewing data from a small quasiexperimental study of 36 children in a Lisbon kindergarten. The study indicated that the reach of the program was extensive, with as much as 95% of the sample of the target population (3- to 7-year-olds) having some exposure to the program. Regarding parents' perspectives, the researcher noted that a majority of the parents considered the program educational and felt that the children were learning from it. An analysis of the study of children's learning revealed trends similar to those noted in other summative evaluations, with the greatest gains in language and numeracy skills.

Similar gains in numeracy and literacy were also found in a study in Mexico (UNICEF, 1996). The researchers studied 3- to 6-year-olds from low-income families in Mexico City (382 children) and Oaxaca (396 children). In both cities, participants were randomly assigned to a high-exposure group who regularly viewed *Plaza Sésamo* in their school classrooms for a 3-month period, or a low-exposure group that watched cartoons. Comparisons of performance on a battery of curriculum-based tests indicated findings in the area of symbolic representation (letter recognition, numeric skills) and geometric shapes. There was also some evidence of gains in the areas of ecology, nutrition, and hygiene in the Mexico City group.

The study also serves as a reminder of an aspect of general summative research design that must be accommodated by researchers. Although there was an attempt to create "experimental" and "control" groups, at the time of the study the reach of *Plaza Sésamo* was so great that it was not possible to know the degree of incidental exposure children had to the program. In the case of the study in Mexico, it was believed, for example, that it was likely that children in the control group had at least minimal exposure to the program outside of the school setting. To control for this difficulty, researchers used an admittedly imperfect proxy measure of exposure. They included in their analysis a variable that looked at children's familiarity with the *Plaza Sésamo* characters, reasoning that children who demonstrated familiarity with the characters were likely to have had exposure to the program.

In contrast, a study in Russia provided a unique opportunity to address this issue of exposure systematically. The program in Russia was initially broadcast in only some regions of the country. Researchers elected to evaluate the impact of the program in a geographical area beyond the broadcast reach, something that enabled the researchers to compare the performance of children who had viewed videotapes of the 65 episodes to that of children who had watched animated Russian fairy tales. Results of the study indicated that, although the most powerful predictor of children's performance was age, viewers of *Ulitsa Sezam* developed some numeracy and literacy skills at a faster rate than their nonviewing peers (*Ulitsa Sezam* Department of Research and Content, 1998).

Around the world, the pattern of results that has emerged from summative evaluations of *Sesame Street* coproductions is noteworthy, not only for the consistency of effects across coproductions, but also because the pattern is so consistent with effects that have been observed for the original version of *Sesame Street* in the United States. I will return to this point later.

ISSUES RAISED AND LESSONS LEARNED

Over the past three decades, formative and summative research conducted in support of *Sesame Street* has not only helped producers gather children's reactions to the specific segments or episodes tested, but has also contributed in many ways to our broader understanding of the medium. Research on *Sesame Street* has provided insight into a variety of issues relevant to both the study and the production of educational television.

Issues for the Study of Educational Television

Television as Informal Educator.   As noted earlier, when *Sesame Street* was conceived in the late 1960s, no one could be sure whether it was even possible for television to succeed in contributing to school readiness. The literature discussed in this chapter stands as powerful testament to the potential for television—and *Sesame Street* in particular—to serve as a tool for informal education.

One might ask how much viewing of *Sesame Street* is necessary to produce an effect. The simplest answer appears to be that it depends on the type of effect being sought. As little as a single exposure to a 2-minute segment of *Sesame Street* has been shown to produce immediate effects in narrowly defined domains, such as replicating a character's solution to a problem. However, such limited exposure was not sufficient to produce more generalized effects, such as transfer of the solution to a new problem (Hodapp, 1977). By contrast, when children have engaged in more sustained viewing of *Sesame Street* over a longer period of time, a sizable literature indicates that such viewing contributes to educational benefits that not only transfer to new tasks and contexts, but also can endure for years.

Clearly, long-range effects of such prolonged duration cannot be explained simply by imitation. Teenagers in the recontact study were not directly applying information learned from *Sesame Street* to their classwork in high school. Rather, Anderson, Huston, Wright, and their colleagues attributed the effects to an *early learning model* in which three facets of early development were proposed as pathways by which long-term effects could result: (a) learning preacademic skills, particularly related to language and literacy, (b) developing motivation and interest, and (c) acquiring behavioral patterns of attentiveness, concentration, nonaggressiveness, and absence of restlessness or distractability (Anderson et al., 1998, 2001; Huston et al., 2001). (Note that these mechanisms directly counter claims by Healy [1990] and others that *Sesame Street* reduces children's attention spans and inhibits the development of language.) These factors contribute to early success in school, which then plays a significant role in determining children's long-term academic trajectories; children who demonstrate good skills early on are likely to be placed in higher ability groups, to be perceived as more competent by teachers, to receive more attention, to feel successful, and to be motivated to do well (Entwistle, Alexander, & Olson, 1997). In addition, these early successes may also affect the types of activities in which children choose to engage; for example, good readers may choose to read more on their own. Each of these outcomes can then result in further success over time. In this way, the model posits a cascading effect in which early exposure to educational television leads to early academic success, which in turn, contributes to a long-term trajectory of success that can endure for years.

Effectiveness of the Coproduction Model. As noted earlier, summative research on international versions of *Sesame Street* found highly consistent effects in Mexico, Turkey, Portugal, Russia, and the United States. Such consistency, in the face of the cultural differences that exist among these societies, speaks to the effectiveness of the coproduction model. It appears that the care taken to ensure the cultural relevance of each coproduction has been successful in helping the series reach and exert a positive impact on its particular target audience.

Hendershot (1998, 1999) argued that, despite attempts to localize *Sesame Street* coproductions, the elements that are common across all such coproductions (e.g., high-quality puppets, the inclusion of some form of the word "*Sesame*" in each title)[2] make them a well-intentioned part of a unidirectional flow of U.S. media that disseminates American culture worldwide. Whether that is true remains to be seen; research to date has not addressed the question of whether children perceive of these programs as "American," or whether viewers become more "Americanized" as a result of watching the series. However, the existing research does indicate that the educational impact of these series is considerable.

Issues for the Production of Educational Television

More than three decades' worth of formative research on *Sesame Street* has been oriented toward identifying approaches and techniques that can make the series as appealing and educationally powerful as possible. The lessons learned from these studies could easily fill a book by themselves. Indeed, they have already filled more than one (e.g., Fisch & Truglio, 2001a; Lesser, 1974). Without attempting to present an exhaustive discussion here, let us review just a few key points.

Appeal. As noted earlier, a key element in making *Sesame Street*'s educational content available to children is making the series appealing enough to motivate viewers to watch. Fisch and Truglio (2001b) sug-

---

[2]Some of the elements that Hendershot uses in her argument are actually misconceptions. Contrary to her claims, theme songs for coproductions of *Sesame Street* do not employ the same music as the U.S. version of the series; the music is composed locally to reflect the musical styles of the region. Nor is the majority of each episode comprised of dubbed segments from the U.S. series; the actual figure is less than 50%. However, *Open Sesame* (an alternate version of *Sesame Street* that is sold for international use) does rely on the U.S. library of segments.

gested that the relationship between appeal and comprehension is most likely reciprocal; just as children will only attend to (and, thus, comprehend) a television program if they enjoy it, they are also likely to enjoy a program more if they find its content to be comprehensible and not over their heads. Thus, for example, Anderson et al. (1981) found that English-speaking preschoolers attended more to *Sesame Street* segments in English than to the same segments dubbed into Greek. A parallel effect was found in measuring Japanese children's attention to a *Sesame Street* segment presented in either English or Japanese (cited in Kodaira, 1990).

Over the years, various elements have been found to contribute consistently to appeal. One such element is humor. Yet, for humor to be successful in promoting appeal, children in the target audience must find the intended humor to be funny. Children's appreciation of various types of humor is affected by their age and developmental level. Early formative research on *Sesame Street* found that preschool children consistently enjoyed certain types of humor (e.g., incongruity and surprise, slapstick, adult errors, silly wordplay), but not more sophisticated forms of humor such as puns that required viewers to appreciate the double meanings of words.

A second element that can contribute to appeal is the inclusion of visual action, such as slapstick, fast-motion, or simply prominent activity or movement on the screen. Numerous studies have shown that preschool (and school-age) children prefer television programs that feature visual action over lengthy "talking heads" scenes (i.e., static scenes focusing on dialogue spoken among characters or directly to the camera). Similarly, a Swedish study by Rydin (cited in Greenfield, 1984) found that when a film about plant growth was animated, 5- and 7-year-olds showed greater comprehension than when the film presented a series of still images. For 7-year-olds, the advantage of motion seemed to elicit a greater understanding of the dynamic process of growth, whereas for 5-year-olds, the advantage reflected children's paying more attention to the animated version.[3]

A third factor in appeal is the use of appealing characters. Numerous formative research studies have found that children point to appealing characters as reasons for liking television programs. Among the traits that make characters appealing are viewers' perceptions of them as funny, nice, smart, and/or helpful. In addition, children often enjoy seeing other children as characters on screen, particularly child characters who are a bit older than themselves (e.g., Fisch, in press-a).

---

[3]In a different medium, a series of computer-based studies by Calvert and her colleagues also found visual action to be associated with appeal and recall. Based on these data, Calvert (1999) concluded that action facilitates children's processing of both visual and verbal information.

Clear and Child-Centered Presentations.   Typically, children's comprehension has been found to be strongest when the subject matter is simple, direct, and concrete rather than abstract. Children are better able to follow narratives on television when they are explicit, rather than requiring viewers to draw inferences, and when they are linear and temporally ordered. Interestingly, this same pattern of results has been found internationally, in formative research on the first Israeli coproduction of *Sesame Street, Rechov Sumsum* (cited in Kodaira, 1990).

In addition, comprehension is generally stronger when the situations and settings that characters encounter are child-centered—that is, when they relate to familiar parts of children's lives. The use of familiar settings or issues that are prominent in children's lives allows children to apply their own prior knowledge to the program. As a result, they can construct a richer understanding of the material.

Music and Sound Effects.   Lesser (1974) catalogued a lengthy list of functions that music can serve in television programs, such as conveying a range of emotions (e.g., joy, sadness), action (e.g., chases, thinking), and situations (e.g., danger, magical occurrence). Apart from conveying meaning and promoting comprehension, music and sound effects repeatedly have been found to capture children's attention and to contribute to the appeal of television programs (e.g., Bryant, Zillmann, & Brown, 1983; Lesser, 1972, 1974; Levin & Anderson, 1976).

Music and sound effects can be particularly effective in promoting attention and appeal when they signal the arrival of a familiar character or program element (Lesser, 1972, 1974) or when music is lively and has a fast tempo (Bryant et al., 1983). However, to be effective in sustaining children's attention to television, music and sound effects must also be carefully integrated with visual movement; as Lesser (1974) observed, consistent with the data on visual action discussed earlier, music may capture attention but probably will not sustain it if the visual that accompanies it is static (e.g., a seated orchestra or stationary folk singer playing their instruments).

Repetition and Reinforcement.   As Lesser's (1974) discussion of the "James Earl Jones Effect" and research on repeat viewing by Sell et al. (1995) demonstrate, children's comprehension can be enhanced by viewing the same material more than once. Repeat viewing can encourage comprehension by providing viewers with a "second chance" to understand content that they may have failed to grasp the first time around. Alternately, if children have begun to grasp a new concept during their first viewing, a second viewing can help to reinforce mastery of the concepts presented. In addition, the data from Lesser and Sell et al. suggest that the nature of subsequent viewings may be different from the first viewing, as children begin to anticipate events in the narrative and isolate central content from the incidental content that surrounds it.

Similarly, comprehension can also be aided by children's viewing several different segments that all address the same underlying educational content (e.g., the letter *B* might be presented and labeled in the context of the words *Bed*, *Bath*, and *Bird*). Indeed, the earliest summative research on the impact of *Sesame Street* found that the educational content areas that had received the greatest emphasis within the series also produced the greatest effects on children's learning (Ball & Bogatz, 1970). Fisch and Truglio (2001b) argued that over time, seeing the same content presented in multiple contexts may help to encourage generalization; because they have seen these concepts at work in several different contexts, children may become sensitized toward looking for the letter *B* in a variety of words (perhaps even words that have not been included in the segments viewed).

For such benefits to emerge, however, children must recognize that, in fact, the content presented in these different segments or contexts is the same. Without that realization, it would be difficult (if not impossible) for the segments to reinforce each other. International support for this conclusion comes from a preschool television study conducted jointly by researchers from the United States and Japan, in which reinforcement appeared to be effective among 5- and 6-year-olds only if the segments included a "clue" to their connection, such as a verbal explanation of the link or the presence of the same characters in the different segments (cited in Kodaira, 1990). I return to these points in chapter 11's discussion of transfer of learning from educational television.

The Sesame Workshop Model.   Together, data from early and later summative studies of *Sesame Street* point to a consistency of effects that have been found over a period of decades; the same types of effects found among children in the early 1970s continued to be found among a new generation of children in the 1990s. The reason for this likely stems from the fact that *Sesame Street* has not remained static over the years. Production techniques and formats have been updated on an ongoing basis, as typified by the introduction of "Elmo's World" at the end of each episode in Season 30 and a subsequent restructuring of the format of the entire hour-long program into a set of recurring formats that appear in the same order in every episode. Curriculum goals have been continually revisited to reflect current thinking in educational practice. Formative research has been used on an ongoing basis to help ensure that material is appealing and comprehensible to its target audience. All of these have contributed to an underlying foundation that has allowed *Sesame Street* to educate children for more than 30 years.

ACKNOWLEDGMENT

Portions of this chapter are adapted from Fisch (1998) and Fisch, Truglio, and Cole (1999).

3

Other Preschool Series and School Readiness

You see a clue? Where? ... Oh! It's a clue! It's our third clue!

—Steve (talking to viewers), *Blue's Clues*

As discussed in the beginning of chapter 2, the pioneering efforts of series such as *Sesame Street* in the late 1960s were driven by an atmosphere in which national attention was focused on the educational needs of preschool children. The decades that followed saw significant changes in society—changes that affected the world in which young children live today. From the perspective of an American preschooler, one of the most important demographic shifts is the marked increase in the number of children in child care. In the year 2000, an estimated 13,000,000 children under the age of 6 spent part or all of their day cared for by someone other than their parents (Children's Defense Fund, 2000; for more detail on the current landscape of child care, see chap. 9, this volume.)

Although demographics may have changed, however, many of the basic educational needs of young children remain the same. The importance of early childhood education is recognized at least as widely now (if not more widely) as it was when *Sesame Street* was conceived. Some of that interest is motivated by the greater availability of empirical data demonstrating the impact of early education. Numerous studies have shown that high-quality early childhood programs can produce short-term gains in IQ and sizable long-term effects on school achievement, grade retention, placement in special education, and social adjustment (see, e.g., Barnett [1995] for a review). In recent years, interest has also been generated by renewed attention to the study of neural development in the brain. The brain activity of 3- to 10-year-olds is more than twice that of adults; more connections are made among brain cells at these ages than at any other time of life (e.g., Chugani, 1996). The degree to which these connections change as a function of children's interactions with their environments has led some educators to argue even more strongly for the need to pro-

35

vide children with enriching educational experiences at the earliest ages (e.g., Carnegie Task Force on Learning in the Primary Grades, 1996; National Education Research Policy and Priorities Board, 1997).

Indeed, the importance of early childhood education has been acknowledged on the Presidential level as well. In 1989, President George H. W. Bush and the National Governor's Association established a set of national goals for education, the first of which was that "by the year 2000, all children in America will start school ready to learn" (Action Team on School Readiness, 1992; Boyer, 1992). His successor, President William Clinton, reinforced this commitment by announcing initiatives centered around the issue of early childhood education in a State of the Union address several years later (U.S. Department of Education, 1997).

The widely acknowledged importance of early education, coupled with the financial success of preschool series such as *Sesame Street* and *Barney & Friends*, has driven many producers and broadcasters to create television series that are intended to promote school readiness among preschool children. In fact, a content analysis by Schmitt (1999) found that even though more television series were targeted at school-age than preschool children in 1998, a greater percentage of the preschool series were educational. Even the phrase "Ready to Learn" has been adopted by PBS as an umbrella title for its preschool programming and associated outreach efforts (e.g., Bryant, Stuart, & Maxwell, 1999).

THE POTENTIAL ROLE OF TELEVISION

As noted in chapter 1, the tremendous reach of television among children invests television with the potential to serve as a powerful vehicle for informal education. Its reach among preschoolers is no different. Parent reports indicate that even children as young as 2 to 3 years old spend more than 18 hours per week watching television (Jordan & Woodard, 2001; see chap. 1, this volume).

Furthermore, as described in chapter 2, research has shown that 3- to 5-year-olds can comprehend and benefit greatly from watching *Sesame Street*. However, that research does not speak to the issue of whether other television series would produce comparable effects on school readiness, or whether significant effects might be possible among younger children. To answer these questions, we must turn to research on other television series for preschool children.

To date, there has been little, if any, longitudinal research to assess the effects of preschool television series other than *Sesame Street* once children have entered school. However, research on several preschool series has revealed more immediate effects that, if sustained, also could contribute to later school readiness.

IMPACT ON SCHOOL READINESS

Before examining the impact of educational television on "school readiness," we must first define what we mean by the term. As Lewit and Baker (1995) pointed out, the concept of "readiness" is poorly defined and used very differently in different contexts. In various instances, it has been used to refer either to helping children become ready to enter school, to helping schools better address children's needs, or to encouraging society to support both children and schools.

For the purposes of this discussion, "school readiness" is used in the sense of children's preparedness to succeed in school. Certainly, it is true that, as the National Association for the Education of Young Children (1990) has argued, all children enter school ready to learn, barring extreme cases of abuse, neglect, or disability. Yet, it cannot be denied that, when children first enter school, some are better equipped to deal with the demands of the school environment than others.

Success in school does not only depend on children's mastery of skills that are traditionally considered academic (e.g., literacy or numeracy), but also rests on a broad range of factors, such as good communication skills, a disposition toward engaging in challenging tasks, and socioemotional skills such as self-confidence and cooperation with peers (e.g., Bredekamp & Copple, 1997; Raver, 2002; Zero to Three/National Center for Clinical Infant Programs, 1992). This chapter reviews research on the impact of educational television on four facets of school readiness among 3- to 5-year-old children: knowledge of typical preschool academic content, problem solving, motivation to pursue challenges, and language acquisition. Impact on socioemotional development is addressed in chapter 8.

Knowledge

Preschool academic curricula for 3- to 5-year-olds typically include content that introduces children to material related to language and literacy (e.g., reading, vocabulary), mathematics (e.g., numbers, shapes), science (e.g., plants, animals), and social studies (e.g., roles of people in neighborhood), among others (e.g., Bredekamp & Copple, 1997). Several of these subjects were included among the measures used in a series of studies that Singer, Singer, and their colleagues conducted to assess the educational effectiveness of *Barney & Friends* (see Singer & Singer, 1998 for a review). The studies simultaneously examined the series' impact on children's social development, as will be discussed in chapter 8.

Barney & Friends (Fig. 3.1) stars a purple dinosaur named Barney who changes from a stuffed doll to a human-sized character when a group of

FIG. 3.1. *Barney & Friends*. (Photo © 2003 Lyons Partnership, L.P. All rights reserved. *Barney & Friends* and all related titles, logos, and characters are trademarks of Lyons Partnership, L.P.)

children need him. Key to the series is the prominent use of songs set to familiar children's tunes (e.g., "I love you, you love me ..." to the tune of "This Old Man"). At its peak, Nielsen ratings showed *Barney & Friends* to be the most widely viewed series in America among children aged 2 to 5.

The Singers' line of research began with series of content analyses that counted the number of instances of educational content in each season of *Barney & Friends*. They coded each episode for several categories of content: cognitive (e.g., vocabulary, numbers, colors), emotional awareness (e.g., joy, anger, excitement), social/constructive attitudinal (e.g., sharing, cooperation, self-restraint), physical (e.g., fine motor skills, nutrition, personal grooming), music and entertainment (e.g., singing, dancing,

games), and multicultural exposure (e.g., language, food, reference to ethnic group). Results from the first two seasons indicated that, on average,
each 30-minute episode contained approximately 100 instances of such
content (J. L. Singer & D. G. Singer, 1993; D. G. Singer & J. L. Singer,
1994a). This figure is somewhat inflated by the fact that an individual
event in an episode could be coded under multiple categories (e.g., a song
about emotions would count as both music and emotional awareness),
but its sheer magnitude is staggering nonetheless.

Indeed, the total was even higher several seasons later; a content analysis of the sixth season of *Barney & Friends* found an average of slightly
more than 200 instances of educational content per episode (J. L. Singer
& D. G. Singer, 2000). The classes of content that were represented most
heavily in the first two seasons were music, emotional, and social content,
followed by cognitive. Less emphasis was placed on physical and multicultural content.

The simple presence of so much educational content does not, by itself, guarantee that viewing will result in learning. Although such effects
are possible, it is also possible that the high density of content would allow for too little focus on any one point to produce significant effects
among viewers. Thus, Singer and Singer also conducted a series of experimental studies to gauge the educational impact of *Barney & Friends*
among children of various ages and demographic backgrounds, and under various conditions (e.g., unassisted viewing versus viewing accompanied by follow-up lessons with a teacher). Each study employed a
pretest–posttest design in which children were tested on a variety of
measures concerning subjects such as numbers, shapes, colors, and occupations. Data were compared between children who were shown episodes of *Barney & Friends* and a control group of nonviewers who were
not shown the episodes.

The Singers' first study found that after watching 10 episodes of the
series without teacher-driven follow-up lessons, a largely White, middle-SES sample of 3- and 4-year-old viewers performed significantly
better than nonviewers on several measures of counting skills, identifying colors, vocabulary, and knowledge of neighborhood, but not in
identifying shapes or labeling emotions (J. L. Singer & D. G. Singer,
1994). However, a replication of the study with a greater representation of 3- and 4-year-olds from low-SES and minority families found
that, for this population, viewing 10 episodes of the series without
teacher follow-up produced only a small advantage over nonviewers (J.
L. Singer & D. G. Singer, 1995). In both studies, stronger effects were
obtained when *Barney & Friends* was combined with teacher-driven lessons, as is discussed in greater detail in chapter 9, which explores adult
mediation of educational television.

Complementary studies with older and younger samples of children found no significant effects for 5½-year-old kindergarten students. This was attributed to ceiling effects; because children in the pretest already knew much of the educational content presented in *Barney & Friends*, significant gains could not be obtained. However, a study with younger children suggested that prosocial effects could exist for children as young as 2 years old, as is discussed in chapter 8 (D. G. Singer, J. L. Singer, Miller, & Sells, 1994; J. L. Singer & D. G. Singer, 1998).

Problem Solving

Apart from a substantive base of knowledge, success in school also requires children to be armed with a repertoire of problem-solving skills that they can apply to a broad range of tasks and situations. The impact of educational television on preschoolers' ability to engage successfully in problem solving was assessed in research on several series that were aimed at 2- to 5-year-olds and aired as part of Nickelodeon's "Nick Jr." programming block. In addition to a prominent prosocial component, the television series in the Nick Jr. block attempt to address cognitive, problem-solving-based goals that Nickelodeon has termed *flexible thinking*. Flexible thinking is defined as providing:

> the foundation for *adaptive behavior* ... [It] depends upon learning that is characterized by openness, authenticity, and a plurality of viewpoints and styles. It requires the ability to examine information independently, critically, from many perspectives, and to be sensitive to the opinions of others and the social context within which learning is taking place. It assumes that the "right answer" is not right for every situation (quoted by Bryant, Bryant, Mulliken, McCollum, & Love, 2001, p. 422).

Impact on Problem Solving. The first Nick Jr. summative study focused on two series: *Allegra's Window* (a live-action series featuring a little girl puppet named Allegra) and *Gullah Gullah Island* (a live-action series about a Black family set on a tropical island). A study by Bryant et al. (1997) examined effects of 2 years' worth of viewing *Allegra's Window* and *Gullah Gullah Island*. During this time, 202 preschool children either viewed or did not view the two series, and nine assessments were conducted over the course of the two years. The bulk of the data consisted of caregivers' ratings of their children, rather than direct assessments of the children themselves, so these data must be interpreted with caution. Still, over the course of the 2 years, caregivers perceived viewers as showing significantly greater increases than nonviewers on scales of flexible thinking (e.g., taking multiple points of view, showing curiosity) and problem solving (e.g., trying different approaches, concentrating, not giving up). The greatest gains appeared within the first month of viewing, and the difference between viewers and nonviewers remained fairly constant over the entire 2-year viewing period.

More direct support for these trends came from a study that compared 61 viewers' and nonviewers' performance in a set of hands-on problem-solving tasks after 2 years of viewing (Mulliken & Bryant, 1999). The tasks, adapted from prior literature, were a spatial reversal task (similar to a carnival shell game), a modified version of the Tower of Hanoi problem in which simpler and more difficult versions of the task were created, and a Go–NoGo task (akin to signal detection) in which response time and accuracy were measured as children distinguished between shapes and/or colors. Data indicated that viewers produced significantly more correct answers in the spatial reversal task. In the modified Tower of Hanoi task, viewers were significantly more likely than nonviewers to be successful in three of the six problems presented (including the two most difficult versions); they also solved four of the six problems (including all of the most difficult problems) in fewer moves than nonviewers. Finally, viewers performed more accurately in the Go–NoGo task than nonviewers, although no significant difference was found for response time.

A subsequent, parallel set of studies assessed the impact of *Blue's Clues* on preschool children's knowledge and cognitive development during a comparable 2-year viewing period (Anderson et al., 2000; Bryant, Mulliken, et al., 1999). *Blue's Clues* (Fig. 3.2) is a popular, participatory series about an animated dog named Blue and her human friend Steve (or,

FIG. 3.2. *Blue's Clues*. (Photo © 2003 Viacom International Inc. All rights reserved. Nickelodeon, Nick Jr., *Blue's Clues*, and all related titles, logos, and characters are trademarks of Viacom International Inc.)

subsequently, Steve's younger brother, Joe), who asks viewers directly for assistance in solving games and puzzles. Throughout each episode, as Steve and the viewers solve various puzzles, Blue leaves her paw print on three objects (clues) that Steve prompts viewers to consider in combination; by figuring out what the objects have in common, viewers are invited to infer what Blue wants.

Results of the research indicated that, on the most basic level, viewers recalled what they had seen; when asked to solve the same puzzles seen in particular episodes of *Blue's Clues* (which involved educational content such as matching, sequencing, and relational concepts), viewers provided significantly more correct answers than nonviewers. More broadly, using subscales from the Kaufman Assessment Battery for Children (K-ABC) and the Kaufman Brief Intelligence Test (K-BIT), Bryant, Mulliken, et al. (1999) found that viewers performed significantly better than nonviewers in solving nonhumorous riddles (e.g., "What is small, has two wings, and can fly?"),[1] Gestalt closure of incomplete inkblot drawings, and a matrices task that tapped nonverbal problem solving; these effects were sustained throughout the 2-year viewing period. No effect was found for children's expressive vocabulary or self-esteem.

It should be noted that, in all of the Nick Jr. studies that presented preschool children with problem-solving tasks, the primary data of interest centered around the number of children who solved each problem correctly and/or the amount of time or number of moves it took to do so. Unlike school-age research on the impact of *Square One TV* on mathematical problem solving (see chap. 5, this volume) or *Bill Nye the Science Guy* on scientific experimentation (chap. 6, this volume), these studies did not also assess impact on the strategies and heuristics that children used in approaching the problems. This is, perhaps, understandable in light of the fact that preschoolers are generally less articulate than school-age children, so it is more difficult for them to discuss their strategies. As a result, the data from these studies demonstrate that sustained viewing of series such as *Allegra's Window*, *Gullah Gullah Island*, and *Blue's Clues* can produce gains in preschoolers' ability to solve problems correctly. However, the mechanism through which these effects arise (e.g., greater motivation or persistence, acquisition of a broader repertoire of heuristics) remains an open question.

Viewer Participation: Solving Problems While Viewing.   A unique feature of *Blue's Clues* is the degree to which it attempts to elicit viewer participation in the puzzles and games presented in the series, thus engag-

---

[1]Note that this task is quite similar to the type of puzzle that is woven through each episode of *Blue's Clues*, as described earlier.

ing viewers actively in the series' educational content. Participation is further encouraged by airing the same episode every weekday during a given week; indeed, participation by 3- to 5-year-old viewers has been found to increase over the course of the week (Crawley, Anderson, Wilder, Williams, & Santomero, 1999).

Generally, it is assumed that the active engagement inherent in viewer participation produces better comprehension and learning among children. However, based on observation data during viewing, Anderson and his colleagues (2000; Crawley et al., 1999, 2002) hypothesized that (at least among preschoolers) the relationship actually may proceed in the opposite direction—that is, viewer participation may reflect mastery *after* children have comprehended educational content. This would explain why participation occurred at lower levels during viewing of *Blue's Clues* early in the week, but increased over repeated exposures to the same episode (as more children, presumably, learned the answers).

This position may gain further support from a subsequent pair of studies by Crawley et al. (2002). Data from the first study indicated that regular viewers of *Blue's Clues* participated more than inexperienced viewers during a single viewing of a new episode of the series. In particular, participation by experienced viewers was most prevalent when the participatory behaviors were standard responses to ritualized prompts that appear in virtually every episode (e.g., responding with the word "notebook" when Steve talks about needing his "handy dandy ..."). As in the case of the puzzles shown in *Blue's Clues*, it appears that prior knowledge of the on-screen prompts and desired responses led to greater participation by viewers.

Participation may also increase, not only when children already know the specific answer that is requested, but also as they become more accustomed to the notion of viewer participation itself. The second study reported by Crawley et al. (2002) found that experienced *Blue's Clues* viewers participated significantly more than nonviewers when shown an episode of a novel, participatory preschool series called *Big Bag*. However, in keeping with Anderson et al.'s (2000) hypothesis about participation and mastery, increased participation was not accompanied by greater comprehension of the *Big Bag* program. I will return to viewer participation and its implications for education in the "Issues Raised and Lessons Learned" section at the end of this chapter.

Language Development

An aspect of school readiness that has been examined across several different preschool television series is language development (see Naigles & Mayeux, 2001 for a review). Let us consider the impact of preschool educational television as it pertains to both first- and second-language acquisition.

First-Language Acquisition.   The potential for television to serve a role in language development was explored in a series of content analyses by Rice and her colleagues. These analyses compared the spoken language used in television series such as *Sesame Street, Mister Rogers' Neighborhood,* and *The Electric Company* to the language parents use in child-directed speech for young children (Rice, 1984; Rice & Haight, 1986). In contrast to situation comedies such as *Gilligan's Island,* the researchers found that the language in the educational television series contained many of the same features that are believed to promote language development in child-directed speech: short length of utterance, repetition, language tied to immediate, concrete referents, and so on. Thus, the potential seemed to exist for such television series to contribute to language development.

In fact, however, subsequent data supported this hypothesis with regard to some aspects of language development but not others. Although not every study has found effects on children's vocabulary acquisition (e.g., Bryant, Mulliken, et al. [1999] did not find a significant effect of *Blue's Clues* on children's expressive vocabulary), many studies have shown that preschool children can acquire new words from television (e.g., Rice et al., 1990; Rice & Woodsmall, 1988; J. L. Singer & D. G. Singer, 1994; cf. Naigles & Mayeux, 2001). By contrast, fewer studies have examined the role of television in children's acquisition of grammar, and they provide little evidence for a significant effect of television (J. L. Singer & D. G. Singer, 1981; cf. Naigles & Mayeux, 2001). Drawing on the more general literature on language development, Naigles and Mayeux (2001) hypothesized that grammatical development may require a socially based construction of meaning that the one-way communication of television does not provide.

In addition, it is worth noting that, under some conditions, educational television programs also may have unintended negative effects on language development. Naigles et al. (1995) found that, after exposure to 10 episodes of *Barney & Friends,* children demonstrated *decreased* understanding of the difference between the mental-state verbs *know* (which reflects certainty) and *think* and *guess* (which are less certain). A subsequent examination of the 10 *Barney & Friends* episodes pointed toward an explanation: The episodes included numerous instances in which *guess* or *think* were used in situations that actually conveyed certainty. Thus, just as exposure to novel words in appropriate televised contexts can have positive effects on young children's vocabulary, consistent misapplications of words can raise misunderstandings as well.

Second-Language Acquisition.   The fact that several studies have shown children to acquire new vocabulary from television raises the question as to whether this might also be true in second-language learning. Aimed at a slightly older audience of first and second graders, *Carrascolendas* was targeted at bilingual Mexican-American children in the Austin, Texas area. Set in the mythical town of Carrascolendas with a bilingual cast of humans and puppets, each episode presented a mixture of segments that were primarily in Spanish and English. A pretest–posttest evaluation with 88 bilingual children (of varying levels of English and Spanish dominance) found that, after exposure to 30 episodes of the series, viewers showed significantly greater English and Spanish fluency than nonviewers. In addition, viewers outperformed nonviewers in three out of five aspects of their use of English (though not Spanish): physical environment (i.e., recognizing objects in the immediate environment), concept development (e.g., size, weight), and multicultural social environment (e.g., understanding the value of speaking both English and Spanish). No effect was found for numbers and figures, or for vocabulary, syntax, or sound features of English or Spanish. Thus, the results suggested that, in some but not all respects, exposure to the series contributed to Mexican-American children's knowledge of English (Williams & Natalicio, 1972).

Conversely, many American preschool series with Latino characters have included individual Spanish words or phrases in their dialogue (e.g., *Sesame Street*, *Puzzle Place*, *Dragon Tales*, *Big Bag*), but the introduction of Spanish words to English-speaking children is a central curriculum goal in *Dora the Explorer* (Fig. 3.3). Shown as part of the Nick Jr. preschool block, *Dora the Explorer* is a participatory series about Dora, a 7-year-old, bilingual Latina girl who lives inside a computer. Aided by her talking backpack and a monkey named Boots, Dora uses her knowledge of Spanish and English as tools in solving problems and puzzles.

To determine whether children learned Spanish words from sustained viewing of *Dora the Explorer*, Linebarger (2001) conducted a pretest–posttest study with 152 3- and 4-year-old children. Vocabulary measures were administered before and after the children watched 24 episodes of the series, with each episode seen at least twice over the course of a week. No control group of nonviewers was included in the study, so results must be interpreted with caution. (However, it should be noted that English-speaking children did not show pretest–posttest differences on Spanish words that were not presented in *Dora the Explorer*).

Results indicated that pretest–posttest gains among children from Spanish-speaking families were associated more strongly with their general language development than with their viewing of *Dora the Explorer*, but English-speaking children did appear to learn some Spanish vocabulary

FIG. 3.3. *Dora the Explorer*. (Photo © 2003 Viacom International Inc. All rights reserved. Nickelodeon, Nick Jr., *Dora the Explorer*, and all related titles, logos, and characters are trademarks of Viacom International Inc.)

from the series. Gains among English-speaking children were small but significant, and were stronger among older children. Those children who were 4 years old at the beginning of the study gained one Spanish word per 14 episodes viewed; 3-year-olds gained one word per 58 episodes viewed. As might be expected from literature on language acquisition, significant gains were most likely to be found for nouns, concepts such as numbers, and for words that were either repeated frequently in the series, connected more frequently to their English equivalents, and/or common in daily life (e.g., *gracias*). Thus, it appears that television can play some role in introducing children to vocabulary from a second language, but clearly, television is far from the only factor.

Pursuing Challenges

A long tradition of theory and research posits that cognitive growth arises through children's engagement in challenging tasks (e.g., Inhelder & Piaget, 1964; Vygotsky, 1978). This idea continues to be prominent in education today, as seen in recommendations that schools must present children with challenging experiences and curricula, and that children must be motivated to pursue such experiences (e.g., Bredekamp & Copple, 1997; National Education Research Policy and Priorities Board, 1997).

The pursuit of physical, cognitive, social, and emotional challenges is at the heart of *Dragon Tales*, a highly popular series for children aged 2 to 6 (with a primary emphasis on 4-year-olds) that is produced by Sesame Workshop and airs on PBS (Fig. 3.4). *Dragon Tales* features the adventures of a pair of Latino siblings, Max and Emmy, who use a magic dragon scale to visit their young dragon friends (Ord, Cassie, and the two-headed Zak and Wheezie) in the fantasy world of Dragon Land. Three broad curriculum goals were defined for the series, with each goal subsuming a set of more specific subgoals:

- To encourage young children to pursue the challenging experiences that support their growth and development.
- To help young children recognize that there are many ways to approach and learn from the challenging experiences in their lives.
- To help young children understand that to try and not succeed is a natural and valuable part of learning.

These goals serve as the base for all of the stories in *Dragon Tales*. The themes of persistence and challenge are further reinforced in that each

FIG. 3.4. *Dragon Tales*. (Photo © 2003 Sesame Workshop and Columbia TriStar Television Distribution. All rights reserved. *Dragon Tales* and all related titles, logos, and characters are trademarks of Sesame Workshop and Columbia TriStar Television Distribution.)

dragon wears a "dragon badge" that glows when he or she grapples successfully with a difficult issue.

Summative research on *Dragon Tales* evaluated whether sustained viewing of the series led to significant gains in children's disposition to engage in challenging tasks and their establishment of collaborative relationships with others. An experimental, pretest–posttest study by Rust (2001) compared data from 340 4- and 5-year-old viewers and nonviewers, before and after viewers watched 20 episodes of *Dragon Tales*. Nonviewers watched 20 episodes of a control series whose curriculum did not overlap with that of *Dragon Tales*.[2] Data on challenge, goal orientation, and collaboration were gathered via multiple measures: (a) a rating scale (adapted from the Devereaux Early Childhood Assessment) in which researchers, teachers, and parents rated the children on several dimensions of goal orientation and collaboration; (b) a task-based interview in which children built structures with blocks; and (c) observations of naturalistic behavior during free play. To prevent any possible bias that might influence the data, researchers and teachers were blind as to which television series (*Dragon Tales* or *Between the Lions*) was the one of interest.

Converging data from multiple tasks and multiple types of observers pointed to the success of *Dragon Tales* in encouraging children to pursue challenges. When ratings from researchers, teachers, and parents were combined, *Dragon Tales* was found to have a significant, positive impact on the frequency with which children chose challenging tasks, initiated or organized play with others, and asked others to play. (A significant effect was also found for sharing and cooperating with others, as is discussed in chap. 8.) Similarly, data from the task-based interviews indicated that exposure to the series had a significant impact on children's tendency to describe their block building in terms of a coherent goal (as opposed to a set of discrete, unrelated pieces). In addition, viewers showed significantly greater gains than nonviewers in the degree to which they spontaneously chose to make things during free play. Thus, it appeared that 2 weeks' exposure to *Dragon Tales* was sufficient to influence viewers' goal orientation, as well as their inclination to initiate and engage in cognitive and social tasks.

Educational Television and Very Young Children

With rare exception, virtually all of the research on the educational impact of preschool television has been conducted with 3- to 5-year-old children.

---

[2]The control series was a literacy series, *Between the Lions*. For information on *Between the Lions*, see chapter 4 (this volume).

As we have seen, this body of literature consistently demonstrates the educational power of television among this age group. However, the lack of research with younger children leaves open the question of whether parallel effects might be found among children below the age of 3.

Yet, outside the laboratory, very young children are exposed routinely to educational television. For example, Schmitt's (2001) analysis of data collected in the early 1980s found that the program that aired most frequently when 0- to 3-year-olds were in the room was *Sesame Street*. Indeed, some preschool television programs and home videos are produced specifically for this younger age group, as in the case of the television series *Teletubbies* or the videos *Baby Einstein* and *Baby Bach*. Do such programs hold educational benefits for very young children? Or are toddlers not yet cognitively ready to comprehend and learn from educational television programs? Certainly, the latter point of view would be consistent with the American Academy of Pediatrics' (1997, 2001) recommendation that television be avoided completely for children under 2 years of age.

To date, no research has addressed these questions directly. However, some insight into comprehension of television among very young children can be gained from several studies that assessed the degree to which children below the age of 3 are able to imitate simple actions or acquire rudimentary bits of knowledge from television. Meltzoff (1988) found that, after watching a videotape of an experimenter pulling apart and reassembling a dumbbell-like toy, even 14- and 24-month-old children could imitate the actions they had seen. In fact, the level of imitation was consistent with that found in another study using live models (Meltzoff, 1985).

Other studies, which compared live and video presentations directly, have suggested that toddlers' imitation from video increases with age and depends on the complexity of the behavior being imitated. McCall, Parke, and Kavanaugh (1977) found that, among 18-, 24-, and 36-month-olds, only 36-month-olds imitated a sequence of actions as frequently when it was presented on video as when it was demonstrated live. Barr and Hayne (1999) manipulated the complexity of the behavior being modeled; they found that, one day after watching an adult model a simple behavior (either live or on videotape), 15- and 18-month-olds produced similar levels of imitation from the live and videotaped presentations, but 12-month-olds did not. By contrast, when the model demonstrated a longer sequence of behaviors, only the 18-month-olds showed as much imitation from the videotape as from the live model.

Further support for this pattern of developmental differences come from parallel studies by Schmitt and Anderson (2002) and Troseth and DeLoache (1998). In each series of studies, 24- and 30-month-olds (and, in the Schmitt and Anderson study, 36-month-olds) watched an experimenter hide a toy in a neighboring room, either on video or through a window (or a video monitor that the children believed was a window). Results indicated that, after the demonstration, 24- and 30-month-olds were less accurate in finding the toy if they watched the video than if they watched the equivalent scene live; 36-month-olds were equally accurate in both conditions, but faster after the live presentation.

Taken together, these studies suggest that, below the age of 2 or 3 years, children can acquire simple behaviors or information from television, but they are less able to learn from a televised portrayal than from a live demonstration. Several possible explanations have been proposed to account for these data, as is discussed in the "Issues Raised and Lessons Learned" section of this chapter. For the moment, it is sufficient to note that toddlers' ability to acquire and use information from television may differ significantly from that of 3- to 5-year-olds, let alone older children or adults.

Naturally, the videos used in these studies are far simpler than anything that would be seen on broadcast television, as is the "educational content" that they present. To date, no summative research has gauged the impact that *Sesame Street* or other series aimed at 3- to 5-year-olds might have on the cognitive abilities of younger children (although one study did examine the impact of *Barney & Friends* on the social behavior of a small sample of 2-year-olds; see Singer & Singer, 1998). Nor has there been any substantive research on toddlers' learning from series such as *Teletubbies*, although small-scale qualitative research in Australia and Germany provided anecdotal reports of individual children under the age of 2 participating while viewing *Teletubbies* (e.g., dancing along or playing games with on-screen characters), and at least one 2-year-old child counting while viewing (Höller & Müller, 1999; Howard & Roberts, 1999). Still, in the absence of more rigorously controlled research, the question of whether toddlers learn substantive educational content from television must remain unanswered for the present.

ISSUES RAISED AND LESSONS LEARNED

Not all of the television series reviewed in this chapter have produced equally strong effects, nor have their effects been equally strong in all domains. For example, series that have shown effects on vocabulary acquisition typically have not produced parallel effects on children's acquisition of grammar (Naigles & Mayeux, 2001).

Nevertheless, this body of literature points to a broad range of effects that are related to numerous aspects of school readiness. Apart from documenting the educational impact of each specific television series individually, the research also speaks to broader issues regarding preschoolers' learning from educational television. These include the means by which these series might contribute to school readiness, the role of viewer participation, and whether educational television can be crafted in ways to fit the cognitive capabilities of children younger than the typical preschool age group of 3 to 5.

Multiple Routes to School Readiness

As noted at the beginning of this chapter, research has not yet assessed the long-term impact of series other than *Sesame Street* on school readiness. Although some studies have been conducted longitudinally over a period of as much as 2 years (e.g., Bryant et al., 1997; Bryant, Mulliken, et al., 1999), children continued to view the television series throughout the 2-year period. Thus, the results found at the end of the studies reflect relatively immediate effects of sustained viewing, rather than long-term effects that endured long after the viewing ceased.

As a result, we cannot be certain whether the significant immediate effects that have been found for preschool exposure to these series would also lead to measurable advantages later, after children have entered elementary or even high school (as Anderson et al., 2001, and Wright, Huston, Scantlin, et al., 2001, found in the case of *Sesame Street*). However, it is informative to speculate on why those sorts of long-term effects might or might not occur.

Summative research has shown these series to produce effects that reflect several different aspects of preparing children for school: providing knowledge (as in research on *Barney & Friends*), encouraging the development of either language (as seen in various series) or problem-solving skills (as in *Allegra's Window*, *Gullah Gullah Island*, and *Blue's Clues*), and motivating children to pursue challenges and goals. All of these would be expected to contribute to school readiness, but each is likely to help children in different (though complementary) ways once they enter school.

With that in mind, let us revisit the early learning model discussed in chapter 2. The early learning model (Anderson et al., 2001; Huston et al., 2001) posits that long-term effects of educational preschool programming stem from a cascading effect in which early exposure to educational television leads to early academic success, which, in turn, contributes to a long-term trajectory of success that can endure for years. The model suggests three pathways through which long-term effects might arise: (a) preacademic skills, particularly related to language and literacy, (b) motivation and interest, and (c) behavioral patterns of attentiveness, concentration, nonaggressiveness, and absence of restlessness or distractibility. The first two classes of effects are clearly evident in the studies reviewed here, and evidence for the third is discussed in chapter 8.

Inasmuch as the observed effects correspond to those prescribed by the model, it is reasonable to imagine that the potential exists for long-term effects to result from sustained viewing of many of these series. Obviously, though, further research would be necessary to determine whether this potential might be actualized.

If such effects do exist, then the existing research suggests that different series might actually produce long-term effects via different avenues. For example, viewers of *Barney & Friends* might receive praise in kindergarten for factual knowledge (e.g., names of colors), whereas regular viewers of *Dragon Tales* might achieve early success by taking on challenging activities and persisting in them until they succeed. Both classes of success would be seen as beneficial under the early learning model. However, it remains to be seen whether one route to early success might be more effective than others in promoting long-term impact.

Viewer Participation and Learning

Participation: Cause or Effect?   Traditionally, when attempts to elicit viewer participation have been woven into educational television series, it has been for one or both of the following reasons: to draw viewers into the program, with the intent of maximizing engagement and appeal, and/or to stimulate viewers to not only attend to the educational content, but also to practice the targeted skills or information actively while viewing. Implicit in the latter goal is the assumption that the educational impact of the material is likely to be stronger if viewers engage with it actively during viewing than if they simply view the program without participating.

However, as discussed earlier with regard to *Blue's Clues*, Anderson and his colleagues (e.g., 2000) suggested that the function of viewer participation may actually be somewhat different (at least among preschool children). Rather than promoting comprehension of the material, these researchers believe that viewer participation reflects mastery of the material after it has been comprehended.

Anderson and his colleagues (2000) framed their approach in terms of cognitive load. When the content of a program is new (and particularly if it includes challenging games), it requires more attention from children. With repeat viewing, children become familiar with the specific content of a given episode and begin to recognize recurring formats. As familiarity grows, less attentional resources are required for comprehension, so children are more free to engage in participatory behavior. In this way, growing tendencies toward viewer participation signal an underlying mastery of the content.

To that explanation, I would add that, over the course of repeated viewing, the relationship between comprehension and participation might be seen as reciprocal. Even if comprehension of challenging content initially precedes participation, the fact remains that once participation occurs, it serves as a rehearsal of the content. Indeed, a long history of theory in information processing argues that information is retained for longer periods of time when learners work actively with the material than when they do not (e.g., Craik & Lockhart, 1972). Thus, as participation increases over the course of repeated viewing, the participation should serve to strengthen viewers' retention of the material. In turn, the stronger comprehension and retention should make participation even more likely to occur during the next viewing.

Relationship to Educational Content.   For viewer participation to serve as rehearsal and reinforcement, the participatory behavior must itself involve the educational content. As Hall, Miller, and Fisch (1990) commented in discussing fifth graders' participation during *Square One TV,* viewer participation meant that these children were not only viewing mathematics but actively *doing* mathematics while they watched. Yet, not all participation during educational television programs is tied closely to educational content. Crawley et al. (2002) distinguished between segments of *Blue's Clues* whose intent is primarily educational or primarily entertaining; a similar distinction could be also made for viewer participation during those segments. For example, viewer participation in playing a pattern-matching game would be an example of rehearsal of educational content (i.e., practicing problem-solving skills and information regarding patterns). However, singing along with the opening theme song would not, because the theme song does not convey information about patterns, and singing it does not require the use of problem-solving skills. (In chapter 10, I use the term *distance* to refer to a similar concept regarding the integration of narrative and educational content.)

It seems reasonable to believe that participation would be more effective in promoting learning of educational content when the participatory behavior involves that content than when it does not. Thus, in considering the potential contribution of participation to retention and learning, it may not be sufficient to look merely at the amount of participation that is elicited. Rather, the nature of the participatory behavior (and its relation to the educational content of the program) is critical as well.

Production Features That Promote Participation.   The occurrence of viewer participation is influenced not only by characteristics of the viewer (e.g., prior knowledge of the content or format of a program), but also by characteristics of the television program. A review of research on participatory segments in *Square One TV* (Fisch & McCann, 1993) pointed to four characteristic features of segments that were successful in eliciting

viewer participation among school-age children. The segments themselves were appealing, which encouraged children to attend to them. The
problems that characters and viewers solved were clear and well-defined.
Sufficient time was provided to allow viewers to respond before on-screen
characters supplied the correct answer. And segments were designed in
ways that allowed viewers to make educated guesses if they were not sure
about an answer; instead of open-ended questions whose answers required viewers to possess a particular bit of knowledge, problems typically
were presented with defined sets of response options from which viewers
could choose (e.g., a multiple-choice question or a given set of suspects in
a mystery). All of these features are likely to promote participation when
built into preschool programming as well. Indeed, all of them can be
found in *Blue's Clues*.

In addition, research on series such as *Blue's Clues* and *Sesame Street* suggests several other features that can be added to this list. One consistently
powerful feature, as discussed earlier, is repetition. This can be repetition
of a single segment or episode, as in the 5-day-a-week broadcast schedule
of *Blue's Clues* or the *Sesame Street* "James Earl Jones" effect described in
chapter 2. Alternately, the same prompt and desired response may be repeated several times within a single episode, or repeated across consecu-
tive episodes, as in the case of *Blue's Clues'* ritualized prompt regarding
Steve's "handy dandy ... " (with viewers responding, "Notebook!").

Another feature lies in the nature of the desired participatory behavior.
Clearly, in creating these programs, producers must choose participatory
behaviors that children can reasonably be expected to perform within a
fairly short period of time. Formative research has been used extensively
in the production of series such as *Blue's Clues* or *Big Bag* to help ensure
that those choices are successful (e.g., Anderson et al., 2000; *Big Bag* Research, 1997; cf. Fisch, 1998).

Together, these factors point toward a single, common sense conclusion: The more that viewers understand what they are being asked to
do—and the more they are given the opportunity to do it—the more likely
it is that they will participate.

Educational Television for Toddlers?   Several explanations have been
offered as to why, up to the age of 2, children have been better able to imitate behaviors or find hidden objects after watching live models than the
same models on videotape. Troseth and DeLoache (1998) suggested that
it may be due to young children's believing that television is "unreal" or
failing to understand that a televised image may represent current reality.
Barr and Hayne (1999) added that it may be due to children's paying
greater attention to a live model, or to perceptual factors, such as the de-
graded image on a television screen or the fact that the televised image is

typically smaller than the true size of the objects shown. Schmitt and Anderson (2002) attributed it to the television image providing poor cues to the 3-D layout of the space where objects were hidden. They argued that the cognitive burden entailed in constructing a 3-D mental representation caused children to have less cognitive capacity available for processing the information that was presented. This resulted in a weaker mental representation of the space, so children took more time and were less accurate after watching the videotape than after seeing a live demonstration.

Without additional research, it is difficult to say which of these explanations is most likely to be true. In any case, however, both the empirical data and the theoretical explanations suggest that children below the age of 3 are better able to learn from live experiences than from television.

This is not to say, of course, that very young children are unable to learn from television at all. Indeed, in the first trial in the Schmitt and Anderson (2002) study, 60% of the 2-year-olds found the object after seeing it hidden on television. The point is merely that television may be less effective than live interactions, at least for this age group.

It remains to be seen whether this also holds true (or, perhaps, might be even more true) for professionally produced television programs, such as *Teletubbies*, or for programs that carry more substantive educational content. If so, then it also remains to be seen whether some types of educational content are better or less well suited to television programs for very young children. For example, in light of researchers' explanations for performance in search tasks, it is possible that content that does not rely on size relations or three-dimensional representations (e.g., colors, letters of the alphabet) might be easier for young children to comprehend.

I would not argue strongly in favor of targeting large quantities of television at toddlers. Certainly, television should not be the only—or even the primary—medium through which children under 3 are educated. Yet, the American Academy of Pediatrics' (1997, 2001) recommendation that television be eliminated entirely for children under the age of 2 may be an overstatement as well. It is possible that very young children, too, can learn some kinds of content from age-appropriate educational television. However, this learning is likely to differ from that of older preschoolers, and it is probably best conceived as a supplement to other enriching activities that children can experience hands-on.

4

Literacy

Faster than a rolling O! Stronger than silent E! Able to leap capital T in a single bound! Look—up in the sky! It's a word! It's a plan! It's Letterman!

—The Electric Company

As we saw in chapters 2 and 3, many of the effects of educational television for preschool children (particularly *Sesame Street*) concerned aspects of literacy. These range from fairly immediate effects on letter recognition to long-term effects on subsequent reading performance. This chapter turns to the effects of literacy series targeted at school-age children.

Literacy education has long been an area of major concern to American educators, researchers, and parents alike. Over the past several decades, numerous government reports have pointed to the crucial role literacy plays in children's success, both in school and in their later lives (e.g., Bennett, 1988; Binkley, 1988; National Commission on Excellence in Education, 1983; National Research Council, 1998). Yet, research in the 1980s indicated that, although 84% of the 17-year-olds who remained in school were reading at an "intermediate" level, fewer than 5% were reading at a level often needed to achieve success in academic, business, or government environments (National Assessment of Educational Progress, 1986). More recent research has shown no meaningful improvement in the reading performance of 9-, 13-, or 17-year-olds between 1980 and 1999, and consistent performance gaps have been found as a function of SES and ethnicity (Federal Interagency Forum on Child and Family Statistics, 2001).

Moreover, book reading traditionally has not been a significant leisure activity in most children's lives. At age 9 (typically regarded as the height of the "reading craze"), almost one half of American children spend at least some time reading each day. However, interest then declines rapidly; less than one quarter of 17-year-olds report spending some free time reading books. Indeed, research studies from the 1940s through the 1980s showed that, on average, children spent only about 15 minutes per day reading (Neuman, 1991).

56

In light of this state of affairs, it is not surprising that considerable re-sources have been devoted to both formal and informal literacy educa-tion. Nor is it surprising that a number of educational television series have been created with the aim of encouraging the development of liter-acy among school-age children.

These series' approaches toward literacy have varied along with educa-tors' conceptions of "best practices" in teaching children to read and write (see, e.g., Rayner, Foorman, Perfetti, Pesetsky, & Seidenberg, 2001 for a review of trends in educational methods). In the 1970s, literacy education was dominated by an emphasis on *phonics*, that is, the correspondence be-tween letters and their related sounds. The 1980s and early 1990s saw de-bate between proponents of phonics and those who preferred a *whole-language* approach in which reading (like spoken language) was seen as developing from reading and writing in context, without explicit teach-ing of phonics (e.g., Goodman, 1989). Subsequent data refuted many of the assumptions of the whole-language approach, which has been sub-sumed into current approaches that incorporate elements of both philoso-phies. Initial reading instruction is now seen as requiring a number of components, such as exposure to spelling–sound relationships, reading for meaning, learning about the alphabetic writing system, and frequent, intensive opportunities to read. Further mastery is seen as requiring a working understanding of how sounds are represented alphabetically, suf-ficient practice to attain fluency, the background knowledge and vocabu-lary necessary to make written texts meaningful, metacognitive processes to monitor comprehension, and continued interest and motivation to read (National Research Council, 1998).

Just as the focus of educational television series about literacy has var-ied along with educational theory, so too has the research that gauged their effects. The following review encompasses impact in three areas: ba-sic reading skills, reading comprehension, and motivation to engage in reading and writing. Typically, assessments were made within a period of days or weeks after viewing. However, longer term effects of viewing *The Electric Company* are discussed as well.

IMPACT ON SCHOOL-AGE LITERACY
IN THE UNITED STATES

To the best of my knowledge, most research on the impact of literacy pro-gramming among school-age children has been conducted in English among children in the United States. Before summarizing this research, it is worth noting the parameters of the programming included in this review. Many American television series for school-age children have claimed to be "literacy shows," but the term has been used quite broadly. Often, producers or broadcasters have labeled television series as serving literacy simply because their characters have been taken from books, regardless of whether the series is designed to model reading or writing skills. For example, *The New Adventures of Winnie the Pooh* was labeled as a literacy series, even though the content of its storylines focused on socioemotional issues and had not been adapted directly from the plots of books.

In fact, such claims probably are not completely without merit. Anecdotal evidence suggests that the existence of television series based on books can stimulate greatly increased sales of the books on which they are based, a point to which I return later in discussing effects on motivation. However, this review focuses more narrowly on television series that explicitly attempt to promote reading and/or writing among children.

Basic Reading Skills

The earliest substantive research on the impact of a literacy series for school-age children was a pair of summative studies on *The Electric Company* (Fig. 4.1) in the early 1970s. *The Electric Company* employed a magazine format, with a number of comedy sketches, songs, and animations comprising a complete show. Among its more familiar elements were

FIG. 4.1. *The Electric Company*. (Photo © 2003 Sesame Workshop. All rights reserved. *The Electric Company* and all related titles, logos, and characters are trademarks of Sesame Workshop.)

"Letterman," a superhero who solved problems by changing letters in words (and thus, their referents, such as transforming a "broom" into a "groom"), and "Silhouette Blends," in which silhouettes of two profiles faced each other, with print appearing on screen as the actors pronounced partial and complete words (e.g., "bl-," "-ack," "black"). *The Electric Company* targeted poor readers in the second grade, and, in keeping with leading educational practice of the time, much of its focus lay in demonstrating the correspondence between letters (or combinations of letters) and their associated sounds.

After the first season of *The Electric Company* was produced, researchers from the Educational Testing Service conducted an experimental/control, pretest–posttest study in which more than 8,000 first- through fourth-grade children participated (Ball & Bogatz, 1973). Approximately one half of the children were shown *The Electric Company* in school for 6 months, while the remaining children were not. Before and after the 6-month exposure period, all of the children completed a paper-and-pencil battery of assessments that addressed all of *The Electric Company*'s 19 goal areas (e.g., the ability to read consonant blends, digraphs, sight words, and final E, among others); a subset of more than 1,000 children were also tested orally in one-on-one sessions with researchers.

The data showed that exposure to *The Electric Company* resulted in significant gains in almost all of the 19 goal areas, thus covering a broad range of reading skills associated with phonics instruction, as well as gains in children's ability to read for meaning. These gains were greatest for younger children (first and second graders), presumably because they had shown the lowest initial performance in the pretest. (Recall also that *The Electric Company*'s target audience was poor readers in the second grade.) The effects held across sex, ethnicity, and native language (English or Spanish). These results were confirmed by the similar, though less pronounced, effects seen in a subsequent summative study that assessed the impact of *The Electric Company*'s second season (Ball, Bogatz, Karazow, & Rubin, 1974).

Parallel effects were found more than 25 years later for another PBS early literacy series, *Between the Lions* (Fig. 4.2). Similar in approach to *The Electric Company*, *Between the Lions*, too, is a humorous, magazine-format series whose goals include promoting concepts of print, phonemic awareness, and letter–sound correspondences (plus other topics, such as whole-language elements) among early readers. Linebarger (2000) presented 17 half-hour episodes to children in kindergarten and first grade over a period of 3 to 4 weeks. Using an experimental/control, pretest–posttest design, viewers' and nonviewers' reading performance was assessed on several levels: specific program content (e.g., ability to read words that had been presented in the episodes viewed), three particular emergent literacy skills (i.e., letter naming, phonemic segmentation flu-

FIG. 4.2. *Between the Lions*. (Photo © 2003 WGBH Educational Foundation and Sirius Thinking Ltd. All rights reserved. *Between the Lions* and all related titles, logos, and characters are trademarks of WGBH Educational Foundation and Sirius Thinking Ltd.)

ency, nonsense word fluency), and more generalized early reading ability, as measured via a standardized test (including knowledge of the alphabet and its functions, and print conventions such as reading left to right).

At the posttest, after controlling statistically for a variety of background variables, kindergarten viewers performed significantly better than nonviewers on three out of five measures of specific program content, all three measures of emergent literacy skills, and the test of early reading ability. However, apart from one significant effect in phonemic segmentation fluency, there were no significant differences among first graders. This appeared to be due, in large part, to ceiling effects; it seemed that the first graders in the sample already possessed the bulk of the skills modeled in *Between the Lions,* perhaps because the data were collected near the end of the school year.

Reading Comprehension

The impact of literacy-based programming on reading comprehension was assessed in unpublished dissertation research involving *Reading Rainbow* (Leitner, 1991). Aimed at a target audience of 5- to 8-year-olds, each episode of *Reading Rainbow* presents a specific children's book that is read on-air as the camera shows illustrations taken from the book; other segments in the episode then deal with related topics in a variety of formats (e.g., documentaries, songs, interviews with children). In this study, 96 fourth graders read a book about cacti in the desert after one of three treatments: (a) watching a 30-minute episode of *Reading Rainbow* that featured the book along with other segments about the desert and animals that live there, (b) a hands-on opportunity to touch and examine a potted cactus, or (c) a verbal prereading discussion in which groups of children were told that they would be reading a book about the desert and asked to imagine the kinds of things that might appear in the book. Among the results of the study, children who had watched the relevant episode of *Reading Rainbow* showed significantly greater comprehension than those who engaged in prereading discussions; no difference emerged between the prereading discussion and hands-on conditions.

Leitner explained the data in terms of modality effects. However, her alternate explanation—that the effect was due to previewing the book through *Reading Rainbow*—seems at least as likely, as only the children in the *Reading Rainbow* condition heard the book read before they read it themselves. Thus, the crucial factor may not have been television per se, but rather, the fact that the television program provided an additional exposure to the book. Yet, whereas this presents a confounding factor in the design of the research, its implications may be less serious in drawing conclusions about the impact of *Reading Rainbow* in the real world. Indeed, this is much of the idea behind *Reading Rainbow*: to expose children to books with the intent that, subsequently, they will be inspired to read these books themselves.

Motivation to Read and Write

As noted earlier, anecdotal evidence suggests that the existence of popular television series based on books can stimulate greatly increased sales of the books on which they are based. This has been seen with regard to both educational series such as *Arthur* and noneducational series such as *Goosebumps*; in each case, sales of the preexisting book series increased greatly when their television versions gained popularity. Indeed, more systematic research on *Reading Rainbow* has reported increases of 150% to 900% in the sales of books featured in the series, and a survey of librarians found that 82% reported children asking for books they had seen on *Reading Rainbow* (Wood & Duke, 1997). However, it is not clear in these cases whether the television programs stimulated increased levels of reading among viewers—that is, whether they led to reading that would not have occurred otherwise, or whether the television-related books simply displaced reading of other books by children who would have been reading anyway.

Anecdotal evidence also points to the power of popular television characters in serving as models for literacy-related behavior. For example, one day after ABC broadcast an episode of the situation comedy *Happy Days* in which the character Fonzie got a library card, there was a fivefold increase in the number of children requesting library cards in the United States (Singer, 1982).

More systematic assessments of the motivational impact of educational television were conducted in research on *Between the Lions* and *Ghostwriter*. Data on the motivational effects of *Between the Lions* have been mixed, with significant effects in some areas but not others, and they have varied by age. Among kindergartners, parents and teachers reported no difference in children's looking at books or magazines alone, talking with others about books, writing during free time in school, or the frequency with which they asked others to read to them. However, parents reported kindergarten viewers' going to libraries or bookstores more and writing significantly more letters, notes, and stories than nonviewers at posttest. The only significant effects for first graders were in parents' ratings of the frequency with which children read books alone and teachers' reports of writing during free time (Linebarger, 2000).

Providing compelling opportunities to read and write was an explicit goal of *Ghostwriter*, a television series and multiple-media initiative for children aged 7 to 10, that included outreach materials, magazines, books, promotional activities, and software. The *Ghostwriter* television series featured a multiethnic team of children who used literacy to plot their way out of jeopardy and solve mysteries (Fig. 4.3). They were aided by Ghostwriter, an invisible ghost who could communicate with them only via reading and writing.

To date, there have been no experimental/control studies of the impact of *Ghostwriter*. However, findings from several pieces of *Ghostwriter* research suggest success in encouraging positive attitudes toward reading and writing, and in providing children with compelling opportunities to engage in such behaviors. On the most basic level, a central component of the *Ghostwriter* television series was on-screen print (e.g., in the form of the characters' messages to and from *Ghostwriter*, a variety of print-based clues, and characters' writing information in their "casebooks"). Several studies have shown that viewers typically chose to read this on-screen print; one national survey found that 83% of respondents said they read

FIG. 4.3. *Ghostwriter*. (Photo © 2003 Sesame Workshop. All rights re-served. *Ghostwriter* and all related titles, logos, and characters are trade-marks of Sesame Workshop.)

along, and an additional 8% "sometimes" did so (Nielsen New Media Ser-vices, 1993). Many viewers also kept *Ghostwriter* casebooks in which they recorded clues along with the characters on screen; one study found that approximately 25% of the girls who viewed *Ghostwriter* kept casebooks, and about 20% of the children said they regularly wrote in code (KRC Re-search & Consulting, 1994).

Yet, perhaps the clearest evidence of *Ghostwriter*'s impact on literacy lay in the large numbers of children who wrote letters to *Ghostwriter* and par-ticipated in mail-in contests that required them to engage in complex ac-tivities such as writing songs or creating their own original superheroes. Such activities were almost completely self-motivated on the part of chil-dren, and some reported that it was the first time they had written a letter. Children's participation in such activities required substantial effort—not only in writing the letters themselves, but also in learning how to address an envelope, obtaining the necessary postage, using zip codes, and so on. Despite all of these potential obstacles, more than 450,000 children wrote letters to *Ghostwriter* during its first two seasons (Children's Television Workshop, 1994). The fact that so many children chose to engage in these types of activities stands as powerful evidence of *Ghostwriter*'s ability to motivate children to become engaged in reading and writing.

Long-Term Effects

As discussed in chapter 2, longitudinal studies of *Sesame Street* found pre-school viewing of educational television to carry long-term effects on literacy behavior in first and second grade (Wright, Huston, Scantlin, et al., 2001; Zill, 2001) and as late as high school (Anderson et al, 1998, 2001; Huston et al., 2001). Very little longitudinal research has assessed the long-term impact of school-age television programs on literacy.

Nevertheless, the summative evaluation of the second season of *The Electric Company* suggested that such series can hold long-term benefits (Ball et al., 1974). Participants in the study included a subsample of children who had also participated in Ball and Bogatz's (1973) prior study when they were in first or second grade; the measures were largely identical to those used in the earlier study (described earlier). Data from the pre-test (i.e., before children saw any additional episodes of *The Electric Company*) indicated that the effect of viewers' initial exposure sustained itself during the several-month interval between studies. This continued difference could be attributed to long-term effects of viewing (rather than viewers' continuing to watch *The Electric Company* after the end of the first study) because local television stations were not broadcasting the series at that time. Interestingly, however, posttest data showed that the effect of viewing two seasons was not considerably greater than the effect of viewing one. Thus, it seems that the major impact of *The Electric Company* came from the children's initial 6-month exposure to the series, and this impact was sufficiently enduring to sustain itself several months after viewing.

IMPACT ON SCHOOL-AGE LITERACY IN OTHER COUNTRIES

As discussed in chapter 2, summative research on international coproductions of *Sesame Street* has shown these series to produce significant effects on early literacy skills (e.g., letter recognition) in Mexico, Turkey, Portugal, and Russia. However, outside of the United States, very little research has attempted to determine whether school-age television programs might hold similar potential to enhance more advanced literacy skills.

Palmer (1993) reported data on one such study, which assessed the educational impact of a literacy series that was produced in Jordan for use throughout the Arab region. Like the international series reviewed in chapter 2, *Al Manaahil* (*"The Sources"*) was a coproduction of an indigenous production company, the Jordan Company for Television, Radio, and Cinema, Ltd., and the Children's Television Workshop. Unlike those other series, however, *Al Manaahil* was targeted at school-age children in first through fourth grade (with a primary focus on early second graders) and was not adapted directly from an existing CTW series in the United States. The curriculum goals of the series centered on promoting children's literacy in Modern Standard Arabic (MSA). This presented particular challenges, because MSA is a formalized dialect of Arabic that is used in classroom reading, but is not heard or spoken in day-to-day conversation.

Research on the impact of *Al Manaahil* was conducted in collaboration by researchers from the University of Jordan and the Educational Testing Service in the United States. More than 5,000 first- through fourth-grade children in Jordan, Morocco, and Tunisia participated in the evaluation. Viewers and nonviewers of *Al Manaahil* completed a test battery of over 200 items, either once or in a pretest–posttest design. Unfortunately, Palmer did not provide a detailed account of the results of the study, which makes it impossible to evaluate the data in any depth. However, he reported that *Al Manaahil* was found to have a positive impact on children's reading skills, and that the effects held across different tests and across children who attended different types of schools.

ISSUES RAISED AND LESSONS LEARNED

Formative and summative research on school-age literacy programs has contributed greatly to our understanding of children's interaction with print shown on-screen, as well as their learning from educational television. Let us consider three areas of interest: factors that contribute to viewers' reading on-screen print, the notion of educational "content on the plotline," and possible mechanisms that might contribute toward the effects of educational television on children's subsequent motivation to engage in reading and writing.

Print-on-Screen

A frequent attribute of television programs designed to promote literacy is the presentation of print on-screen during the program. Typically, this is intended to provide viewers with concrete examples of print concepts (e.g., environmental print, letter sounds), to match words to their referents, and/or to provide compelling opportunities for children to practice reading while they watch the program. For example, highlighting parts of a word in different colors can call attention to letter–word correspondences or the blending of individual letter sounds into words. Showing a page of a book, a sign, or a shopping list on-screen can emphasize day-to-day opportunities for reading environmental print and encourage viewers to read the on-screen text along with the characters.

Clearly, however, such efforts can succeed only if the print is presented in ways that make it both possible and inviting for children (particularly poor or reluctant readers) to read it. In attempting to make print attractive to children, producers often employ bright colors, set text at unusual angles, and use animation to "liven up" the print. However, these conventions must be employed with care, or they may actually make the text more difficult for children to read. For that reason, a great deal of formative research for *The Electric Company* and *Ghostwriter* was devoted to identifying techniques by which print could be presented effectively on television.

Some of the critical factors that emerged in this research seem almost like common sense. Data pointed to the importance of large fonts, high contrast between print and backgrounds, and standard orientations of print. Print also must remain on-screen long enough to be read, and if animated, it must stay still long enough for target-age children to read it (Fisch, in press-a; Williams et al., 1997).

An innovative line of research in support of *The Electric Company* employed devices that measured children's eye movements to identify the parts of the screen that children were looking at while watching particular segments. This research was extremely valuable in identifying techniques to maximize the likelihood that children would look at (and read) the print that was shown on-screen, rather than any extraneous objects that might have been on the screen at the same time. One interesting example lies in the development of the "Silhouette Blends" format described earlier, in which silhouettes of two profiles faced each other, with print emerging from their lips as the actors pronounced partial and complete words. Early in development, a test version of one segment was produced in which full profiles of the actors were used, rather than silhouettes. Data indicated that, in this condition, children tended not to look at the on-screen print, but rather at the actors' facial features (particularly their eyes). By contrast, children's attention focused on the print when silhouettes were used in place of faces, and so the decision was made to use silhouettes in the version that was broadcast (Gibbon, Palmer, & Fowles, 1975).

Finally, research has shown that, although on-screen print must be legible, legibility alone is not sufficient to guarantee that viewers will choose to read it. Rather, print must be incorporated into the narrative of a segment or program in a way that makes it compelling for children to read it. This points to a concept that Sesame Workshop staff have taken to calling *content on the plotline*.

Content on the Plotline

The term *content on the plotline* was coined by the staff of *Ghostwriter* (e.g., Hall & Williams, 1993; Williams et al., 1997), although the principle it describes was in use long before. Educational content is considered to be "on the plotline" if it is integral to the narrative of a television program, so that the characters cannot achieve their goals without considering and/or applying the educational content. If the educational content is tangential to the narrative, it is not considered to be on the plotline.

One might expect that viewers would be more likely to attend to, process, and retain educational content when it is on the plotline than when it is not. In fact, formative research for *Ghostwriter* found that, after viewing an early episode of the series, children showed better recall of literacy-based material that was on the plotline than of other such material that was not (Hall & Williams, 1993). This finding was supported in another subject area by similar trends regarding retention of science content in *Cro* (Goodman, Rylander, & Ross, 1993; cf. Fisch, Goodman, McCann, Rylander, & Ross, 1995 and chap. 6, this volume).

Several approaches were used to place literacy on the plotline in *Ghostwriter*. On one level, the clues that the characters used to solve mysteries all hinged on literacy, so that literacy inevitably "saved the day." In addition, characters used literacy to help them deal with emotions and overcome difficult situations, such as writing (and rewriting) a note to someone when they were too upset to speak to them directly. Finally, literacy was key to the central conceit of the series, as the characters could only communicate with their supernatural friend Ghostwriter by writing messages to him and reading the messages he wrote to them.

Variations on some of these methods had also been used in *The Electric Company*, such as Letterman saving the day by changing a letter in a word, or Fargo North, Decoder puzzling out the missing letters in a written clue. Some segments featured familiar characters such as Spider-Man or Wile E. Coyote, who (like Ghostwriter) communicated only via speech balloons or written signs that were not read aloud. Thus, the only way for viewers to know what these characters were saying was to read the on-screen print.

Together, these various methods accomplished several purposes simultaneously. On one level, because reading and writing were essential to the characters' attaining their goals, such portrayals demonstrated the usefulness of literacy. On another, because the on-screen print was integral to the narrative (and, in some cases, the stories could not be fully understood without reading), these series not only provided the opportunity for children to read brief examples of print, but also gave them a reason to do so.

Promoting Motivation

As noted earlier, relatively little research has evaluated the impact of school-age programming on children's motivation to engage in literacy.

Moreover, Linebarger (2000) found inconsistent effects on motivation, with significant effects emerging in some domains of literacy but not others. Clearly, more study is needed to provide definitive answers regarding the extent to which educational series can motivate children to engage in reading and writing. However, it seems that some impact does exist, as reflected both in the presence of some significant effects in Linebarger's experimental study, and in real-world examples, such as children's letters to Ghostwriter and increased demand for books featured on television.

These effects suggest several means by which educational television programs might contribute to motivation. First, television may take advantage of the existing appeal of particular books. By making children aware of appealing or interesting books, television programs can stimulate children to obtain those specific books from a library or bookstore. Indeed, part of the process involved in selecting books for *Reading Rainbow* consists of reading books to beginning readers in schools in the New York area; only those books that elicit an enthusiastic reception from the children are included in the series (Liggett & Benfield, 1994). This process appears to have been successful, given children's increased desire for books seen in *Reading Rainbow* (Wood & Duke, 1997). Yet, as previously noted, the existing data do not indicate the *reason* for this increased demand—whether it is due to greater numbers of children reading, existing readers spending more time reading, or the same number of readers simply choosing these particular books instead of others. The first two explanations could be taken as indicators of increased motivation regarding literacy. However, the third explanation would not, because it reflects subject-matter preferences rather than increased amounts of reading.

A second, more indirect means by which educational television programs might contribute toward motivation is as a side benefit of their impact on emergent literacy skills. Viewing *The Electric Company* and *Between the Lions* has been shown to result in significantly improved performance in a variety of reading skills (Ball & Bogatz, 1973; Ball et al., 1974; Linebarger, 2000). It is possible that, as children's reading improves, they find reading to be easier and, perhaps, more enjoyable—or, at least, less effortful and aversive. If that is the case, then a significant barrier toward reading (particularly leisure reading) might be lowered.

Other means by which effects might occur stem from the way literacy is integrated into the narrative of a given educational television program. Yotive and Fisch (1998) proposed two possible ways by which television programs might contribute to interest in academic subjects such as literacy, science, or mathematics. One possibility (based in the idea of content on the plotline) is that seeing on-screen characters using literacy or other academic content in fun and important ways might cause viewers to think of these subjects as more important and interesting for themselves as well. For example, seeing literacy "save the day" in a *Ghostwriter* mystery might help viewers to appreciate the importance of literacy and thus generate further interest. Another alternative (which does not require content to be on the plotline) is that placing educational content in the context of appealing and entertaining elements might create a "halo effect" that leads viewers to perceive the educational content itself as appealing as well. Under this hypothesis, for example, a child who is not interested in reading but enjoys rap music might come to think of reading as more appealing after hearing a rap song about reading in *Ghostwriter*. In Yotive and Fisch's first hypothesis, interest is generated by demonstrating the inherent importance or enjoyability of the educational content. The latter hypothesis suggests that interest is generated less via the inherent value of the educational content itself than through its repeated association with an appealing context. Presumably, the former approach would result in more enduring effects because the critical factor is inherent in the child's construct of literacy, rather than an association with something more appealing.

Finally, the potential contribution of modeling and identification with characters should not be overlooked. Characters are often one of the factors children cite most as a reason for the appeal of series such as *Ghostwriter* (e.g., Fisch et al., 1994). If viewers identify with characters in a television program, then seeing those characters consistently engage in, value, and enjoy literacy-based activities might lead viewers to be more disposed toward engaging in such activities themselves.

Because only a limited amount of research has explored the motivational effects of literacy-based programming, it is not yet possible to say which explanation is most correct. However, this point will be revisited in chapters 5 and 6, as attitudinal effects have been studied somewhat more deeply in the areas of mathematics and science.

5

Mathematics
and Problem Solving

Announcer: The story you are about to see is a fib—but it's short.
The names are made up, but the problems are real.
Kate Monday: ... I was working the day watch out of Mathnet.
My partner's name is George Frankly. The boss is Thad Green.
My name's Monday. I'm a mathematician.

—Introduction to "Mathnet," *Square One TV*

Over the past several decades, a great deal of attention has been paid to the state of mathematics learning among American children. Concern over mathematics education is perhaps typified by the reform movement that arose in the 1980s. Motivated by several complementary factors—the United States' disappointing standing in international comparisons of mathematics achievement, significant gaps in achievement across ethnic and socioeconomic lines, and widespread attrition from mathematics classes in high school—organizations such as the National Council of Teachers of Mathematics (NCTM) and Mathematical Sciences Education Board of the National Research Council (NRC) spoke of a "crisis" in mathematics education, documenting the problems that existed and prescribing changes in the way mathematics should be taught (e.g., NCTM, 1989; NRC, 1989, 1990). Indeed, one of the eight National Education Goals that were established in 1990 stated that, "by the year 2000, United States students will be first in the world in mathematics and science achievement" (National Education Goals Panel, 1997, p. 3).

One of the features that characterized the reform movement was the recommendation that mathematics content be embedded in a context of problem solving, as opposed to decontextualized drill and practice. Another was a recognition of the need not only to convey mathematical knowledge, but also to foster positive attitudes toward mathematics. This included enhancing children's enjoyment of mathematics, their recognition of its usefulness in the real world, and their motivation to engage in mathematics.

In the years since these efforts began, positive change has been found in some aspects of mathematics performance, but not others. Nationwide data from the National Assessment of Educational Progress has shown improvement in mathematics scores among fourth-, eighth-, and twelfth-grade students between 1982 and 2000 (Barton, 1997; Federal Interagency Forum on Child and Family Statistics, 1999). However, performance gaps between ethnic and socioeconomic groups have not narrowed, and international data continue to show U.S. performance falling at or below the international average (Barton, 1997; National Educational Goals Panel, 1997).

Driven by widespread concern over mathematics education, several television series have addressed the subject of mathematics for school-age children. This chapter reviews research on their impact in three areas: knowledge of mathematics, mathematical problem solving, and attitudes toward mathematics. To my knowledge, there has been no research to date on the long-term impact of educational television in these areas, nor has substantive research been conducted outside the United States. Thus, the present review is concerned with the immediate effects of sustained viewing of mathematics programs among school-age children in the United States.

In addition to the research reviewed here, several studies have also shown that educational television programs can provide contexts for children to engage in rich mathematical activities guided by a teacher or researcher (Lampert, 1985; Sanders & Sonnad, 1980; Schauble & Peel, 1986), and that effects can be aided by the inclusion of accompanying hands-on materials or teacher guides (e.g., The Cognition and Technology Group at Vanderbilt, 1997; Foundation for Advancements in Science and Education, 1997). Research on teacher-assisted learning is discussed in chapter 9. The focus here is on children's learning from unaided viewing of educational television.

IMPACT ON SCHOOL-AGE MATHEMATICS AND PROBLEM SOLVING

In keeping with broader educational theory and practice, summative research on educational television series about mathematics has assessed impact in three primary areas: children's knowledge of mathematics, their performance in mathematical problem solving, and their attitudes toward mathematics. Let us consider each of these areas in turn.

Knowledge of Mathematics

Perhaps the most basic level on which television might exert an impact is in enhancing children's understanding of mathematical concepts. Effects on knowledge of mathematics have been found across studies and across school-age television series. Harvey, Quiroga, Crane, and Bottoms (1976; cf. Bryant et al., 1983) evaluated the impact of eight episodes of *Infinity Factory*, a mathematics series for 8- to 11-year-old children with a particular focus on African American and Latino children. The series employed a magazine format, and was intended to facilitate children's understanding of mathematical concepts (e.g., measurement, scaling) and to provide models of creative problem solving. Over the course of a trial broadcast season, a research study was conducted with more than 1,000 children to gauge the impact of the series. The study found that viewers showed significant gains in mathematics performance at posttest, although White children showed greater gains than minority viewers.

Knowledge of mathematics was also the focus of one early summative study of *Square One TV* (Fig. 5.1). Aimed at 8- to 12-year-olds, *Square One TV* employed a magazine format that included comedy sketches, game shows with real children, short films, music videos, animation, and an ongoing mathematical detective serial, "Mathnet." The goals of the series were to promote positive attitudes toward mathematics, to promote the use and application of problem-solving processes, and to pres-

FIG. 5.1. "Mathnet," *Square One TV*. (Photo © 2003 Sesame Workshop. All rights reserved. *Square One TV* and all related titles, logos, and characters are trademarks of Sesame Workshop.)

ent sound mathematical content in an interesting, accessible, and meaningful manner.

Peel, Rockwell, Esty, and Gonzer (1987) assessed children's comprehension of 10 mathematical problem-solving segments taken from the first season of *Square One TV*. Although limited by the absence of a pretest or nonviewing control group (because the study was intended to measure comprehension rather than learning per se), the study is notable for measuring comprehension on three different levels: *recall* of the problem and solution in each segment, *understanding* of the mathematics that underlay the segment, and *extension* of the mathematics content to new, related problems (a phenomenon that is generally referred to as *transfer of learning*; see chap. 11, this volume). For example, one segment, "I Love Lupy: Licorice," was a parody of *I Love Lucy* in which the lead character was hired to cut 24-inch strands of licorice into 5- and 7-inch strands with as little waste as possible. Recall questions asked children to recount Lupy's problem and the way she solved it. Understanding questions concerned the mathematics that underlay the segment, including the function and purpose of the mathematics used (e.g., "Why did Lupy line up the pieces of licorice next to the two-foot strand?"). Extension questions presented children with hands-on materials and asked them to solve similar problems with strands of different lengths.

As one might expect, comprehension at all three levels varied somewhat across the segments tested. However, a general trend emerged: The highest performance was found on the level of recall (with 88% of children providing satisfactory answers, on average), followed by understanding (71% satisfactory), which was followed in turn by extension (66% satisfactory). In this way, the study's approach and data raise an important issue that must be considered in evaluating the effectiveness of educational television: Different results may be found depending on the way in which "comprehension" is defined. This point is revisited later in the "Issues Raised and Lessons Learned" section.

Further evidence for television's ability to impart mathematics knowledge comes from research on *Cyberchase*, an animated adventure series about mathematics that premiered on PBS in 2001 and is produced in partnership by Thirteen/WNET and Nelvana (Fig. 5.2). Aimed at children aged 8 to 11, the series features three young heroes who use mathematics to thwart the schemes of The Hacker, a would-be tyrant who intends to take over an electronic cyberworld.

At the time of this writing, summative research on the impact of *Cyberchase* is underway. However, data from a pretest–posttest pilot study, conducted with more than 450 third and fourth graders, are suggestive. The pilot study did not include a control group of nonviewers, so the data must be interpreted with caution. However, the study found significant increases in knowledge of five areas of mathematical content (navigation, estimation, area, fractions, and surveys) after children watched five episodes of *Cyberchase* that covered these topics. The effects were consistent across grade, sex, and ethnicity (Rockman Et Al, 2002).

FIG. 5.2. *Cyberchase*. (Photo © 2003 Educational Broadcasting Company and Nelvana International Limited. All rights reserved. *Cyberchase* and all related titles, logos, and characters are trademarks of Educational Broadcasting Company and Nelvana International Limited.)

Effects on Problem Solving

Under the reform movement in mathematics education, effects on children's knowledge of mathematical content are important, but they are not sufficient in themselves. Rather, to be meaningful, effects should also be observed within the context of children's ability to solve mathematical problems (a domain touched on in the aforementioned Peel et al. [1987] study of *Square One TV*).

As discussed in chapters 2 and 3, several studies found significant gains in preschoolers' problem-solving performance as a result of their exposure to educational television series (Anderson et al., 2000; Bryant, Mulliken, et al., 1999; Hodapp, 1977; Mulliken & Bryant, 1999). Thus, the questions to be addressed in this chapter are: (a) whether parallel effects might be found for mathematical problem solving among school-age viewers, and (b) whether such programs might impact on the process of problem solving—that is, the strategies and heuristics children use—as well as the solutions they produce. (Recall that studies with preschool children typically have examined accuracy and/or response time, rather than the heuristics used.)

Problem solving was at the heart of a tightly controlled experimental/ control, pretest–posttest study that assessed the impact of *Square One TV* on its viewers' ability to engage in mathematical problem-solving (Hall, Esty, & Fisch, 1990; Hall, Fisch, et al., 1990). In this study, fifth graders in two public elementary schools in Corpus Christi, Texas (where *Square One TV* had not been broadcast) viewed 30 episodes of *Square One TV* over a period of 8 weeks, while their counterparts in two other schools did not. A subsample of 48 children (24 viewers and 24 nonviewers), individually matched for sex, SES, ethnicity, and performance on a standardized mathematics test, participated in extensive, task-based interviews before and after the 8-week viewing period. Interviewers and coders did not know which children were viewers and which were not, and the children did not know of the interviewers' connection to *Square One TV*.

Problem solving was tested via several hands-on, nonroutine mathematical Problem-Solving Activities (PSAs), each of which could be solved through a number of approaches. For example, one set of problems presented children with a mathematical game and asked them to figure out what was wrong with the game and how to fix it. (In fact, the problem lay in probability—one player had a much greater chance of winning—and there were several valid ways to fix it.) From pretest to posttest, viewers showed significant gains in the number and variety of problem-solving actions and heuristics they used to solve problems (e.g., looking for patterns, transforming problems); at the posttest, viewers used a significantly greater number and variety than nonviewers. Perhaps as a result, viewers also showed significant gains in the mathematical completeness and sophistication of their solutions; that is, their solutions to two of the three sets of PSAs became significantly more complete and sophisticated after watching the 30 episodes of *Square One TV*, whereas nonviewers showed no significant change. Thus, exposure to *Square One TV* affected both the ways children worked on problems and the solutions they reached. Moreover, these effects occurred regardless of the children's sex, ethnicity, SES, or performance on standardized mathematics tests. This was very encouraging, as girls and minority children have been considered to be "at risk" for mathematics education (e.g., National Research Council, 1989).

Attitudes Toward Mathematics

The same study of *Square One TV* also assessed the series' effects on children's attitudes toward mathematics (Hall, Fisch, et al., 1990). In contrast to previous studies in mathematics education, which had assessed attitudes via fairly limited pencil-and-paper scales, attitudes in this study were assessed via in-depth interviews that were then coded under elaborate coding systems by blind coders.

Pretest–posttest comparisons showed significant differences between viewers and nonviewers in several attitudinal domains. Viewers showed significantly greater gains than nonviewers in their conceptions of what "math" is (i.e., beyond rote skills such as basic arithmetic), their motivation to pursue challenging mathematical tasks, and the number of times they spontaneously talked about enjoying mathematics and problem solving throughout the interview (i.e., without being asked directly about enjoyment). Again, there was no consistent mediation of the effects by sex, ethnicity, or SES. The only dimension that failed to exhibit a significant effect was children's conceptions of the usefulness of mathematics; in light of the overall pattern of positive effects, it was unclear whether there was truly no effect or whether the measures were not sufficiently sensitive to detect it.

Some of these effects found parallels in Rockman Et Al's (2002) pilot study on the impact of *Cyberchase*. As noted earlier, the absence of a control group in this study means that the data must be interpreted with caution. With that caveat, though, the study found that, after watching five episodes of *Cyberchase*, viewers showed significant increases in their interest in and attitudes toward mathematics. In addition, viewers reported higher levels of confidence in their ability to solve mathematical problems. Interestingly, however, increases in the breadth of children's definitions of "math" did not achieve significance, even though this was one of the attitudinal dimensions that showed the greatest change in Hall, Fisch, et al.'s (1990) study of the impact of *Square One TV.* Possible reasons for the disparity across series are discussed next.

Notably, both *Square One TV* and *Cyberchase* were targeted at elementary-school children, at ages before attitudes toward mathematics begin their sharp decline. The intent was to "inoculate" children by promoting positive attitudes at a point before negative pressures would begin to come into play. Conversely, a series of 15-minute programs called *Futures* was targeted at students already in junior high school. Hosted by noted mathematics teacher Jaime Escalante, *Futures* premiered in 1990 and presented interviews with scientists, engineers, and other professionals (e.g., athletes, fashion designers) in an attempt to stimulate interest in careers that involve mathematics and science.

The impact of the series was evaluated via an experimental/control, pretest–posttest study with 176 children aged 12 to 14 (Research Communications Ltd., 1992; cf. Chen, 1994a). Data were collected before viewers watched the series, after the completion of the viewing period, and again one month later. The richness of the data is limited by the fact that the study relied on paper-and-pencil measures in which children indicated the degree to which they agreed with a series of printed statements (e.g., "Careers that use math can be creative"). With that in mind, however, the series was found to have a significant impact on viewers' attitudes.

Unlike *Square One TV* and *Cyberchase*, however, the significant effects produced by *Futures* did not take the form of increases in viewers' attitudes. Rather, the effect was to mitigate a decline in viewers' attitudes. That is, both viewers and nonviewers showed declines from pretest to posttest, but nonviewers' attitudes declined more than viewers'. It is not clear whether the difference between the effect of *Futures* and the other two series is due to the older target age group for *Futures*, the measures used in the studies, or features of the programs themselves.

ISSUES RAISED AND LESSONS LEARNED

Parallel to research on the impact of educational television on literacy (chap. 4, this volume), research in the area of mathematics has demonstrated the potential for educational television to hold significant benefits for school-age viewers. Educational television series have been found to promote growth in children's knowledge of mathematics, their problem-solving skills, and their attitudes toward mathematics. These effects have been found to hold across gender, ethnicity, SES, and past performance on standardized tests of mathematics.

In light of the significant effects on literacy that have already been reviewed, one might imagine that data reported in this chapter serve merely to prove that television can also produce significant effects in the domain of another academic subject area. Certainly, part of the value of this research does lie in its application of educational television to mathematics and problem solving. However, when considered alongside research in literacy, the studies reviewed here also serve to deepen our understanding of the nature of the impact of educational television, as well as the means by which effects might occur.

Defining "Comprehension"

Typically, one of the chief foci in research on the impact of educational television lies in evaluating children's comprehension of or learning from the programs they watch. In many ways, this would seem to be a fairly straightforward variable to measure, providing an objective criterion for judging the success of the program.

However, by assessing comprehension on three different levels—recall, understanding, and extension (i.e., transfer)—the Peel et al. (1987) study of *Square One TV* highlighted the degree to which even seemingly objective evaluations rely on implicit assumptions. When can we say that children have comprehended something that they saw in an educational television program (or, indeed, in their classroom or elsewhere)? Is it when they can recall the content for a tester or evaluator? Is it when they can demonstrate a deeper understanding of the underlying concepts? Or is it only when they can apply the same principle to a new problem or situation? The criteria and measures that one uses to assess impact reflect the assumptions of the teacher or researcher who is conducting the evaluation—assumptions that are often implicit rather than explicit. Yet, these implicit assumptions can exert a significant impact on the results that are obtained, as illustrated by Peel et al. (1987) finding different rates of performance in response to questions designed to measure recall, understanding, and extension. Similarly, as discussed in chapter 2, Hodapp (1977) found that, after a single exposure to a problem-solving segment from *Sesame Street*, preschool viewers could replicate the solution shown (analogous to Peel et al's level of "recall" or "understanding") but could not apply the same solution procedure to a novel problem (analogous to Peel et al's level of "extension").[1]

This point takes on even more importance when we consider the fact that research on the impact of a given educational television series often is

---

[1]Possible reasons for this phenomenon are discussed in the context of science and technology in chapter 6. A broader theoretical mechanism to help explain transfer of learning from educational television is proposed in chapter 11.

not conducted purely out of theoretical interest, but also for the sake of accountability to funding agencies and other interested parties. In that context, then, we can conceive of "success" as dependent not only on the observed impact of the series itself, but also on the criterion set by the judge or evaluator.

Exploring Mechanisms for Impact

Impact on Problem Solving.   Several studies of the impact of educational television on problem solving among preschoolers were reviewed in Chapter 3 (Anderson et al., 2000; Bryant, Mulliken, et al., 1999; Mulliken & Bryant, 1999). Whereas those studies examined impact on children's solutions, the Hall, Esty, et al. (1990) and Hall, Fisch, et al.(1990) summative studies of *Square One TV* examined both the mathematical sophistication of children's solutions and also the problem-solving heuristics that they used to reach those solutions. As a result, the *Square One TV* study lends greater insight into the means by which effects arose.

In attempting to explain the effects of *Square One TV*, Esty, Hall, and Fisch (1990) looked at the relationship between heuristics and solutions, as well as the relationships between both of these variables and exposure to *Square One TV*. It is not surprising that they found a highly significant, positive correlation between the number and variety of heuristics children used and the sophistication of their solutions; in other words, the use of a greater number and variety of heuristics was associated with reaching more sophisticated solutions. A statistical model-fitting analysis indicated that *Square One TV* actually had a threefold effect. Sustained viewing of the series produced: (a) a direct effect on children's use of problem-solving heuristics, (b) a direct effect on the sophistication of children's solutions, and (c) an indirect effect on solutions, mediated by its effect on heuristics—that is, increasing the number and variety of heuristics also allowed children to reach more sophisticated solutions (Fig. 5.3).

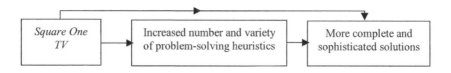

FIG. 5.3. Model of the impact of *Square One TV* on children's mathematical problem solving (after Esty et al., 1990).

Given that viewing *Square One TV* led to children's using a greater number and variety of heuristics, the question remains as to how that effect came about. Esty et al. (1990) proposed three possible mechanisms by which the effect might have occurred:

1. Exposure to the series might have caused children to add new heuristics to their repertoires of behaviors.
2. The number of heuristics in children's repertoires could have remained unchanged, but children might have come to see their existing heuristics as applicable to a broader array of problems.
3. The heuristics themselves might have been unchanged, but children could have become more motivated to use them.

Esty et al. hypothesized that the effects of *Square One TV* were most likely attributable to some combination of these factors, rather than one factor in isolation. In particular, however, they observed that the role of motivation was supported by a significant correlation between children's use of heuristics and their motivation (as measured in the attitudinal portion of the study). However, subsequent analysis suggested that the notion of motivation leading to the use of problem-solving heuristics did not quite fit the data, as we shall see in the next section.

Relationships Among Dimensions of Attitude.   After the Hall, Fisch, et al. (1990) study was completed, Fisch and Hall (1991) conducted a series of qualitative and quantitative post hoc analyses to examine relationships among various aspects of attitudes and problem solving. These analyses were designed to lend insight into the ways in which the various dimensions of attitude related to each other, the ways in which they related to children's problem-solving performance, and the paths by which each variable was affected by viewing *Square One TV.*

One set of analyses examined relationships among these dimensions in the pretest, before viewers were exposed to *Square One TV.* Two findings were particularly notable. One was a close relationship between children's enjoyment of mathematics and their motivation to pursue it. The relationship appeared to be bidirectional, with children citing each dimension as contributing to the other—that is, children explained that they were motivated to engage in mathematics because they enjoyed it, and the sources of their enjoyment reflected an engagement orientation toward motivation. The second notable finding was that children's constructs of mathematics (i.e., their conceptions of what "math" is) played a central role in their enjoyment, motivation, and perceptions of the usefulness of mathematics. Broad conceptions of mathematics were associated with more positive attitudes in each of these dimensions.

Thus, it would seem that one potential route by which educational television (or even formal education) could enhance children's attitudes toward mathematics would be to expand children's conceptions of what "math" is. Like the Hall, Fisch, et al. (1990) study, past research in mathematics education has shown children's conceptions of "math" to be limited to a set of memorized, rote procedures involving numbers that are applied to problems with only one answer (e.g., Schoenfeld, 1988). As educational television helps viewers develop a broader view of mathematics that reaches beyond arithmetic and decontextualized number skills, they can come to see mathematics as useful and more widely applicable in the real world, they may enjoy it more, and they may become more motivated to pursue mathematics themselves.

With that in mind, it is worth revisiting some of the research on attitude that was discussed earlier. In particular, both *Square One TV* and *Cyberchase* were found to produce significant effects on children's attitudes toward mathematics. However, the effects of the two series differed in that *Square One TV* produced significant effects on children's constructs of mathematics, whereas *Cyberchase* led to only a nonsignificant trend in this area.

To what can we attribute the disparity? An examination of the two series suggests that the answer may actually be quite simple. Both series exposed viewers to numerous instances of characters using a broad range of mathematics to solve problems in meaningful contexts. However, *Square One TV* frequently labeled those instances explicitly as "math," whether in songs such as "That's Math," video game parodies like "Mathman," or the exploits of crimefighting mathematicians in "Mathnet." *Cyberchase* took a different approach; it also presented various examples of mathematics, but without using the word "math" as often. Given children's naive tendency to define mathematics in very narrow terms, it is possible that viewers learned about and grew interested in the specific topics presented in *Cyberchase*, but did not necessarily recognize all of them as mathematics. A similar phenomenon appeared in a study on attitudes toward science and technology, as is discussed in chapter 6.

Relationship Between Attitude and Problem Solving. In their analysis of data from the summative study of *Square One TV*, Fisch and Hall (1991) found significant positive correlations among children's motivation, their ability to generate real-life applications for mathematics, and the number and variety of heuristics they used when working on problem-solving tasks. As noted in the previous discussion of problem solving, it would be reasonable to imagine that increases in motivation led to increases in children's use of heuristics. However, a statistical model-fitting analysis suggested that, in fact, the causality was in the opposite direction:

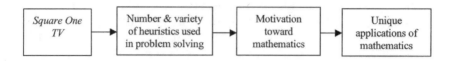

FIG. 5.4. Model of the relationship among *Square One TV*, motivation, and perceived usefulness of mathematics as reflected in ability to gener-

Exposure to *Square One TV* led to increases in problem solving, which contributed to higher levels of motivation. In turn, the effect on motivation contributed to children's ability to generate unique applications for mathematics (Fig. 5.4) Thus, it appears that providing children with a richer repertoire of problem-solving tools also served to strengthen their inclination to put these skills to work, and helped children recognize a wider range of situations in which those skills can be applied.

More broadly, this example illustrates the degree to which effects of educational television often are not simple, unitary causal relationships. Salomon (e.g., 1991; Salomon, Perkins, & Globerson, 1991) wrote of the need to consider a "cloud of correlated variables" in educational research, and the same is true here. Mental constructs such as repertoires of heuristics or attitudes toward academic subjects are complex in themselves, so it stands to reason that the paths toward effects in these areas would be complex as well.

The curriculum goals of most educational television series have taken multidimensional approaches that strive for impact in attitudinal or affective domains at the same time as they address knowledge or cognitive skills. However, even when research has assessed impact on both cognition and affect, the studies have typically tested for effects on each outcome variable individually, without also looking at relationships among them. As a result, there is little empirical evidence to provide insight into the role that attitude and affect might play in television's effects on academic knowledge or skills. Similarly, there is equally little evidence to speak to the role of knowledge and cognition in the impact of educational television on attitude toward academic subjects. Future research is required to explore these relationships more fully, and to yield a more complete understanding of the impact of educational television.

6

Science and Technology

Well, as I always say, sometimes you have to do the wrong stuff
to find out what the right stuff is.

—Ms. Frizzle, Scholastic's *The Magic School Bus*

There is a long history of science programming on children's television, from the debut of *Mr. Wizard* in 1951 through more recent efforts, such as *Beakman's World* and *Science Court*. To date, science programming has taken many forms and employed many formats, ranging from presenters speaking fairly directly to the camera, to documentary-based series, to narratives presented as animated cartoons.

As in the case of literacy and mathematics (see chaps. 4 and 5, this volume), the motivation behind many science series stems from broader calls for widespread informal science education. As society becomes increasingly dependent on technology, the need for effective science education becomes ever more critical. Yet, from the 1970s through the 1990s, numerous studies pointed toward deficits in science education in the United States. For example, a series of national assessments found steady declines in the science performance of 17-year-olds between 1969 and 1977, and performance in 1986 remained substantially lower than it had been in 1969 (National Assessment of Educational Progress, 1991; National Commission on Excellence in Education, 1983). An international study in 1992 showed the performance of U.S. students to be disappointing in comparison to children from other countries (Postlethwaite & Wiley, 1992). And although 1997 data from the Third International Mathematics and Science Study showed American fourth graders to outperform children in 19 out of 25 countries, the picture was very different in eighth grade, where children in 20 out of 40 countries outperformed American students (National Education Goals Panel, 1997). Motivation and general attitudes toward science also declined between grades 6 and 10, as reflected in a consistent trend of large numbers of students (particularly girls and minority students) choosing not to take three or more years of science classes in high school (e.g., Jones, Mullis, Raizen, Weiss, & Weston, 1992; Simpson & Oliver, 1990; U.S. Department of Education, 1982).

In response to these issues, the 1980s and 1990s saw the growth of a reform movement that called for changes in the way science is taught in the United States. This movement has been typified by efforts such as Project 2061 and the *Benchmarks for Science Literacy*, both produced by the American Association for the Advancement of Science (AAAS), and by the *National Science Education Standards* created by the National Research Council (AAAS, 1993; National Research Council, 1995; Rutherford & Algren, 1990). All of these efforts are characterized by a greater emphasis on hands-on experiments and activities, tying science to real-life contexts and children's prior knowledge, and finding ways of teaching that actively engage children and foster positive attitudes toward science. In addition, many have stressed the need not only for renewed efforts in school, but for informal science education outside the classroom as well (e.g., Falk, Donovan, & Woods, 2001; Rutherford & Algren, 1990; Tressel, 1988).

IMPACT ON SCHOOL-AGE SCIENCE AND TECHNOLOGY

Over the course of television's many years of science programming, a great deal of anecdotal evidence has supported the notion that children can acquire science knowledge and be motivated to conduct their own experiments as a result of watching educational television programs. For example, Don Herbert (1988), a.k.a. "Mr. Wizard," reported that many adults have told him that their childhood exposure to *Mr. Wizard* taught them to think scientifically, kindled an interest in science, or motivated them to pursue careers in science or technology. Similarly, Mielke (1988) told the story of a boy who brought a scale into an elevator and weighed himself as the elevator moved up and down, after watching a similar experiment on *3-2-1 Contact*.

These sorts of anecdotes, although suggestive, do not provide concrete proof of television's power in science education. This chapter reviews more systematic research on the educational impact of several science-based television series. In particular, the review covers the impact of educational television programs on children's knowledge regarding science and technology, their exploration and experimentation, and their attitudes toward science and technology. It is interesting to note that the series to be considered span several very different genres—presenter-based demonstrations, magazine-format documentary, and Saturday morning cartoon—but have all produced a consistent pattern of significant effects.[1]

---

[1]It is worth noting that a similar pattern of effects was also found for the 1990s science-based children's radio series, *Kinetic City Super Crew*. Like the various television series discussed here, *Kinetic City Super Crew* presented both a fictional story (as in Scholastic's *The Magic School Bus* or *Cro*) and informational features *(con't.)*

Knowledge of Science

Numerous educational television series have been found to produce significant gains in viewers' knowledge of specific science content. Science learning from television has been documented among audiences ranging from preschool viewers of *Sesame Street* (Truglio et al., 2001) to older adults viewing the science documentary series *Nova* or news inserts featuring Mr. Wizard (Gagne & Burkman, 1982; Research Communications Ltd., 1987).

Among television series aimed at school-age children, perhaps the greatest number of studies has concerned *3-2-1 Contact*, a magazine-format series targeting 8- to 12-year-olds, particularly girls and minority children (Fig. 6.1). *3-2-1 Contact* relied heavily on live-action, mini-documentary segments in which teenage hosts investigated scientific topics or interviewed real scientists in a variety of fields and settings. In addition, the series included animations, songs, and a dramatized mys-

FIG. 6.1. *3-2-1 Contact*. (Photo © 2003 Sesame Workshop. All rights reserved. *3-2-1 Contact* and all related titles, logos, and characters are trademarks of Sesame Workshop.)

(as in *3-2-1 Contact* or *Bill Nye the Science Guy*). Here, too, exposure led to significant differences between listeners' and nonlisteners' knowledge of science content and engagement in home science activities (Flagg, 1994).

tery serial called "The Bloodhound Gang." Each week of shows was built around a specific theme, such as scaling, electricity, or outer space, with many of that week's segments corresponding to some aspect of that theme.

Research on the impact of *3-2-1 Contact* is somewhat limited by the methods used. Almost all of the studies relied largely on paper-and-pencil (typically multiple-choice) quizzes to assess comprehension, and on pencil-and-paper checklists (e.g., concerning occupations that children would like to have or that they saw as involving science) to assess impact on science interest, rather than on interview methods that might provide richer portraits of children's knowledge and attitudes.

Despite this limitation, however, a consistent pattern of effects was observed with regard to comprehension. Studies varied in the number of episodes presented to children (from 10 to more than 40). At all levels of exposure, however, these studies were unanimous in demonstrating that viewing *3-2-1 Contact* resulted in positive effects on children's comprehension of the science topics presented, as reflected in significant increases in viewers' performance on pencil-and-paper quizzes (Cambre & Fernie, 1985; Johnston, 1980; Johnston & Luker, 1983; Wagner, 1985). The effects of *3-2-1 Contact* were often strongest among girls, one of the populations that has often been found to be underrepresented in science (e.g., Levin, Sabar, & Libman, 1991).

Other studies, using either pencil-and-paper measures or task-based interviews, have found parallel effects for the science content of other television series. In the United States, similar effects have been seen among 8- to 10-year-old viewers of *Bill Nye the Science Guy* (Rockman Et Al, 1996) and 6- to 10-year-old viewers of two animated series, *Cro* and Scholastic's *The Magic School Bus* (ARC Consulting LLC, 1995; Fay, Teasley, Cheng, Bachman, & Schnakenberg, 1995a; Goodman, Rylander, & Ross, 1993; cf. Fay, Yotive, et al., 1995; Fisch et al., 1995). Outside the United States, viewers have acquired science knowledge from the Australian series *Australia Naturally* (Noble & Creighton, 1981), and an assortment of individual episodes of *Owl TV, Know How, Tomorrow's World, Body Matters*, and *Erasmus Microman* in the United Kingdom (Clifford, Gunter, & McAleer, 1995).

As one might expect, several studies have shown comprehension to vary as a function of characteristics both of the viewers and of the specific material tested. Older children often have shown better comprehension of science content than younger children, presumably because of their greater base of prior knowledge, stronger comprehension skills, and/or greater articulation in responding to the measures used. At the same time, even within a given television series, comprehension and learning also have been found to be stronger for some episodes than others (ARC Consulting LLC, 1995; Goodman et al., 1993). Potential reasons for differences among episodes are discussed in the "Issues Raised and Lessons Learned" section at the end of this chapter.

Exploration and Experimentation

In addition to measuring children's recall and understanding of science content, research on Scholastic's *The Magic School Bus* also asked children to describe how the characters in the series learn. In each animated episode of the series (aimed at children ages 6 through 9), a flamboyant teacher named Ms. Frizzle used a magical school bus to take her class on a "field trip" to learn about a science concept; for example, they might venture undersea to explore marine life or shrink to microscopic size to examine the workings of the human body from the inside. Data from focus groups found that some viewers recognized the characters as active learners who engaged in exploration, experimentation, and doing things (ARC Consulting LLC, 1995).

Research on another series, *Bill Nye the Science Guy*, focused more directly on viewers' own use of the process of science. Parallel to research on *Square One TV* and mathematical problem solving (chap. 5, this volume), a study by Rockman Et Al (1996) assessed the impact of exposure to *Bill Nye the Science Guy* on children's hands-on science experimentation. Designed for children aged 8 to 10, each episode of *Bill Nye the Science Guy* featured real-life comedian and scientist Bill Nye conducting experiments and demonstrating scientific concepts (often with surprising effects) in a variety of settings. In this study, a series of hands-on science tasks (e.g., classifying animals, figuring out interesting ways to use tops) were presented to 387 viewers or nonviewers before an extended viewing period in which children viewed at least 12 episodes of the series in school or at home; the same problems were presented to another 462 viewers and nonviewers after the viewing period. After viewing, viewers scored higher in their process of exploration (e.g., making more observations and comparisons) and in the sophistication with which they classified animals (e.g., using categories such as "mammals" instead of number of legs). Thus, consistent with problem-solving data on *Square One TV* (Hall, Esty, & Fisch, 1990; Hall, Fisch, et al., 1990), exposure to *Bill Nye the Science Guy* held significant benefits for both the processes children used and the sophistication of their solutions.

Attitudes Toward Science

Apart from conveying knowledge and modeling process, the goals of *3-2-1 Contact*, *Bill Nye the Science Guy*, and *Cro* all include stimulating positive attitudes toward science and/or technology as well. As in the research on knowledge described earlier, research on the impact of *3-2-1 Contact* on children's attitudes toward science is somewhat limited by its reliance on pencil-and-paper measures. Nevertheless, significant effects on children's interest in science and images of scientists were found across these studies, although they were moderate in size and less consistent than effects on knowledge (Cambre & Fernie, 1985; Johnston, 1980; Johnston & Luker, 1983; Wagner, 1985). It is not clear whether *3-2-1 Contact* had less impact in this area, or whether the more moderate effects were a function of the relatively limited measures used.

A wider array of measures was employed to measure interest in science and technology in a summative study of *Cro*, a Saturday-morning animated series for children aged 6 to 11 (Fay, Teasley, et al., 1995; cf. Fay, Yotive, et al., 1995). *Cro* featured the adventures of a Cro-Magnon boy and a group of talking mammoths (Fig. 6.2). It was designed to promote knowledge of and interest in technology (i.e., simple machines such as levers and gears).

Methods used in the study included pencil-and-paper measures, in-depth interviews, and behavioral observations of children as they

FIG. 6.2. *Cro*. (Photo © 2003 Sesame Workshop. All rights reserved. *Cro* and all related titles, logos, and characters are trademarks of Sesame Workshop.)

chose to engage in technology-related versus -unrelated activities. Under an experimental/control, pretest–posttest design, children who viewed eight episodes of *Cro* were compared to nonviewers, who watched eight episodes of another animated, educational series that did not concern science (*Where on Earth Is Carmen Sandiego?*). Results pointed to a variety of significant effects concerning interest. Some of these were: *Cro* viewers showed significantly greater pretest–posttest gains than nonviewers in their interest in doing technology activities related to episodes of *Cro* that they had seen (e.g., making a catapult). They exhibited greater interest in learning more about the technology content of particular episodes. And they were significantly more likely to engage in hands-on activities connected to two of the episodes when given a choice among these activities and other, nontechnology activities. However, gains were not significant for interest in technology activities that had not been presented in *Cro*, perhaps because the children did not possess a mental construct of "technology" that was sufficiently broad to encompass all of these types of activities (Fay, Teasley, et al., 1995; along similar lines, see chap. 5 for a discussion of effects of *Square One TV* and *Cyberchase* on children's constructs of mathematics.)

Finally, Rockman Et Al's (1996) evaluation of *Bill Nye the Science Guy* found little change in viewers' attitudes toward science as reflected in pencil-and-paper measures, but this was attributable to ceiling effects, as children achieved high scores even in the pretest. By contrast, parent reports suggested the presence of some positive effects on motivation: 61% believed that their children's interest in science increased to some degree after watching *Bill Nye the Science Guy*, almost all believed that their interest in participating in science activities increased, and 35% reported that their children talked with them about the content of specific episodes of the television series. Naturally, however, the latter data must be interpreted with caution as they are based on parent perceptions rather than direct assessments of children.

ISSUES RAISED AND LESSONS LEARNED

In many ways, the consistent pattern of significant effects across science-based television series replicates the effects that were reviewed in the domains of school-age literacy and mathematics (chaps. 4 and 5, this volume). Just as in the case of mathematics, educational television programs were found to produce significant effects on children's knowledge of science and technology, processes of exploration and experimentation, and attitudes toward science and technology.

In addition, this research, coupled with published accounts of experiences in producing television programs about science, also lends insight into the constraints and opportunities posed by a variety of television genres (e.g., documentary, animated cartoon), as well as characteristics that can be built into educational television programs to maximize their effectiveness.

Genres of Television: Constraints and Opportunities

Children's television series about science have been produced in a wide range of genres, including minidocumentaries (e.g., *3-2-1 Contact*), presenters speaking directly to camera (e.g., *Mr. Wizard, Bill Nye the Science Guy*), live-action mystery stories (e.g., the "Bloodhound Gang" segments in *3-2-1 Contact*), and humorous narratives in animated cartoons (e.g., *Cro*, Scholastic's *The Magic School Bus*), among others. As the aforementioned research demonstrates, programs within all of these genres have been found to yield significant benefits among their target audiences. Thus, it is not the case that any one genre is best suited to the treatment of science (or, perhaps, other academic subjects) on television. Rather, if executed properly, many different genres can be employed to convey science content effectively.

That said, it is also the case that each genre has its own particular strengths and weaknesses. Each genre operates within its own set of production-based assumptions and constraints, and when the program is broadcast, viewers come to the screen with different sets of expectations for different genres.

To illustrate this point, Fisch, Yotive, McCann, Cohen, and Chen (1996) compared the treatment of science in the documentary segments of *3-2-1 Contact* and the Saturday-morning cartoon narrative of *Cro*. Although the curriculum goals of the two series overlapped greatly, their formats made them very different television shows. It would be as difficult to imagine the teenage hosts of *3-2-1 Contact* jumping back in time to the Ice Age to rescue a talking mammoth from the other side of a gorge as it would be to imagine *Cro*'s prehistoric cast leaping forward in time to interview a doctor about hypothermia. Such incongruities of format would likely be jarring to viewers, and could interfere with engagement and/or learning.

As a result, although all of these genres may serve as effective vehicles for science content as a whole, some *types* of science content might be better suited to one genre than another. In addition, the presentation of science content also must be tailored to fit the genre of the program.

Presentation of Content. In comparing *3-2-1 Contact* and *Cro*, Fisch et al. (1996) noted several ways in which genre affected the framing and presentation of science content. Where fairly straightforward demonstrations and explanations could be fit into *3-2-1 Contact* simply by having characters address the audience or host/interviewers directly, these had to be fit into a fictional narrative in *Cro*, and the fit had to seem natural. Characters in *Cro* could not suddenly break the "fourth wall" and interrupt the ongoing story to give a lengthy explanation to viewers; rather, such explanations needed to occur in the course of conversation among characters. To seem natural, this often meant that explanations had to be broken up and spread over the course of the story, rather than taking place in a single, lengthy speech.

For example, the topic of light and refraction was approached in *3-2-1 Contact* through demonstrations of the effects of different-shaped lenses (with a teenage host speaking directly to camera) and a visit to a lighthouse to learn how beams of light are focused to be visible at greater distances. By contrast, *Cro* approached light and reflection through a story in which the prehistoric characters discovered some shiny, reflective rocks that they dubbed "see-myselfers" (i.e., natural mirrors).

In addition, as an animated cartoon, the episode of *Cro* included numerous jokes, instances of visual humor and slapstick, and an emotionally compelling "B-story," none of which were present to the same degree in *3-2-1 Contact*. As a result, the "density" of the science content probably felt heavier to viewers of the *3-2-1 Contact* segments than to viewers of *Cro*.

Matching Topics to Genres.   Although it is true that a particular topic might be handled differently across genres, it is also true that some topics may lend themselves more easily to one genre than another. In some ways, animated cartoons allow for greater freedom and flexibility in choosing topics. For example, because *Cro* was animated, the series was free to present tremendous, intricate machines (e.g., catapults, windmill-powered ski lifts, wheel-and-belt systems) that would have been prohibitively expensive to build for presentation in a live-action television series. Similarly, Scholastic's *The Magic School Bus* has set its stories in settings ranging from deep space to the inside of a loaf of bread (to explore food chemistry and changes that occur during baking), which would require a lavish special effects budget to replicate in live-action.

Conversely, the documentary format offers freedom of a different kind. Narrative genres are limited by the fact that the science topic must lend itself to serving as the center of a compelling story. The *Cro* production team, for example, demonstrated remarkable creativity in producing engaging stories set in prehistoric times that could convey the workings of machines such as windmills or sophisticated concepts such as storage of energy. However, creating such stories is not always easy. For some topics, it may be easier—and perhaps more effective—to use the more direct, matter-of-fact presentation provided in a documentary format.

Another strength of the documentary format lies in its ability to portray real-life applications of science. Segments in *3-2-1 Contact* have portrayed people using science in real-life occupations ranging from doctors to lighthouse keepers to glass blowers, and have explicitly labeled these as applications of science. This breadth of applications was a natural outgrowth of the documentary genre, in which viewers expected to see different types of people interviewed each day. By contrast, the prehistoric setting of *Cro* made it more difficult to ground applications in the real, modern-day world.

Industry Considerations and Reach.   Finally, on a practical level, it is also worth noting that the choice of genre holds implications for broadcast and reach as well. One of the primary motivations for producing *Cro* as an animated cartoon was so that it would be broadcast on Saturday-morning network television, which reaches a larger and different audience of school-age viewers than PBS. Because Saturday-morning commercial television consists primarily of animated cartoons, *Cro* was much more likely to be aired by a major network if it, too, fell within this genre. Indeed, subsequent efforts to syndicate episodes of *3-2-1 Contact*—a live-action, documentary-style series—on commercial television met with limited success.

Characteristics of Effective Science Programs

Although research has found evidence of children's learning science content from various television series, it is also the case that not all treatments of science on television are equally effective. Summative research on both *Cro* and Scholastic's *The Magic School Bus* found that children understood the science or technology content in some episodes better than others (ARC Consulting LLC, 1995; Goodman et al., 1993). Based on examinations of the relevant episodes, the researchers drew conclusions as to the characteristics of the episodes that may have made some episodes more effective than others. Complementary sets of characteristics were identified on the basis of formative research on *3-2-1 Contact* (Mielke & Chen, 1983) and the experiences of the production team in creating *Les Débrouillards* ("*The Resourceful Ones*"), a magazine-format science series produced in Canada (Frenette, 1991).

Interestingly, many of the characteristics identified in these various series are the same. In addition, they also parallel characteristics identified in preschool and school-age television programs in other academic subject areas (e.g., Fisch, in press-a; chap. 2, this volume). Indeed, some of these characteristics were subsequently built into all of the *Cro* episodes produced in Season II, and significant differences between viewers and nonviewers were found for all of the episodes tested (Fay, Teasley, et al., 1995a).

Taken together, experiences with these series point to the following characteristics as contributing to effective treatments of science and technology on television. The television series listed beside each entry are the ones for which it has been discussed explicitly in past literature. However, the same characteristic certainly may be applicable to other series as well:

- Focusing on concrete, visual phenomena or devices, as opposed to abstract principles (*Cro*, *Les Débrouillards*, Scholastic's *The Magic School Bus*)
- Using unusual or action-filled, rather than static, visuals (*3-2-1 Contact*)
- Choosing topics that are inherently interesting to children and relevant to their lives (*Les Débrouillards*)
- Presenting content via age-appropriate language and at levels of difficulty that are tailored to children's knowledge and developmental level (*Les Débrouillards*)
- Enhancing appeal through age-appropriate humor (*3-2-1 Contact*, *Les Débrouillards*)
- Including characters whom viewers see as competent and intelligent, and with whom they can identify—particularly characters who are slightly older than the target audience (*3-2-1 Contact*, *Les Débrouillards*)
- Embedding science content in a dramatic narrative (*3-2-1 Contact*, *Les Débrouillards*)
- Making educational content integral, rather than tangential, to the narrative plotline—a notion that is similar to "content on the plotline" in *Ghostwriter* (chap. 4, this volume) or "distance" in the theoretical model proposed in chapter 10 (Scholastic's *The Magic School Bus*, *Cro*)
- Focusing an individual episode or segment tightly on conveying a small number of ideas (Scholastic's *The Magic School Bus*)
- Repeating concepts across an episode or segment (Scholastic's *The Magic School Bus*)
- Drawing explicit connections among conceptually related segments (*3-2-1 Contact*)
- Balancing straightforward delivery of science content with a process of discovery (*Les Débrouillards*)
- Embedding content in a context of problem solving in which characters continually revisit and refine their solutions to make them more effective (*Cro*)

- Presenting experiments in ways that children can replicate at home (*Les Débrouillards*)

I return to these characteristics in chapter 10, proposing a theoretical model to explain some of the mental processing that contributes to children's comprehension of educational television. Naturally, however, this list also holds implications on a more practical, applied level: By incorporating these features into the production of an educational television series, producers can increase the likelihood that it will have the desired impact on its target audience. As we have seen, the end result can be significant benefits for children's knowledge, skills, and attitudes regarding science and technology.

7

Civics and Social Studies

I'm just a bill.
Yes, I'm only a bill,
And I'm sitting here on Capitol Hill.

—"I'm Just a Bill," *Schoolhouse Rock*

Parallel to trends in subjects such as science or mathematics, the National Council for the Social Studies (NCSS) and other organizations have attempted to promote social studies education that does not merely require rote memorization. The recommended approaches involve helping students to develop a deeper understanding of the material, cognitive skills necessary for thinking critically, and attitudes that lead them both to learn more about the subject and to take active roles in their communities. As stated in the curriculum standards for social studies, a major purpose of social studies education is the promotion of *civic competence*—that is, the knowledge, skills, and attitudes necessary to become good, informed citizens (NCSS, 1994).

Efforts toward reforming social studies education in the United States have been motivated, in part, by the results of national assessments that pointed to severe deficits in children's knowledge. For example, in 1986, the National Assessment of Educational Progress (NAEP) showed that one third of 17-year-old students did not know that the Declaration of Independence signaled the American colonists' break from England, and more than one fifth could not identify George Washington as the commander of the colonial forces during the American Revolution (Bennett, 1988).

NAEP assessments in 2001 suggested that new efforts in social studies had begun to bear fruit. The number of fourth and eighth graders who scored above the "basic" level in geography and U.S. history (indicating at least a partial mastery of the subject) increased slightly between 1994 and 2001, although twelfth graders showed no change (National Center for Educational Statistics, 2002a, 2002b). The 1998 civics assessment showed that 65% to 70% of children in all three grades scored at or above "basic" in civics as well (National Center for Educational Statistics, 1999).

Effective social studies education draws on a broad array of disciplines, such as archaeology, anthropology, economics, geography, history, law, philosophy, political science, psychology, religion, and sociology, among others. Such programs foster individual and cultural identity, promote understanding of the forces that hold society together or tear it apart, address critical issues, prepare students to make decisions based on democratic principles, and lead to citizen participation in public affairs (NCSS, 1993, 1994).

Over the years, educational television programs for children have addressed many topics that can be considered to fall within the purview of social studies. These include such diverse series as the geography game show *Where In the World Is Carmen Sandiego?* (and the subsequent animated adventure series, *Where on Earth Is Carmen Sandiego?*), children's news specials produced by networks such as ABC or Nickelodeon, and historically based animated series such as *Liberty's Kids* or *Histeria!* However, research in this area has focused more narrowly on two topics: children's recall and understanding of current events material presented in television news programming, and the impact of televised *Schoolhouse Rock* songs on children's understanding of topics related to civics.[1] Unlike research on television series about literacy, mathematics, or science (chaps. 4, 5, and 6, this volume), far less attention has been devoted to the impact of such programming on children's attitudes toward or interest in such material.

NEWS AND CURRENT EVENTS

Television news programming is widely recognized as the major source of news for adult viewers (e.g., Gunter, 1987; Gunter, Sancho-Aldridge, & Winstone, 1994). Although television news programs in the United States typically target adult audiences, they are watched by significant numbers of children as well. Several studies conducted in the late 1970s found that many elementary school children watched news programs at some point during the week (e.g., Atkin, 1978; Drew & Reeves, 1978; Egan, 1978). More recently, Nielsen ratings indicated that, each day, approximately half a million 2- to 11-year-olds watch the news (Stipp, 1995), and a national poll found that 65% of 11- to 16-year-olds reported watching a news program on the previous day (Children Now, 1994). Indeed, Comstock and Paik (1991) observed that children get most of their

---

[1]A fair amount of research has also investigated the impact of educational television on children's appreciation of cultural diversity. This research is reviewed in the discussion of the effects of prosocial programming in chapter 9.

news information from television, as opposed to newspapers, radio, or discussions with others.

Most of the research on viewers' comprehension of and learning from television news has focused on adults rather than children. This is understandable, as the primary audience for news programming is typically adults. However, the fact that so many children watch the news raises questions as to the information that children acquire from watching the news. Moreover, these issues take on even greater significance when we consider news programs produced specifically for children. Let us consider children's learning from each type of news programming in turn.

Knowledge Acquisition From Adult News

A handful of studies have examined children's learning from adult news programs. In the United States, Atkin and Gantz (1978) found that elementary-school children who watched adult news programs over the course of one year showed moderate increases in knowledge of political affairs and current events.

In Great Britain, Cairns and his colleagues conducted a series of studies in Northern Ireland and Scotland to examine the impact of adult news programs on children's knowledge about unrest in Northern Ireland. Results of the first study indicated that Scottish children who watched Northern Irish television newscasts knew more about the unrest than those who did not, suggesting that children had learned from viewing the news programs. However, higher levels of awareness were found (not surprisingly) among children living in relatively peaceful sections of Northern Ireland. It is not clear whether this was due to their greater learning from television or greater knowledge acquired through other sources, such as newspapers or word of mouth (Cairns, Hunter, & Herring, 1980). Subsequently, a correlational study found that the Irish children who knew the most about the unrest were boys, those who lived closer to the violence, and those who watched more adult news on television; a follow-up study found an advantage for 11-year-old viewers of the news but not 8-year-old viewers (Cairns, 1984). Because the data were correlational, however, it is unclear whether children learned about the unrest from the newscasts, or whether children who already knew about the unrest from other sources were more inclined to watch the news.

Finally, although the focus of their study was on fear reactions rather than knowledge acquisition, it is worth noting that when Smith and Wilson (2002) interviewed children in grades K through 6, they found that 52% could recount a television news story that had frightened them. Thus, at least one half of their sample demonstrated long-term recall of news stories. Indeed, if the researchers had asked children to recall any news story at all (not only frightening ones), it is quite possible that performance would have been higher. Taken together, then, the data from these studies suggest that, at least to some degree, children can acquire knowledge from adult newscasts.

Several factors affect children's learning from adult newscasts. Furnham and Gunter (1985) found that male teenagers recalled violent television news stories better than females, whereas females showed better recall of nonviolent stories; the sex difference did not appear for written or audio versions of the same stories. Using a sample of 8- to 13-year-olds, Drew and Reeves (1980) found that younger children recalled a news story better when it was embedded among other news stories, whereas older children showed better recall when it was embedded among cartoons. They also found greater recall when children liked and believed the story, and (consistent with Salomon's [1983] theory of Amount of Invested Mental Effort, or AIME) when they thought its purpose was to inform rather than entertain. Drew and Reese (1984) found recall to be stronger among 10- to 16-year-olds when the story was accompanied by visuals in film footage, as opposed to being conveyed by "talking heads." A greater understanding of the role of visuals in children's recall of television news is provided by research on news programs produced for children, as we shall see shortly.

Knowledge Acquisition From Children's News

Several studies have supported the notion that adult audiences recall news presented in print form better than television news, perhaps because print allows readers the opportunity to slow down or reread difficult passages (Browne, 1978; DeFleur, Davenport, Cronin, & DeFleur, 1992; Faccoro & DeFleur, 1993; Furnham & Gunter, 1985; Gunter, Furnham, & Gietson, 1984; Wilson, 1974). However, the situation appears to be very different for younger audiences.

A series of studies in the Netherlands compared fourth and sixth graders' recall of news stories presented in a news program aimed at children, *Jeugdjournaal* ("*Children's News*"), with print and audio versions of the same stories (Walma van der Molen & van der Voort, 1997, 1998, 2000). These studies found consistently that immediate recall of the news stories was greater when they had been presented on television than in any other form. Interestingly, the effects of television were greatest when the information in the televised visuals was redundant with (rather than complementary to) information in the audio track—an advantage that also appeared when redundant visuals were included in the print condition. This led the researchers to explain the advantages of the televised presentations using Paivio's (1971) dual-coding hypothesis, which posits a greater likelihood of recall when the same material is presented in two modalities (audio and visual) than when it is presented in only one. The effect was replicated with children in England (Gunter, Furnham, & Griffiths, 2000), lending further support to the theory. The role of visuals, and its implications for children's learning from educational television in general, are discussed in greater detail in the "Issues Raised and Lessons Learned" section at the end of this chapter.

In the United States, perhaps the most prominent—and certainly the most controversial—recent example of American news programming for children is *Channel One*, a 10-minute news program (plus 2 minutes of commercials) that is fed, not to homes, but directly to middle and high schools. In exchange for delivering the program to their students on at least 90% of school days, schools receive a satellite dish, two VCRs, and televisions in each classroom from the producers of *Channel One*. Several studies have measured learning from *Channel One* via forced-choice, paper-and-pencil assessments. Although one study found no effect (Knupfer & Hayes, 1994), most found that exposure to *Channel One* resulted in viewers' knowing more about the news topics covered in the broadcasts than nonviewers did (Greenberg & Brand, 1993a; Johnston & Brzezinski, 1994). However, even when effects were found, some were not significant for children with grade-point averages of C or D, or were stronger for students who were motivated or whose teachers discussed the news on a regular basis (Johnston & Brzezinski, 1994). Although some have questioned the frequency with which teachers actually follow up on *Channel One* broadcasts with further discussion (see Bachen, 1998 for a review), the latter finding raises a question as to the degree to which effects are attributable to the program per se as opposed to the discussions it might stimulate.

Fueling controversy more, though, was the finding that children not only learned from the news portion of the program, but also from the commercials embedded in the program. Viewers of *Channel One* evaluated products more highly and expressed greater intent to buy products (although they were not significantly more likely to actually buy them) if they had seen these products advertised on *Channel One* (Brand & Greenberg, 1994; Greenberg & Brand, 1993a). The effectiveness of such in-school advertising, coupled with the increasing presence of advertising in schools, has given rise to debate over the propriety of such efforts (e.g., Richards, Wartella, Morton, & Thompson, 1998; Wartella & Jennings, 2001).

Interest in News

Interest in and motivation to seek out news beyond the programs viewed was assessed only in research on *Channel One*. Self-report data showed that students and teachers reported examples of seeking out information or contributing to dinnertime conversation because of *Channel One* (Ehman, 1995). However, quantitative comparisons of viewers and nonviewers found no significant difference in students' reports of talking about news stories outside class or using other media to learn about news stories (Johnston & Brzezinski, 1992; Johnston, Brzezinski, & Anderman, 1994). The latter findings, coupled with the potential confounding effects of classroom discussions that might have followed up on the program, shed doubt on *Channel One*'s having caused increases in children's interest in seeking out news. To paraphrase Johnston et al. (1994): To the degree that *Channel One* held benefits for its viewers, it appeared to satisfy, rather than stimulate, their need to know.

AMERICAN HISTORY AND GOVERNMENT

In the 1970s, a series of 3-minute educational interstitials, *Schoolhouse Rock*, aired between children's programs on ABC. Each interstitial was animated and presented a song about a topic in English, mathematics, science, or American history. At the time, no research was conducted to assess the educational effectiveness of *Schoolhouse Rock*. However, when the series was rebroadcast in the 1990s, a series of studies by Calvert and her colleagues (Calvert, 1995, 2001; Calvert & Pfordresher, 1994; Calvert, Rigaud, & Mazella, 1991; Calvert & Tart, 1993) assessed children's and adults' comprehension of two *Schoolhouse Rock* interstitials: "I'm Just a Bill" (the steps through which a bill passes to become a law) and "The Shot Heard 'Round the World" (the Revolutionary War). In addition, a third interstitial, "The Preamble" (verbatim text of the Preamble to the Constitution) was tested only with adults. Together, the data from these studies suggested that the interstitials were less effective than alternate versions of the same interstitials with the audio track spoken in prose rather than sung. Repeated exposure to the original, musical versions improved verbatim recall of the text of the Preamble; indeed, greater viewing of *Schoolhouse Rock* as a child was associated with greater recall of the Preamble as a young adult. However, research on the other two songs indicated that the songs were less effective than prose in promoting deeper comprehension of the educational content among children.

Calvert and her colleagues attributed this to modality effects, with songs simply better suited to verbatim recall, and/or to a better match between the prose presentation and verbal recall measures. Yet, others who found poor comprehension for particular songs in educational television programs have pointed to factors that were more specific to the individual songs involved. For example, Palmer concluded that poor comprehension of one song in *Sesame Street* was due to the drum beat inadvertently obscuring key words in a song about rhyming (Palmer & Fisch, 2001). In any event, it is clear that these three *Schoolhouse Rock* interstitials succeeded only on the level of verbatim recall.

ISSUES RAISED AND LESSONS LEARNED

As noted earlier in this chapter, the field of social studies is broad and multidisciplinary. Yet, compared to research in subjects such as literacy, mathematics, or science, the existing research on educational television in the area of civics and social studies has focused on a far narrower slice of the pie.

Nevertheless, data on news programming and *Schoolhouse Rock* speaks to issues concerning the use of visuals and songs in educational television. These issues extend beyond civics and social studies to carry implications for children's learning from educational television as a whole.

Songs as Vehicles for Educational Content

As already discussed, Calvert (2001) concluded, on the basis of her research on *Schoolhouse Rock*, that songs may be an effective medium for promoting verbatim recall among school-age children, but not deeper processing. Proponents of this position might draw additional support from formative research on a Mexican coproduction of *Sesame Street*, which found one song to be effective in engaging preschoolers' attention, but not in conveying educational content (reported in Cole et al., 2001).

Conversely, others have maintained that it is not music per se that is ineffective in conveying educational content. Rather, the educational effectiveness of a given song depends on its execution, as in Palmer's attribution of the failure of an early *Sesame Street* song to the orchestration obscuring key words in the lyrics (Palmer & Fisch, 2001).

From my own experience in the production of educational television, I believe that the truth probably lies somewhere between the two positions. Certainly, all agree that songs can provide effective mnemonics for verbatim recall, as seen not only in *Schoolhouse Rock* promoting recall of the Preamble to the Constitution (Calvert & Tart, 1993), but also in common, non-television examples such as using songs to teach children the alphabet or the months of the year. Beyond the level of verbatim recall, however, I feel that the medium of songs does present challenges for the presentation of educational content on television, but that songs still can be effective if executed properly.

The challenges stem from the fairly rigid structure of songs, which constrains the freedom of the writer and performer. In spoken dialogue, a writer can spend more time expanding on complex points or less time on points that are likely to be familiar to the audience already. Moreover, the writer can use whatever combination of words he or she wishes, in an attempt to deliver the educational message as clearly as possible. In songs, on the other hand, lyrics must adhere to a particular meter and rhyme scheme, which restricts the combinations of words that the writer can use. Tempo, too, constrains the treatment of educational content because a steady tempo makes it less feasible to slow down during a complex point or speed up during simple material.

At the same time, though, the medium of songs carries strengths that lend themselves well to the treatment of educational content. Not the least of these is the natural opportunity for repetition and reinforcement that lies in repeating a chorus, verse, or refrain. Research on series such as *Sesame Street* has shown that comprehension is enhanced by repetition of material within segments, or repeated exposure to the same segment over time (e.g., Lesser, 1974; chap. 2, this volume), and there is every reason to expect this to hold true for repetition over the course of a song as well. However, the song must be crafted to take advantage of that opportunity, as in the case of a song created for a *Sesame Street* outreach program in fire safety (see chap. 9, this volume), whose chorus consisted almost entirely of multiple repetitions of the phrase, "Stop, drop, and roll." Similarly, as in Palmer's example, the song must be structured such that the music and rhyme scheme draw children's attention to the educational message, and not away from it.

From this perspective, there are several reasons why children might not have learned more from the *Schoolhouse Rock* songs, "I'm Just a Bill" and "The Shot Heard 'Round the World." First, the educational content presented in each of these songs (the steps by which a bill becomes law and the history of the Revolutionary War) is fairly complex. Second, the complexity is compounded by the fact that both songs are upbeat, with fairly fast tempos that result in the information being presented quickly. Third, unlike the song about the Preamble (in which the text of the Preamble is repeated several times over the course of the song), the educational content in each of these two songs is presented in the verses and not the chorus, so the content is never repeated to provide reinforcement. Indeed, although the lyrics in each chorus are thematically related to the educational content, there is little concrete information in the chorus itself.

Thus, one can easily see how the tempo, meter, and rhyme scheme of songs might pose challenges for the effective treatment of educational content on television. However, further research will likely be necessary before we are able to settle the question of whether songs simply are not suitable vehicles for educational content, or whether their effectiveness depends on more specific aspects of their execution.

The Role of Visuals

Walma van der Molen and van der Voort's (1997, 1998, 2000) research on news programming demonstrated clearly that children's recall of news is enhanced by the use of visuals that convey the same information as the audio track. This effect finds parallels in research in other subject areas as well. Within the domain of science and technology, summative research on *The Magic School Bus* and *Cro* suggested that the use of visuals could contribute to viewers' comprehension, as did formative research on *3-2-1 Contact* (ARC Consulting LLC, 1995; Goodman et al., 1993; Mielke & Chen, 1983; see chap. 6, this volume). Similarly, on the preschool level, research on *Sesame Street* found comprehension to be stronger when the subject matter was concrete and visual (e.g., Fisch, in press-a; Fisch & Truglio, 2001a; Lesser, 1974).

Nor is the effect limited to factual or educational content; Calvert, Huston, Watkins, & Wright (1982) found that redundant visual and auditory information led to increased story comprehension as well. Thus, the effect observed by Walma van der Molen and van der Voort appears not to be specific to television news. Rather, it holds implications for children's comprehension of educational television as a whole.

As the reference to early *Sesame Street* research (Lesser, 1974) suggests, the advantages of visuals have long been recognized in research on viewers' comprehension of television. A series of studies by Hayes and Birnbaum (1980) presented preschool children with videotapes in which the visual and audio tracks were mismatched (i.e., they came from different programs), and found that viewers' recall of the visual information was stronger than their recall of the audio. This led Hayes and Birnbaum to propose the *visual superiority hypothesis*, which posited that children prefer visual information, and that visual information interferes with comprehension of any auditory information that is presented simultaneously. However, their claim was refuted by subsequent research that demonstrated that when the visual and audio tracks were not mismatched, the difference in recall disappeared (e.g., Pezdek & Hartman, 1983; Pezdek & Stevens, 1984). As television uses both visual and auditory modalities to convey information, it is likely that, as Rolandelli (1989) argued, children's reliance on one or the other may depend more on which modality presents the most useful and comprehensible information at the moment than on a more general preference for visual information.

Walma van der Molen and van der Voort's (1997, 1998, 2000) use of the dual-coding hypothesis provides a compelling explanation for the greater recall found in the case of redundant visuals and audio. Indeed, their position is strengthened by the fact that their research carefully controlled for factors associated with alternate explanations, such as deficits in children's reading ability or the possibility that the effect might be due to listening to the television program rather than watching (neither of which was supported by the data).

Of course, the benefits described by the dual-coding hypothesis come into play only when visuals are redundant with auditory information. I would suggest that, under the proper conditions, visuals also carry two additional advantages, even if they are not redundant with the audio track. First, as discussed in chapter 2, children (particularly preschoolers) pay more attention to television when it shows visual action than when it shows static "talking heads" (e.g., Lesser, 1974). This greater attentiveness to the program could contribute to greater comprehension. In fact, Calvert (1999) has taken this point even further, arguing that action provides a code that facilitates children's processing of verbal and visual information. Second, the fact that a given concept can be captured in visuals often indicates that the concept is concrete rather than abstract. Research on *Sesame Street* and school-age science series has suggested that viewers show better comprehension of educational content on television when the concepts presented are concrete rather than abstract (chapters 2 and 6, this volume).

Note that neither one of these points is an exclusive function of the use of visuals per se. By nature, some pieces of educational content are more concrete than others, regardless of whether they are presented visually. Similarly, a narrative can include more or less action regardless of whether that action is portrayed visually. Indeed, Gibbons, Anderson, Smith, Field, and Fischer (1986) found that 4- to 7-year-olds reproduced more of characters' actions than speech, even when they only heard the story without watching it. Thus, whereas the benefits of redundant visual and auditory information grow out of the sensory modalities involved, the benefits of concrete and dynamic visuals may lie as much in their being concrete and dynamic as in their being visual.

8

Prosocial Programming

Do you know you're special, and that people can like you
just the way you are? Well, I do.

—Fred Rogers, *Mister Rogers' Neighborhood*

To address the effects of prosocial television programs properly, we must consider television in the broader context of children's socialization. Children learn social behavior through interactions with and observations of family, peers, and others in a wide variety of contexts, including home, school, and all of the other settings in which children spend time.

Of course, face-to-face interactions with family and peers almost certainly outweigh television and other media in determining children's social development. Thus, for example, Eron, Walder, and Lefkowitz (1971) concluded that, although exposure to aggressive television programs contributes to aggressive behavior in children, the presence of environmental, familial, and cognitive characteristics that promote the learning of aggressive responses probably play more important roles. Nevertheless, as discussed in chapter 1, American children spend tremendous amounts of time watching television—more than in any other activity except sleeping. The sheer amount of time spent in front of the television set suggests, at least, the potential for television to serve as a socializing agent.

In fact, several studies have confirmed that children not only acquire social behavior from television, but consciously look to the medium as a source of social learning. For example, one study of 180 9- to 15-year-old children found that approximately 20% of the children reported using television to learn about social behavior or "themselves" (Greenberg, 1974). Similarly, Noble and Noble (1979) found that a sample of 136 Australian teenagers overwhelmingly reported learning a broad range of social behaviors from the American situation comedy *Happy Days*, including aspects of dating behavior and how to "be cool."

Given findings such as these, it is not surprising that exposure to negative television would be found to result in negative effects on children's behavior, or that positive television would result in positive effects. Indeed, reviews and meta-analyses of the relevant literature indicate that

105

both classes of effects are significant (e.g., Hearold, 1986; Lovelace & Huston, 1983; Mares, 1996; Mares & Woodard, 2001, in press; Noble, 1983; Paik & Comstock, 1994; Rushton, 1982; Wilson et al., 1997).

Among the meta-analyses, Hearold (1986) analyzed 230 studies on television and social behavior conducted before 1978, and concluded that positive effects were approximately twice as strong as—and more enduring than—negative effects. Subsequent meta-analyses have taken narrower slices of the literature, examining effects of either prosocial or antisocial television (e.g., violent television) without examining the two simultaneously. Together, though, these analyses suggest roughly equal positive and negative effects, equivalent to a correlation of .32 between exposure to violent television and aggressive behavior (Paik & Comstock, 1994) and .27 between prosocial television and prosocial outcomes (Mares, 1996; Mares & Woodard, in press). Each reflects a small to moderate effect on viewers.

Research on prosocial television programs has paid particular attention to impact on children's social knowledge and behavior in several areas: positive interactions and "friendliness" (including the reduction of aggression), altruism and cooperation, self-control and delay of gratification, and the reduction of stereotypes. Let us consider each of these areas in turn.

POSITIVE INTERACTIONS AND "FRIENDLINESS"

A number of studies have examined the broad impact of prosocial television programs on children's interactions with peers—what Rushton (1982) termed *friendly behavior* and Mares (1996) called *positive interactions*. The vast majority of research on this class of prosocial effects was conducted with preschool children, leaving many questions open with regard to older children.

That said, the literature to date indicates that exposure to prosocial television can result in more positive interactions among preschool children. Mares's (1996) meta-analysis of the relevant literature suggests small to moderate effects in this area.

Consider, for example, two field experiments involving *Mister Rogers' Neighborhood* (Fig. 8.1). For more than 30 years, this gentle PBS television series attempted to help children understand the world and themselves. Host Fred Rogers guided viewers through each episode, with the episode typically divided into two main parts. One, set largely in Mister Rogers' home, consisted primarily of Mister Rogers talking one-on-one with the viewer and, at times, an on-screen visitor or two. The other part was set in the Neighborhood of Make-Believe, in which puppets and live-action cast members encountered a socioemotional issue related to the topic that Mister Rogers had discussed.

Friedrich and Stein (1973) compared the behavior of preschool children in naturalistic settings before, during, and after a 4-week period in which children were exposed to 12 episodes of either *Mister Rogers' Neighborhood*, aggressive cartoons (*Batman* and *Superman*), or programs with neutral content. Results showed that viewers of *Mister Rogers' Neighborhood* showed a variety of prosocial effects, including increased levels of self-controlling behavior, task persistence, and (among low-SES viewers) nurturance, cooperation, and verbalization of feelings. Consistent with

FIG. 8.1. *Mister Rogers' Neighborhood.* (Photo © 2003 Family Communications Inc. All rights reserved. *Mister Rogers' Neighborhood* and all related titles, logos, and characters are trademarks of Family Communications Inc.)

these effects, Coates, Pusser, and Goodman (1976) found that exposure to four 15-minute excerpts from *Mister Rogers' Neighborhood* resulted in significant increases in preschoolers' social contacts with, and giving positive reinforcement to, other children and adults. (Similar effects were found for *Sesame Street*, but only among children who had low scores at pretest.) A third study (Friedrich & Stein, 1975) found effects that were also significant but more limited in scope. In this study, unaided viewing produced significant effects in role play that paralleled the story seen on television, but (in the absence of follow-up training) not more generalized effects on helping behavior in other situations.

This variation in significance across studies has been seen for other television series as well. For example, some studies involving prosocial segments from *Sesame Street* found significant effects only when the testing situation has been similar to the context shown on-screen (e.g., Paulson, 1974; see following text), whereas others found more generalized effects on children's behavior during free play with other children (e.g., Zielinska & Chambers, 1995).

Effectiveness has varied somewhat within the realm of social knowledge as well. For example, Singer and Singer (1994, 1998) found that viewers of *Barney & Friends* demonstrated greater awareness of manners than nonviewers. However, Aidman (1993) found no difference between viewers and nonviewers of *Mister Rogers' Neighborhood* in their knowledge of appropriate host–guest behaviors. I return to these points in the "Issues Raised and Lessons Learned" section at the end of this chapter.

ALTRUISM AND COOPERATION

Taking the literature as a whole, Mares' (1996) meta-analysis found one of the larger effect sizes for altruism, suggesting a moderate to large effect of prosocial programming on children's altruism. Yet, data regarding the promotion of cooperation and altruism (defined here as sacrificing one's own reward to help another) also have been somewhat mixed, with some studies finding significant effects (as in the case of Rust's [2001] summative evaluation of *Dragon Tales*) and others not. Once again, the critical determining factor often seems to have been the degree of correspondence between the prosocial behavior that characters model in the program and the viewer behavior that is assessed subsequently.

Thus, for example, Sprafkin, Liebert, and Poulos (1975) found that after watching an episode of *Lassie* in which Lassie's master rescues a puppy, children were more likely to help some puppies who were ostensibly in distress, even though it meant leaving an activity in which they were earning points toward a prize. However, several studies found effects of unaided viewing of *Sesame Street* and *Mister Rogers' Neighborhood* on measures of cooperative or helping behavior that corresponded relatively closely to the situations shown on screen, but no significant effects in more generalized behavioral measures or free play (e.g., Friedrich & Stein, 1975; Paulson, 1974). When Friedrich and Stein combined viewing with follow-up role playing activities, though, effects appeared in the more generalized measures as well.

Of course, it is worth noting that not all treatments of prosocial behavior on television are the same. In producing prosocial television, a constant question is whether to portray only positive behavior, or whether to begin with a character misbehaving and then learning to behave properly. Silverman and Sprafkin (1980) exposed preschool children to *Sesame Street* segments that took one or the other of these approaches (or neutral segments that contained no social lesson), and then assessed cooperation during a marble game. Results indicated that those children who watched the segments in which conflict preceded a resolution actually showed *less* cooperative behavior than children in the neutral condition; no such effect appeared for the prosocial-only condition. Thus, it seems that, at least for preschoolers, it was best to present only positive modeling. Whether this would also hold true for school-age children is unclear.

SELF-CONTROL/DELAY OF GRATIFICATION

Several studies found that watching televised models delay their own gratification can lead to viewers' doing the same, whether behavior is assessed immediately after a single exposure or as part of a longer term behavioral intervention (e.g., Elias, 1983; cf. Mares, 1996). Mares's (1996) meta-analysis of the literature suggests a small to moderate effect of prosocial programming in this area.

Much of this research employed special films or videos created for the sake of the intervention, rather than broadcast television programs. However, one study that used a broadcast series was the field experiment by Friedrich and Stein (1973) described earlier. Among the effects found in the study was the finding that children exposed to a diet of 12 episodes of *Mister Rogers' Neighborhood* were significantly better at delaying gratification than children who watched a diet of aggressive television programs. However, there was no significant difference between children who watched *Mister Rogers' Neighborhood* and those who watched neutral programs, suggesting that the difference between prosocial and aggressive programs actually may have been due to a negative effect of aggressive programming, rather than the prosocial effects of *Mister Rogers' Neighborhood*.

REDUCTION OF STEREOTYPES

Over the years, a significant amount of research has investigated the role
television plays in the formation and combating of gender and ethnic stereotypes (see, e.g., Christenson & Roberts, 1983 for a review). A long line
of content analyses have documented consistent underrepresentation
and skewed portrayals of female and minority characters in both adult
and children's entertainment programming (e.g., Greenberg & Brand,
1993b; Signorelli, 1993). Furthermore, exposure to such portrayals has
been found to contribute to the formation of children's stereotypes. Indeed, one American study found that White children's perceptions of African-Americans could be influenced—positively or negatively—by as
little as a single exposure to an animated cartoon (Graves, 1975).

Conversely, a number of American television series have been created
in specific attempts to reduce stereotypes among preschoolers and/or
school-age children, such as *Big Blue Marble* and *Vegetable Soup* in the
1970s or *Puzzle Place* in the 1990s. Similar attempts have been made in
other countries, often in parts of the world where significant tensions exist
between ethnic groups. Summative research on some of these series has
shown positive effects, such as increased self-esteem among minority children and improved attitudes toward children of other groups among all
viewers (e.g., Mays, Henderson, Seidman, & Steiner, 1975; Roberts et al.,
1974). Mares's (1996) meta-analysis suggests a small to moderate effect
in this area.

Let us consider, for example, the data obtained for several preschool
and school-age series produced in various parts of the world.[1]

Series for Preschool Children

Diversity has been a defining characteristic of *Sesame Street* since its incep-
tion. Its emphasis on diversity began to grow in Seasons 3 and 4, with the
introduction of goals regarding Latino-American culture and Spanish
words (Lesser & Schneider, 2001; Palmer & Fisch, 2001).

Early on, research suggested that exposure to *Sesame Street* could affect
children's attitudes toward other ethnic groups. Bogatz and Ball (1971)
found that African-American and White preschoolers who viewed the second season of *Sesame Street* expressed more positive attitudes toward other
groups of children (African-American and Latino) than nonviewers did.
In a Canadian study, 3- to 5-year-old children were shown *Sesame Street*
programs containing 12 minutes of inserts designed to promote positive

---

[1]This research is reviewed only briefly here. Further information on these studies
can be found in Fisch (in press-b).

attitudes toward French Canadians, Asians, and Native Americans. After-wards, viewers chose photos of these children as desired playmates signifi-cantly more often than nonviewers did (Gorn, Goldberg, & Kanungo, 1976). As one might expect from the brevity of exposure, Gorn et al. found that the effect did not sustain itself until the next day.[2] Still, the fact that even a short-term effect could be produced by such limited exposure was encouraging.

In the 1980s, *Sesame Street* embarked on a more explicit, 4-year curricu-lar focus on race relations. Each season adopted a different group as its fo-cus: African-Americans, Latinos, Asians, and Native Americans. Material produced under this curriculum was intended to stress both similarities and differences among ethnic groups, and to encourage preschoolers to see peo-ple who look different from themselves as possible friends. Production was informed by an extensive program of formative research conducted with White children and with children from each of the groups covered under the curriculum (see Truglio et al., 2001 for a review). This research estab-lished baselines regarding young children's thoughts and feelings about their own and other ethnic groups, and identified areas of need.

Subsequent formative research assessed viewers' comprehension of some of the race relations segments. For example, one pair of studies ex-amined comprehension of two live-action segments ("Visiting Iesha" and "Play Date") that presented White children visiting African-American friends in their homes. After viewing, the vast majority of Afri-can-American, Puerto Rican, and White children were able to recall activi-ties that the friends in the segment had shared. Most recognized that the White children in the segments felt positively about their visits as a whole and about trying the new foods. However, consistent with the preproduction formative data discussed earlier, less than one half of the children thought that the parents of the children in the segments were happy about the visits (*Sesame Street* Research, 1991, 1993).

As difficult as issues concerning race relations might be in the United States, the challenges were all the more daunting for a joint Israeli–Palestin-ian coproduction of *Sesame Street* entitled *Rechov Sumsum/Shara'a Simsim*. The central goal of the series was to promote mutual respect and under-standing among Palestinian and Israeli preschoolers living in the region.

To evaluate its success in achieving this goal, a set of summative studies was conducted with approximately 600 4- and 5-year-olds, including Pal-estinian, Palestinian–Israeli, and Israeli children. Pretest data collected prior to the broadcast of the series showed that children demonstrated

---

[2]In addition, the observed effect may have been inflated because their measure used photos of children from the video. The fact that these children had appeared on television may have contributed to their attractiveness as playmates.

some knowledge about symbols associated with their own culture (e.g., a menorah for Israelis, a mosque for Palestinians) but minimal awareness of symbols of the other culture. Moreover, even at these young ages, children could already articulate negative stereotypes about the other group (e.g., beliefs about Arabs wanting to hurt Jews or Jews shooting at Arabs).

Four months after the premiere of *Rechov Sumsum/Shara'a Simsim*, posttest data showed that, despite the political tensions that surrounded children, there had been significantly greater changes in viewers' knowledge and attitudes than in nonviewers'. There was an increase in children's positive descriptions of people from the other culture, and more understanding that children in the other culture engage in activities similar to their own (e.g., eat similar foods). Israeli and Palestinian children showed an increased ability to identify symbols from their own culture and (in a later study) the other culture. Moreover, after 4 months' exposure to the series and (in some cases) associated outreach materials, children increased their use of prosocial strategies to resolve hypothetical conflicts (Bernstein, 2000).

It is remarkable indeed that *Rechov Sumsum/Shara'a Simsim* could produce these sorts of effects at a time of such tension and conflict. Given that the level of violence in the region has continued to climb in the time since the series' 1998 premiere, it would be interesting to see whether similar effects would be obtained today, or whether the impact of *Rechov Sumsum/Shara'a Simsim* would now be outweighed by children's experiences in their daily lives.

Series for School-Age Children

Perhaps the largest-scale evaluations of a television series designed to reduce gender stereotypes among school-age children is Johnston and Ettema's (1982) summative research on *Freestyle*, which included a sample of more than 7,000 children in seven sites across the United States. Targeting 9- to 12-year-old children, *Freestyle* aimed to reduce gender stereotypes by portraying characters in nontraditional gender roles and sometimes triumphing over stereotypes held by other characters (e.g., a girl overcoming a potential employer's attitudes to land a job at a gas station). Children were assigned to one of three conditions: viewers (in home or school); nonviewers; or viewers with teacher-led follow-up discussion. Questionnaires were used to assess children's gender-related attitudes toward themselves and others before and after a viewing period including 26 episodes. Moderate positive effects were found for unaided viewing in school, and some weaker effects were found only among the heaviest at-home viewers. Considerably greater effects were found when viewing was combined with follow-up discussion.

Internationally, one example of a school-age series designed to promote positive relations among ethnic groups can be found in *Nashe Maalo*. Aimed at a target age group of 7 to 10, the central goal of *Nashe Maalo* was to promote respect and understanding among ethnic Albanian, Macedonian, Roma, and Turkish children living in the former Yugoslav Republic of Macedonia. Although Macedonia is one of the most ethnically mixed countries in the region, its society is profoundly segregated. Limited contact among ethnic groups gives rise to fear, which has the potential to lead to instability and conflict.

In *Nashe Maalo*, a multiethnic cast of four young friends share a common secret: Karmen, a personification of the building in which they live, reveals herself to them because she believes their minds are sufficiently open to receive her messages of mutual respect and understanding. She magically transports the cast into the realities of others, providing them with insight into each other's lives.

The educational impact of the series was evaluated with a sample of 240 children from the Skopje region, representing all four of the targeted ethnic groups. Children's attitudes were measured before and after a period of several months, during which they watched videotapes of all eight episodes of *Nashe Maalo*.

Because all of the children in the study viewed *Nashe Maalo* and there was no control group, the data must be interpreted with some caution. Still, the data did point to a number of significant effects. Prior to viewing, many children exhibited negative, stereotyped perceptions of Albanian, Macedonian, Romany, and Turkish ethnic groups; the least positive descriptions were directed toward the Roma (including the descriptions provided by Roma children themselves). In the posttest, however, many children provided more positive descriptions when presented with images of people either from other ethnic groups or from their own. Macedonian children showed the greatest positive changes in perceptions of other ethnic groups, whereas Albanians showed the greatest change in perceptions of their own group. In addition, whereas nearly all of the children were able to identify Macedonian (the national language) prior to viewing, exposure to *Nashe Maalo* led to significant increases in children's ability to identify the three minority languages; this gain was strongest among ethnic Macedonian children, who are typically the least exposed to the other languages.

Finally, before viewing, 67% of children indicated a reluctance to invite children from other ethnic groups into their homes. After viewing *Nashe Maalo*, there was an increase in the number of ethnic Macedonian children who said they would be willing to invite Albanians, Roma, and Turks to their homes. Thus, it appeared that *Nashe Maalo* succeeded in affecting children's knowledge of and attitudes toward other ethnic groups (Common Ground Productions et al., 2000).

LONG-TERM EFFECTS

Where effects of prosocial programming have been measured longitudinally, data indicate that the effects of exposure can persist but often grow less strong over time. Not surprisingly, the effects of brief exposure to such programming tend not to endure long after viewing; for example, Gorn, Goldberg, and Kanungo (1976) found that exposure to brief segments of *Sesame Street* resulted in significant effects on children's desire to play with children from other ethnic groups, but Goldberg and Gorn (1979) found that this effect was not sustained one day after viewing. More intensive exposure can lead to longer term effects, but these, too, may decay over time. For example, Friedrich and Stein (1973) found that the effects of sustained viewing of *Mister Rogers' Neighborhood* continued to some extent after a 2-week postviewing period, but were smaller than they had been immediately after the viewing period.

When viewing has been combined with follow-up discussion or other activities, effects can be more enduring. For example, Elias' (1983) video-based treatment for boys with behavioral problems resulted in positive effects that were still evident 2 months after the intervention. Johnston and Ettema (1982) found that combining *Freestyle* with follow-up discussion led to effects that persisted 9 months after exposure. However, it is interesting to note that although they found no decay in effects on children's attitudes (e.g., their feelings toward girls who play football), some decay was evident in their beliefs (e.g., in girls' ability to play football well). The researchers hypothesized that real-life experiences during the intervening 9 months may have challenged children's new beliefs about the way things are, but not their attitudes about how things should be.

Longer term effects have not been investigated in as much depth, but data suggest that these exist as well. As discussed in chapter 2 (this volume), Bogatz and Ball (1971) found that children who viewed *Sesame Street* as preschoolers were rated more highly in school readiness one year later, after they entered school. The teacher ratings used in Bogatz and Ball's study included not only academic indicators, but social factors such as "relationship with peers," too. At the extreme, the "recontact" study conducted by Anderson, Huston, Wright, and their colleagues found that preschool viewing of *Sesame Street* and other educational programs was associated not only with academic outcomes but also lower levels of aggressive tendencies in high school (Anderson et al., 1998, 2001; Huston et al., 2001).

ISSUES RAISED AND LESSONS LEARNED

Just as in the case of the academic subjects discussed in previous chapters, this research suggests that exposure to prosocial programming can lead to significant, positive change in children's social behavior. However, as Mares's (1996) meta-analysis indicates, effects in this area have been significant but small to moderate in magnitude.

Given the strength of some of the effects seen in academic domains such as literacy or school readiness, why would effects be small to moderate with regard to social behavior? Several possibilities seem likely. First, the primary cause could lie in the viewers: It is possible that children's social schemas and behavior are more resistant to change than their knowledge, skills, or attitudes regarding academic subjects. This could stem from either a greater degree of resistance inherent in children's well-practiced social schemas or from external factors in children's social environments, such as the influence of family or friends (a point to which I will return). Second, the primary cause might lie in the television programs used: It is possible that some of the television series used in these studies (or some of the segments or episodes within a single series) were simply more effective than others. Third, it is possible that, because it can be more difficult to measure social schemas than academic knowledge, the measures in some studies may not have been sufficiently sensitive to detect effects. It is difficult to know which of these explanations might be most correct, but I speculate that, in fact, all of these factors play a role.

Nevertheless, the research reviewed in this chapter shows prosocial programming to exert a consistent pattern of significant effects on children's social behavior. This impact—and, in some cases, inconsistency of impact—raises several important issues that can contribute to our understanding of such effects and the production of effective prosocial programming. Each of these issues is discussed in turn.

Exploring Mechanisms for Impact

In general, theoretical explanations for the social effects of television have tended to concern negative effects of television, such as the learning of aggression, more than positive effects of prosocial television programs. Nevertheless, it seems reasonable to assume that many of the same mechanisms can be applied to positive effects as well.

Many early theories to explain the social effects of television were rooted in Bandura's (1971) social learning theory. Such explanations focused on mechanisms such as modeling, imitation, and/or identification with characters on screen to explain children's acquisition of the behaviors modeled on screen. One of the chief factors determining whether a televised behavior will be imitated by viewers is the consequence that the behavior holds for the character on screen; if the character is rewarded for

a given behavior, viewers will be more likely to display the behavior themselves (Bandura, 1965).

A second approach views media effects less in terms of the acquisition
of new behaviors than in the production of a behavioral response—that is,
influencing viewers' selection of existing behavioral patterns that are already stored in memory (Berkowitz, 1984; Berkowitz & Rogers, 1986).
Under this approach, children select strategies or patterns of behavior
from a broader repertoire that is available to them, and apply the selected
behaviors to the given situation at hand. Exposure to televised models
who exhibit prosocial (or violent) behavior produces priming effects that
activate analogous stored behaviors, which thus become more likely to be
selected and exhibited in subsequent real-life situations.

A third approach views the relationship between violent television and
aggressive behavior—or, presumably, prosocial television and positive behavior—as more reciprocal: Violent television promotes aggressive behavior, and aggressive children seek out violent television (Huesmann, 1986).
This model adopts an information-processing approach in which exposure to television can result in the acquisition of new behavioral scripts or
schemas (as in the social learning approach), which produces enduring effects, or in the activation of existing scripts or schemas (as in priming effects), in which case effects are more transitory. Activation effects are seen
as more likely among older children, who have already built up significant
behavioral repertoires, whereas younger children are more likely to add
new scripts or schemas to their repertoires.

A point of intersection among all of these theoretical approaches may
lie in Bandura's (1986, 2002) refinement of his original social learning
theory into social cognitive theory. All of the aforementioned approaches
correspond to aspects of social cognitive theory, in which the path from
observation of televised characters to behavior produced by viewers is believed to proceed through four discrete stages, each of which is subject to
its own influences: (a) attentional processes that determine what is selec-
tively observed by the viewer (due to, e.g., salience or viewer preferences),
(b) retention processes through which modeled information is represented in memory in symbolic form, (c) production processes in which the
viewer translates stored abstract representations into actions, and (d) motivational processes, which can determine whether learned behaviors will
be performed, depending on their functional value or potential risk in a
given situation. Thus, for a child to act cooperatively after viewing a televised character who acts cooperatively, the child would have to attend to
the character's behavior, create and store a schematic representation of
the behavior (or activate a preexisting analogous schema in memory),
subsequently translate that schematic representation into physical action
when faced with an appropriate situation, and be motivated to do so. Fail-

ure at any of these stages could result in the viewer not displaying the behavior in a real-life situation or laboratory assessment. I return to many of these points in chapter 12.

Considering Effects in Context

As noted in the beginning of this chapter, children do not watch television in a vacuum. Children learn social behavior not only from television, but through interactions with and observations of family, peers, and others in a wide variety of contexts. Television may play a role as a socializing agent, but it is far from the only socializing agent in children's lives.

Moreover, the prosocial messages presented in an educational television series are likely to be mediated by lessons learned from family and peers, as well as children's own life experiences. In some cases, these experiences may work hand-in-hand with the prosocial lessons shown on-screen. In other cases, however, the messages from these various sources may conflict with each other. When conflicts emerge, it seems likely that real-life experiences and the opinions of family and friends will dominate, as when the impact of diversity messages in *Sesame Street* or *Freestyle* was limited by children's perceptions of the opinions of their parents or friends. By the same token, it is worth noting that Corder-Bolz (1980) found that children decreased gender stereotyping after watching a relevant episode of the situation comedy *All in the Family,* but Fairchild (cited in Greenfield, 1984) found that liberal adults saw the series' bigoted lead character, Archie Bunker, as an exposé of prejudice, but prejudiced viewers found support in his views.

Thus, in considering the effects of prosocial programming (from the standpoint of either a researcher or producer), it is important to approach such effects with reasonable expectations in mind. Particularly when dealing with sensitive topics, such as promoting respect in the midst of tensions in Macedonia or the Israeli–Palestinian conflict, one would not expect that a single television program would transform opinions overnight. In such cases, even a small effect can be both important and impressive.

Presenting Prosocial Content Effectively

Naturally, apart from the mediating effects of the social context within which prosocial television series are viewed, the impact of such series is largely a function of how effectively the prosocial messages have been presented within the program. As Schmitt (1999) observed in her content analysis, many broadcasters responded to the Children's Television Act by airing far more prosocial series than series with substantive academic content. From my own experience with producers and broadcasters, my sense is that this is due, in part, to two perceptions within the industry: a sense that prosocial series are "easier" to produce because they are more similar to noneducational entertainment programs such as situation comedies, and a belief that more viewers will watch prosocial series than programs with academic content (thereby creating higher Nielsen ratings and advertising revenue).

The latter perception is contradicted by the long-term ratings success of numerous preschool series on PBS and Nickelodeon, as well as highly rated school-age series such as *Ghostwriter*, whose ratings rivaled those of some of the most popular Saturday-morning cartoons. In addition, at least one empirical study demonstrated that children do not necessarily distinguish between educational and noneducational programs on the basis of their educational content, even when they comprehend that content successfully (Fisch, Yotive, McCann, Garner, & Chen, 1997). Certainly, it may be true that viewers will be less likely to watch *boring* or *didactic* educational programs, but the same can be said for boring noneducational programs, too. Engaging educational series can be every bit as appealing as noneducational television.

More pertinent to the present discussion, however, is the perception that prosocial series are "easier" to produce. Based on my personal experience working on both prosocial and academic television series, I argue that this, too, is a misconception. It may be easy to produce poor or mediocre prosocial series, but creating effective prosocial programming is every bit as challenging as creating academic series, if not more so. Much of the challenge lies in the need to ensure that the prosocial message is not overridden by the inclusion of unintentional messages that may conflict with or be more salient than the intended message.

As an analogy, consider the production of *Cro*, an animated cartoon about science and technology (chap. 6, this volume). In producing *Cro*, a central challenge lay in the need to create an appealing, humorous series without employing many of the standard conventions of animated cartoons, such as characters standing or running in midair. The concern was that viewers would fail to discriminate between the educational content of the series (which often concerned physics) and these conventions, which defied physics.[3] At best, a failure to discriminate could have diluted the impact of the factual educational content. At worst, it could have resulted in the series' promoting misconceptions.

By the same token, to convey prosocial content effectively, producers of prosocial programs must exercise care to ensure that the programs do not inadvertently undercut their positive messages by portraying negative so-

---

[3]Indeed, Fisch et al. (1997) found that viewers failed to discriminate between real science and pseudoscience seen in *The Flintstones*.

cial behavior. It is often tempting to include negative behavior in television programs, whether for the sake of humor (e.g., insult jokes) or even in the service of an educational message (e.g., a character misbehaving before learning his or her lesson). Yet, although this approach may seem natural, it also carries the danger of sending mixed messages to the audience. Indeed, there is even the possibility that, after viewing, children may remember or imitate the character's inappropriate behavior instead of the positive messages that follow it.

For this reason, research on *Sesame Street* and other series has suggested that, for preschool audiences, it is best to avoid negative modeling entirely and focus only on positive messages (e.g., Lovelace & Huston, 1983). The greater sophistication of older viewers makes it possible to include moderate amounts of negative behavior in prosocial programs aimed at older audiences, as in some of the segments in *Freestyle*.

Even in series for older audiences, though, great care must be taken to ensure that the presentation of negative and positive behavior achieves the proper balance. All too often, prosocial television programs fall into a stereotypical "sitcom formula," in which a 30-minute episode spends 27 minutes dwelling on the problem, then resolves it via a quick apology or hug and a speech about what the characters have learned. Such presentations may be ubiquitous but are unlikely to be educationally effective. To be effective, the positive messages and behavior must be handled in ways that make them at least as salient and memorable as (if not more memorable than) the initial conflict. Over the course of the program, significant amounts of time and attention must be devoted to the positive behavior. In addition, the positive behavior must be made at least as engaging and visually interesting as the negative behavior that preceded it; the positive message cannot simply be conveyed in a speech. Only then are viewers likely to walk away from the program with the proper message in mind.

Whose Values?

Finally, when dealing with prosocial content, it is important to recognize that not all prosocial messages are equally appropriate for all audiences. When producers select the specific prosocial messages that will be conveyed in a television program, these choices reflect the producers' values, which may or may not be universal. For example, stories in which parents and children communicate as equals might be appropriate (and quite valuable) for Anglo-American audiences. Yet, they may be less appropriate for Asian-American or Latino-American families, where a greater emphasis is placed on the values of filial piety and respect for elders. Such issues become all the more prominent when producing material for international distribution.

It is typically necessary to adhere to a single message and viewpoint in series that target preschool children. For older children, however, one way to overcome this challenge is to acknowledge that multiple viewpoints exist—for example, by including on-screen characters who represent different, but equally valid, approaches to a given issue. Another is to encourage viewers to discuss the relevant issues with their own families.

These challenges came to the fore in the production of a *3-2-1 Contact* special on sex education, *3-2-1 Contact Extra: What Kids Want to Know About Sex and Growing Up*. Aimed at an audience of 8- to 12-year-olds, the special dealt with a variety of issues related to sex, including topics such as puberty, heterosexual intercourse, and homosexuality.

Because of the sensitivity of these topics, the production of the one-hour special was informed by an unusually extensive series of seven formative research studies that involved more than 500 children and more than 200 parents (see Rosen & Sroka [1992] for a review). A significant amount of the research was conducted with parents from religious groups that typically hold conservative views about sexuality and sex education, as it was expected that these groups might be most easily offended by a careless treatment of the subject matter.

Informed by this research, the special took a twofold approach: (a) It was driven primarily by questions that came from children and parents themselves, often seen on-screen during discussion sessions with a trained sex educator, and (b) great emphasis was placed on the importance of preteens discussing these issues with their parents to learn their families' values and beliefs. The latter point was also supported by a publicity campaign and printed parent's guide that accompanied the broadcast.

By adopting this approach, the program was able to deal with sensitive issues without promoting a single set of values or point of view. For example, in discussing masturbation, one of the sex educators explained that it is not physically harmful, but that different families feel differently about whether it is appropriate. In this way, the special was able to convey factual information to children while being responsive to the needs of a broad range of parents. Indeed, even among the more conservative parents who participated in the research, the vast majority saw the special as a valuable means of opening discussion about subjects that they may have been uncomfortable broaching on their own.

As this example illustrates, it is possible to address even sensitive subject matter effectively via educational television. However, it is crucial to be aware of the different values that may be held among a diverse viewing audience. Depending on the subject matter at hand, it may be necessary to accommodate more than one perspective, either by presenting multiple viewpoints explicitly in the program or by encouraging more personalized follow-up with parents, teachers, or other trusted caretakers. The mediating role of parents, teachers, and child-care providers is the focus of chapter 9.

9

Adult Mediation: Parents, Teachers, Child-Care Providers

Sometimes the flowers bloom because of the one who has done the planting.

—Jun, *Sagwa, the Chinese Siamese Cat*

The previous chapters in this volume focused on unaided viewing of educational television—that is, viewing without elaboration by a parent, teacher, or other adult. Yet, children do not watch television in a vacuum. In many cases, watching television is a group activity, whether at home, in school, or in child-care settings.

Recognizing this point, numerous books and publications have offered suggestions for things that adults can do to maximize children's learning from educational television (e.g., Chen, 1994b; Dudko & Larsen, 1993; Family Communications, 1998; KCET, 1997; Stein, 1979). Typically, recommendations include discussions and activities that adults can employ before, during, and/or after viewing to expand on the content of the program.

From one perspective, one might ask why such efforts are necessary. As the prior chapters of this volume amply demonstrate, such intervention is not a prerequisite for children's learning from television. Significant positive effects of unaided viewing have been documented among both preschool and school-age children in a wide variety of academic subject areas. Viewing has led not only to immediate effects, but to long-term benefits as well. What, then, is to be added by adult mediation of educational television?

In fact, the answer is "a lot." Adult mediation can facilitate and enhance the impact of educational television in several ways: by encouraging exposure, by tailoring the material to individual children, and by extending the experience beyond the television screen.

On the most basic level, adults can determine whether children will be exposed to an educational program in the first place (St. Peters, Fitch,

Huston, Wright, & Eakins, 1991). Particularly in the case of preschoolers, this can be as simple as turning on the television set or tuning in a particular channel. Home viewing by older children is typically less heavily controlled by adults (e.g., Woodard, 2000), but here, too, experts on parenting and media have recommended that parents be aware of their children's viewing habits, steer them away from programs with violent or other negative content, and direct them toward appropriate educational television series (e.g., Chen, 1994b). In addition, parents can buy educational home videos, and teachers and child-care providers can elect to show educational television in classrooms, day care centers, or after-school programs.

Beyond simple exposure, parents, teachers, and providers have the opportunity to tailor the viewing experience to children in their care. Because television is a mass medium, producers of educational series do not have the ability to personalize the treatment of a story or a piece of educational content to the needs, prior knowledge, or developmental level of an individual viewer. The same program is seen by children in advanced and remedial classes, and by children of various demographic backgrounds. Adults' discussions during and around the program can elaborate on content that is difficult for a particular child to understand. They can tie televised content to children's own past experiences to build on existing knowledge. And they can expand on the material.

Even after a program ends, adult mediation can help the learning experience continue. Adults can use an educational television program as a springboard to introduce new subject matter and stimulate interest, then expand on the presented educational concepts via follow-up discussion or hands-on activities.

This chapter examines the effects of adult mediation of educational television in three contexts: parent–child coviewing at home, efforts designed to benefit preschool children in child care settings, and school-age efforts in school and after-school programs.

PARENT–CHILD COVIEWING

Although coviewing occurs far more frequently for prime-time family programming, studies have shown that parents and other adults typically coview educational programming with children only about 25% of the time (Carpenter, Huston, & Spera, 1989; St. Peters et al., 1991). Indeed, in light of the growing numbers of parents working outside the home, this figure may be even lower today.

However, several studies have shown that, when coviewing does occur, parents' comments and verbal interpretations can lead to significant increases in preschool children's learning from educational television (e.g.,

Collins, 1983; Corder-Bolz, 1980; Friedrich & Stein, 1975; Salomon, 1977; J. L. Singer & D. G. Singer, 1976; Watkins, Calvert, Huston-Stein, & Wright, 1980). Buerkel-Rothfuss and Buerkel (2001) noted that, in fact, parental comments during coviewing can take several forms. They can refer to either the specific program being viewed, aspects of television in general, or real-life experiences and values.

Effects of Parental Mediation

Research on the impact of parental mediation has examined the role of such interaction on several classes of outcomes: children's learning of the educational content in a television program, their more general language development (independent of the intended goals of the program on the screen), and engagement in participatory activities.

Learning Educational Content.   In some cases, the research question of interest has been whether parent–child interaction can enhance children's comprehension of the educational content in a television program. For example, a pair of studies by Reiser and his colleagues examined the effect of coviewing a set of *Sesame Street* videotapes. They found that 3- and 4-year-olds were significantly better able to identify a set of letters and numbers if they watched the videos with a coviewing adult who asked them to name the letters and numbers during the program. There was no effect if the adult had simply named the letters and numbers themselves while coviewing (Reiser, Tessmer, & Phelps, 1984; Reiser, Williamson, & Suzuki, 1988).

It is interesting to note that this effect may be unique to coviewing with an adult. Haeffner and Wartella (1987) found that first and second graders' comprehension of a prosocial cartoon and adult-oriented situation comedy was not enhanced by watching the programs with an older sibling. Although non-television research has shown that children can learn from older siblings (e.g., Gauvain, 2001), that was not the case here—largely because the coviewing siblings were not trying to teach. Comments among siblings in the Haeffner and Wartella study typically did not take the forms that have been found to promote learning in parent–child interactions. In all likelihood, this can be attributed to older siblings' watching for the purpose of their own entertainment, rather than watching with the intent of enhancing their younger siblings' learning (as a parent might).

Language Development.   Whereas the studies by Reiser et al. examined impact on children's learning of educational content that was embedded intentionally in the programs viewed, Lemish and Rice (1986) examined parent–child coviewing with regard to learning of a different kind. Inspired by studies that showed gains in young children's language development to result from parent–child interaction during joint story-book reading, Lemish and Rice examined the nature of the interactions between mothers and children that occur during coviewing of television programs such as *Sesame Street*. They found these interactions to be quite similar to those documented for book reading: labeling objects on the screen, questioning about television content, repeating dialogue, and ex-panding on material in the program (e.g., relating it to the child's personal experiences). Just as these types of book-related interactions were found to contribute to language development, they argued, the same was likely to be true for interactions in front of a television.[1]

Viewer Participation.   The British television series *Playschool* pro-vides insight into still another type of parental influence. Although the hosts of *Playschool* asked questions of viewers and presented ideas for games to play or crafts to make, children typically did not do these pro-jects while watching the program (which would have been difficult as it required gathering materials and so on). Rather, the intent was for chil-dren to carry out the activities after the episode ended. A key factor in determining whether preschoolers engaged in these postviewing activi-ties was whether the activities were encouraged and supported by the children's mothers (Dunn, 1977).

Training Initiatives

Of course, not all parents are equally concerned with their children's television viewing, equally inclined to elaborate on televised educational content, or equally effective in doing so. For example, a study by NFO Research (1990) found that parents who read books daily were more likely than less frequent readers to encourage their children to watch *Reading Rainbow*.

For that reason, various efforts have been made to educate parents about practices they can use to build on educational television with their children. One such project grew out of the PBS Ready to Learn (RTL) ini-tiative, which is described in more detail in the section on preschool child care. Research by Bryant, Maxwell, Stuart, Ralstin, and Raney (1999) found that simply receiving a mailing of RTL print materials (activity

---

[1]Interestingly, a recent exploratory study suggests that similar interactions can also occur during joint reading of online storybooks (Fisch, Shulman, Akerman, & Levin, 2002). Thus, it appears that the trigger for such interactions may be engage-ment with a narrative, rather than the use of a particular medium.

guides, posters, and information on PBS preschool series) did not make parents significantly more likely to engage in critical viewing efforts or follow-up activities with their children. However, when the materials were combined with a training workshop for parents, results were far more positive. Relative to parents who received either no treatment or the materials alone, parents who attended the RTL workshops watched television with their children more often, guided children toward educational television more often, conducted more hands-on activities related to children's television programs, read more with their children, emphasized more educational selections in their reading, and engaged more in reading-related behavior, such as taking children to the library. A subsequent mail survey found that parents still reported engaging in similar behaviors 6 months after they participated in the workshops.

Thus, it appears that even if individual parents are not already inclined or able to expand upon their children's viewing of educational television, they can learn to do so. However, some training efforts may be more effective than others; in-person training is likely to be more successful than simply sending materials in the mail.

PRESCHOOL CHILD CARE

From the standpoint of a young child in the United States, one of the most important demographic shifts of the past several decades has been the marked increase in families in which both parents work outside the home. Due in part to economic necessity, and in part to the women's movement leading to greater career opportunities for women, far fewer mothers are choosing to stay home and raise their children than in the 1960s. Whereas less than one third of mothers with children under 18 worked outside the home in the early 1960s, more than two thirds did so by 1990. In the year 2000, an estimated 13,000,000 children under the age of 6 spent part or all of their day cared for by someone other than their parents (Children's Defense Fund, 2000).

Child care today comprises a broad spectrum of options, including day-care centers, in-home care, family child care, relative care, and others. Much of this care is unlicensed and unregulated, which has given rise to an equally broad range of quality. In some instances, the care children receive is of high quality, and perhaps even more enriching than the care they might otherwise receive at home. In other cases, however, the child-care environment is not intellectually stimulating, and the providers who work with children are not trained in early childhood education. Indeed, a review by Barnett (1995) found enrollment in high-quality child care programs to be associated with long-term benefits in IQ and aspects of later school performance. However, these benefits were not found uniformly across all of the child-care programs studied, probably because of variation in funding and quality of care.

A number of educational television series for preschool children have been accompanied by outreach materials distributed to child-care providers at little or no cost. Typically, these consist of print materials that provide ideas for activities or discussion that build on the educational content of the television program. In some cases, a kit of videotapes, audiotapes, and/or hands-on materials may be included as well.

Additionally, some outreach efforts include an in-person training component, in which providers are introduced to the materials and educational practices that they can incorporate into their child-care programs. For example, the *Sesame Street* Preschool Education Program (PEP) is intended to combine active viewing of *Sesame Street*, daily reading of children's books, and hands-on activities to enhance the quality of children's educational experiences in child care. PEP is supported by a training component for providers that offers them opportunities to practice and discuss the key elements of the program with other professionals (e.g., Yotive & Fisch, 2001).

Occasionally, such efforts reach beyond a single television series to encompass several different educational series, usually broadcast on the same network. A notable example of this approach is the PBS Ready to Learn (RTL) initiative. Launched in 1994, RTL encompasses on-air television series (e.g., *Sesame Street, Barney & Friends, Arthur*), interstitials that air between programs, Web-based activities, community outreach materials and initiatives (e.g., users' guides, in-person RTL workshops for parents and providers), and informational resources for parents and providers on using television effectively (e.g., Chen, 1994b; for further details on RTL, see Bryant et al., 2001; Bryant, Stuart, & Maxwell, 1999.)

Often, television-based outreach projects are designed broadly, to contribute to the overall quality of child-care programs by giving providers substantive resources that they can use in promoting literacy and other preacademic skills. In other cases, these projects are targeted more narrowly at a specific topic such as fire safety. In both cases, the underlying idea is to use the appeal of familiar television characters to engage and educate children, and to help providers (many of whom may have little or no formal training) foster children's learning effectively.

Effects

Because these sorts of outreach efforts typically target providers as well as children, impact research has examined outcomes on both levels.

Effects on Providers.   Several studies have assessed the impact of *Sesame Street* PEP on the educational practices of child-care providers. Some of these studies employed self-report data rather than observations of providers' behavior, so their results must be interpreted with caution. However, after attending training sessions, providers reported attitudinal effects such as greater pride, sense of purpose, and confidence in themselves as teachers. They also reported improvements in instructional practices, such as spending more time reading to children, using storytelling techniques to make books come alive, and choosing developmentally appropriate books. Impact on the quality of child care was greater in home-based family child care than in day-care centers, probably because training for providers is less common in family child care, and children in these settings are often poorer and in greater need of educational resources. Indeed, an experimental study of *Sesame Street* materials for family child care found that providers who received the materials and attended training sessions subsequently read more books, used educational television more effectively, showed more sophisticated planning of activities, and drew greater links among the books, television, and activities than providers who did not (Acord & Romontio, 1995; Mindel & Dangel, 1990; Program Research Department, 1999; RMC Research Corporation, 1993; cf. Yotive & Fisch, 2001).

Less extensive effects on providers were found in an evaluation of PBS's Ready to Learn outreach initiative (Bryant, Maxwell, Stuart, Ralstin, & Rainey, 1999). Six months after receiving materials and participating in an RTL workshop, providers reported taking a more active role regarding television with the children in their care (e.g., watching and talking about educational television programs). Unlike the *Sesame Street* PEP data, however, no changes were found in providers' reading to children.

Effects on Children.   Naturally, effects on providers' behavior and attitudes are important, but the chief aim of outreach projects based on children's television is to promote learning among the children served in child care. To date, relatively few studies have assessed outcomes for children, but the studies that do exist are enlightening.

For example, as noted in chapter 3 (this volume), several studies by Singer and Singer found that children's learning from *Barney & Friends* was significantly greater when television viewing was accompanied by discussion and activities conducted by a preschool teacher. Children who experienced these additional activities (instead of just watching *Barney & Friends* without follow-up) performed better on a number of dimensions, including counting, vocabulary, and awareness of manners (J. L. Singer & D. G. Singer, 1994; Singer & Singer, 1995; cf. Singer & Singer, 1998).

It is important to note that, in contrast to unaided television viewing, the effects of television-based outreach projects are not simply a function of the television program or hands-on materials that were produced. Rather, effects depend at least as heavily (or, perhaps, even more heavily) on the way those materials are used by a given child-care provider. If they are used effectively, the materials are likely to have their desired impact. Yet, if they are not used to their best advantage by the provider, then the impact is likely to be reduced or even negated.

Indeed, the same set of materials may see very different patterns of use among different child-care providers. For example, consider data from research on *Sesame Street* outreach materials regarding fire safety. This research found that comprehension of the embedded fire safety messages was greatly impacted by three factors: (a) the number of messages presented in a single session (with comprehension enhanced when providers or fire safety educators focused on only a small number of messages at a time), (b) repetition and reinforcement, and (c) the degree to which the presentation of the messages was made interactive (Einzig, Cappella, & Michaelis, 1996; cf. Yotive & Fisch, 2001). When used well by skilled providers, the materials were an effective vehicle for conveying fire safety information; the materials were less effective when they were used less well. Implications of the variability among providers are discussed at greater length in the "Issues Raised and Lessons Learned" section at the end of this chapter.

SCHOOL-AGE CHILDREN: SCHOOL AND AFTER-SCHOOL

Just as untrained and unprompted parents sometimes use coviewing of educational television as a springboard for discussion or activities, teachers sometimes do the same with their students. For example, Roche (1993) reported using a number-based magic trick from *Square One TV* in a first-year algebra class, where the students watched the segment and then collaborated on figuring out the mathematical relationships that made the trick work. Lampert (1985) showed fifth graders a segment from *The Voyage of the Mimi* that involved time and speed, and used it to engage students in exploring the underlying mathematical principles—a process that entailed graphing points on a Cartesian plane and writing computer programs to replicate the situation.

Often, however, school use of educational television does not begin with teachers, but with the producers of the program. As in the child-care projects discussed earlier, ancillary materials are sometimes created to accompany the broadcast of an educational television series. Teachers are provided with print and/or hands-on materials that are designed to spur discussions and activities that can extend children's learning from specific educational television programs.

In the case of video-based projects such as those produced by Galaxy Classroom or the Association for Instructional Television, the video component of these projects was produced not for broadcast, but specifically for use in the classroom. In other cases, these materials are created to accompany existing television programs that were produced primarily for home viewing. For example, teacher guides were published to accompany the broadcast of educational series such as *Square One TV, 3-2-1 Contact*, and *Reading Rainbow* (e.g., Children's Television Workshop, 1981, 1987; Lancit Media Productions, 1995). These guides provided teachers with episode-by-episode descriptions of each season, information on their educational content and connections to classroom curricula, and suggestions for related classroom activities.

Like everything else in the classroom, the use of educational television is highly adaptive to teaching style. Frequently, the experience follows a model in which an educational television program is used to introduce a topic and stimulate children's interest, after which the teacher engages children in discussion or hands-on activities that follow from the program. At other times, the experience may begin with introductory discussion by the teacher that sets up the content of the television program. The teacher also may stop the program in the middle to ask children what they think will happen next, or have them try to solve the problem shown in the program before watching the characters' solution. Forsslund (1990) reported on a British project that found the most positive results to occur when television programs were shown *after* discussion and classroom activities, so that the program served as a summary of the material covered. There is no one "right" way to use educational television in school; the best practice depends on the nature of the materials and subject matter, and on the style of the individual teacher.

Effects

Effects on Children.   A number of studies have demonstrated that classroom exposure to television-based materials can lead to significant gains in children's performance in various academic subjects. One subject area that has been researched around the world is language arts. In the United States, the Galaxy Classroom language arts program for third through fifth graders included a series of television programs (featuring an ongoing drama about a multicultural group of students), along with books, a magazine, a teacher's guide that suggested activities, and audioconferencing among classes that were using the same materials in different schools. Children who were exposed to the Galaxy Classroom materials demonstrated significantly greater reading achievement than control children who did not receive the materials. However, results were weaker with regard to children's writing (Block, Guth, & Austin, 1993).

Studies in several countries have found that children learn language (either their own or a foreign language) from teacher-supported television viewing. An early example is *Téléniger*, which was produced in the country of Niger and targeted at educationally disadvantaged children who did not speak French, the official language that was used in their schools. Supported by live teachers whose only training was their own elementary education and a 3-month training course in using *Téléniger*, the series attempted to teach French by presenting dramatic stories in which words were paired with concrete images of their referents. After 2 to 3 years of instruction, children scored well on standardized French tests and showed a lower than normal rate of being left back at the end of a school year (Greenfield, 1984; Schramm, 1977).

Foreign language learning can also be promoted through the use of television in school. Forsslund (1990) reported that an Israeli study found significant improvement in low-IQ children's comprehension of English after viewing a series of English-language programs in school, and that a Swedish study found similar effects from English-language programs that were subtitled in Swedish. However, the effect of subtitling did not appear if the language in the program was too sophisticated (as in, e.g., BBC news programs).

As in literacy, Galaxy Classroom projects in science have been found to produce comparable gains among children in kindergarten through second grade (Guth, Austin, DeLong, & Pasta, 1995) and third through fifth grade (Guth, Austin, DeLong, Pasta, & Block, 1995). The former study found that most of the young children understood the science content in one of the themes presented, although comprehension increased with age. First and second graders rated themselves as significantly more curious and marginally more self-confident in the posttest, but attitudes toward school did not change significantly. In addition, second graders improved significantly on some items in a measure of observation skills (although first graders did not, probably due to the difficulty of the task). Data from the latter study showed significant improvement in science knowledge and classification skills at all three ages. However, not all of the effects appeared at all ages; fifth (but not fourth) graders demonstrated increased ability to isolate and manipulate variables in experiments, while fourth (but not fifth) graders showed gains in scientific reasoning.

Effects on science performance were also found for video-based *Integrated Science* classroom materials. When Bryant, Cho, Maxwell, and Raney (1999) matched schools on a variety of demographic variables, they found that middle school students performed significantly better on the Stanford Achievement Test in science if their schools used the *Integrated Science* materials than if they had not. However, the difference was not significant when schools were not matched individually, suggesting that the effects of demographic factors such as SES and school budget were stronger than those of the materials.

In the area of mathematics, classroom exposure to the instructional television series *The Eddie Files* resulted in effects on children's knowledge and attitudes toward mathematics. After viewing, children were better able to define concepts shown in the series, answer content-related questions correctly, and offer applications of the curriculum topics. In addition, children reported being more interested in mathematics, and increases were found in the number who said they would like a job that uses mathematics (Foundation for Advancements in Science and Education, 1997). Bransford et al. (1988) used segments from *Raiders of the Lost Ark* as a springboard for having students solve mathematics problems, such as using Indiana Jones's height and the length of his bullwhip to figure out how far he would have to jump to get over a pit. Fifth and sixth graders (who were below average in mathematics) were more successful in solving these problems under these conditions than if the concepts were taught in a more traditional manner. The students were also able to generalize the mathematical concepts to other situations.

Effects on problem solving were documented for two American classroom projects, the instructional television series *Thinkabout* and the multimedia *Jasper* project. In a study conducted at several sites around the United States, Sanders and Sonnad (1980) found that classroom viewing of *Thinkabout* led to teacher-rated gains in children's thinking skills, and to observed increases in the number of alternatives that children offered in solving problems. *Jasper* (also known as *The Adventures of Jasper Woodbury*) revolved around a series of dramatic stories on videodisc. The stories presented characters encountering mathematical problems in meaningful contexts (e.g., calculating weight, fuel, and distance in order to use an ultralight airplane to rescue an injured eagle). The videos did not show solutions to the problems, but used them as springboards for viewers' attempting to solve them in the classroom. Use of the *Jasper* videodiscs and follow-up activities led to pretest–posttest gains in fifth graders' knowledge of the subject matter. Significantly greater gains were found when the project was enhanced by having children also solve analogous problems and by adding teleconferencing among children in different communities. The latter also produced significant effects on several aspects of children's attitudes toward these types of mathematical activities (Cognition and Technology Group at Vanderbilt, 1997).

Finally, Court TV's *Choices and Consequences* initiative (which combined a television series and classroom curriculum) was found to produce significant effects on children's knowledge of legal terms and on some aspects of their social skills related to violence prevention (i.e., empathy, a decrease in self-reported verbal aggression). Due to ceiling effects, no effects were found for perspective-taking, perceptions of risk, or physical aggression (Wilson et al., 1999).

Aided Versus Unaided Viewing.   As these studies demonstrate, classroom video coupled with teacher-led instruction can produce significant effects on children's performance and attitudes across a number of subject areas. However, as discussed in previous chapters, significant effects have also resulted from children's viewing educational television without the benefit of adult coviewing or follow-up activities. Thus, the question arises as to whether teacher-led discussion and/or activities enhances the impact of educational television beyond the effects that would have resulted from unaided viewing.

A few studies have compared the effects of unaided viewing of educational programs with the effects of the same programs supported by teacher-led discussion or hands-on activities. These studies revealed stronger effects from the combination of viewing plus teacher support than from viewing alone—a trend observed for both academic and prosocial content. For example, Witt and Johnston (1988; cf. Forsslund, 1990) found significant effects of the mathematics series *It Figures* on children's subsequent performance. However, neither the television series nor the activities were as effective alone as they were when the two were combined.

In the social domain, summative research on *Freestyle* (see chap. 8, this volume) found the series to produce considerably stronger effects in reducing sex stereotypes when viewing was combined with teacher-led discussion (Johnston & Ettema, 1982). On the other hand, the added benefits of teacher discussion were less ubiquitous in an assessment of the prosocial PBS series *Degrassi Junior High*. When viewing was combined with teacher involvement, children rated the program as more effective in making an impression on them and raising issues to think about for the future, but it did not lead to significant increases in children's comprehension of the basic messages conveyed (Singer & Singer, 1994b).

Taken together, these studies suggest that classroom materials that combine educational television with teacher-led discussion and/or activities can be effective in impacting on children's knowledge and attitudes. Several studies have found that the combination of television plus classroom activities can yield stronger effects than either one alone, although this has not always occurred across every measure. The inconsistency may be attributable to characteristics of either the television program or the teachers; as noted earlier, neither all educational television programs nor all teachers are equally effective. This point is discussed in greater detail in the next section of this chapter.

ISSUES RAISED AND LESSONS LEARNED

Research on adult mediation of educational television points to several conclusions regarding the role of parents, teachers, and child-care providers. The lessons learned from this research enrich our understanding, both of the processes involved and of ways in which materials can be produced to be maximally effective.

Variability Among Adults

The introduction to this chapter noted that parents, teachers, and child-care providers have the potential to play multiple roles with regard to educational television: as gatekeepers who can expose children to the material, as facilitators who help children understand the information presented in a television program, and as educators who engage children in related discussions or activities that extend beyond the program.

As we have seen, empirical research has shown that adults often do play these roles. However, research also indicates that not all adults are equally inclined or equipped to do so. Perhaps this is to be expected among parents at home; most parents are not formally trained as educators, and in comparison to schools, the home setting does not carry the same sort of mandate to provide children with constant educational experiences. Yet, teachers and child care providers also vary widely in their use of such materials. Some of this variability stems from their comfort with and inclination to use television in the classroom. Their level of comfort can spell the difference between the materials' being used with children or left in a closet.

Another contributing factor is the adults' own facility with the academic subject matter and classroom activities, which impacts directly on the effectiveness of the lessons. Some highly skilled and motivated teachers can use television as a springboard to create their own, original classroom activities without outside support, as in the mathematics activities previously discussed (Lampert, 1985; Roche, 1993). However, even when teachers or child care providers are given hands-on or print materials that suggest activities, there is great variability in their use of the materials; this is illustrated by the example of *Sesame Street* fire safety materials mentioned earlier. Data from the *Sesame Street* study found that some educators were highly effective in making lessons interactive, employing repetition and reinforcement, and breaking down fire safety lessons into manageable chunks that were presented over the course of several lessons. Other educators were less so. The effectiveness of the presentation fed directly into the amount that children learned from the experience—even though all of the children were exposed to the same materials (Einzig et al., 1996; cf. Yotive & Fisch, 2001).

As others have noted, this variability speaks to the importance of not simply handing materials to parents, teachers, or providers, but rather, supporting their use with some form of training that shows them how the materials might be used (e.g., Choat, 1988; Eckenrod & Rockman, 1988; Forsslund, 1990; Yotive & Fisch, 2001). As already discussed, Bryant, Maxwell, et al. (1999) found that Ready to Learn parent materials were far more effective when parents participated in training workshops.

Indeed, a study by Eckenrod and Rockman (1988) demonstrated just how important training can be. In this study, teachers attended training sessions and were given a resource guide for instructional television. Results showed that when teachers subsequently returned to their classrooms, they tended to use the videos and activities that were demonstrated as examples during the training sessions. However, they were far less likely to use materials that were in the resource guide but had not been demonstrated during training.

Making Materials Useful

Although parents, teachers, and providers are key in the effective use of these sorts of materials, use is equally dependent on the effective production of the materials themselves. After all, if the materials are not created in ways that make them easily usable in a classroom, then they will not be used, no matter how entertaining, educationally rich, or valuable they may be.

Many factors come to bear in determining the ultimate effectiveness of such materials. For the purposes of this discussion, let us limit ourselves to several factors that are uniquely relevant to school and child-care settings.

Time. The constraints on classroom time, in both school and child care, are formidable. The daily routine of preschool child care (meal and snack times, naps, circle time, story time, etc.) limits the amount of class time that providers can devote to a video or activity. This is even more true in school, where teachers often are accountable for covering a set curriculum over the course of a year, preparing children to perform well on standardized tests, and so on.

Time spent on television-based activities is time that is not being spent on other lessons. As a result, a video or activity is far more likely to be used if its length fits within the constraints of available time in the classroom. Data from numerous studies have indicated the ideal length of a classroom video to be no more than 10 to 15 minutes, and the time spent on a video plus activity or discussion to be no more than approximately 30 minutes (e.g., Gotthelf & Peel, 1990).

Fit to Curriculum. By the same token, given the constraints of the classroom, materials are far more likely to be used if teachers can see easily how they connect to their existing classroom curriculum. If the materials (no matter how educationally rich they may be) do not map onto the curriculum that a teacher is obligated to meet, then the materials are likely to be treated as a nice "extra" to be used only if time permits. On the other hand, if the materials provide a good fit and help teachers meet the demands of their curricula, then the conflict disappears and the materials are more likely to be used.

Still, it is not sufficient for such connections to exist; they also must be immediately apparent to teachers. Because of constrained schedules, many teachers simply do not have the time or inclination to uncover these connections for themselves. For this reason, teacher's guides often provide detailed, episode-by-episode rundowns that are annotated with the educational content covered in each part of every episode (e.g., Children's Television Workshop, 1981, 1987). In some cases, as in the science series *3-2-1 Contact*, a database searchable by topic is also provided.

Some projects have gone still further in adapting broadcast television programs into new forms to make them more classroom-friendly. For example, the broadcast version of the mathematics series *Square One TV* employed a magazine format in which each episode was comprised of several segments that often were connected loosely, if at all. Videotapes for the classroom version of the series (*Square One TV Math Talk*) were reedited so that each video focused on a single topic, such as probability. In this way, teachers could use a given video when they dealt with that topic in the course of the year, without having to search through several different episodes to locate appropriate segments (Yotive, 1995).

Fit to Setting. Just as classroom materials must fit a school curriculum, materials also must fit the nature of the setting for which they are intended. For example, different sets of *Square One TV* outreach materials were developed for use in schools and after-school programs, because of the different needs and constraints inherent in these settings. After-school programs are typically less structured than classrooms and tend toward informal educational experiences rather than formal "lessons." After-school programs also usually serve mixed-age groups, as opposed to schools, which are more often segregated by age and grade. With this in mind, *Square One TV* materials for after-school programs were designed differently from those created for the classroom. After-school activities were based in play (e.g., board games), involved many more physical games and activities, and were designed so that children of different ages or levels of ability could all participate and learn something appropriate to their level (Davis, Friedman, & Martin, 1990).

On the preschool level, too, different types of child care present different constraints and opportunities for the use of these sorts of materials. For example, although the *Sesame Street* PEP program was designed to be used in many forms of child care, the subsequent *Building on Sesame Street* program was targeted more specifically to the needs of family child care. In contrast to center-based care, family child care generally takes place in the provider's home, is less formally structured, and more frequently includes children of different ages in the same group. For these reasons, the *Building on Sesame Street* materials were designed to provide not formal lessons, but activities that built on "teachable moments" that were likely to arise as natural parts of the day (e.g., meal time, activities for rainy days). Activity ideas were presented on cards that hung in a multipocketed holder on the wall; this made the individual activities more immediately accessible than they would have been in a sizable manual such as the one used in the original *Sesame Street* PEP program (Yotive & Fisch, 2001). Design considerations such as these made it far more likely that the materials would not only be distributed to family child care providers, but also used.

Preparation and Materials. Along similar lines, materials for schools and child care settings should not require extensive preparation by the teacher or provider. Certainly, as some have pointed out, television will probably be used more effectively in the classroom if teachers screen videos and plan activities in advance (e.g., Forsslund, 1990). However, that preparation time needs to be limited, or the adults may decide that it is not worth the trouble. Printed background material should be short and to the point, and the time required for physical preparation should be kept to a minimum.

Nor should hands-on activities require teachers or providers to buy expensive materials. Kits that are sent to educators do not need to include every single item that will be used in a given activity; for example, it is perfectly reasonable to expect that teachers or providers already have crayons. Yet, it is important to recognize that teachers and providers work under limited budgets, and that they cannot be expected to buy items that they do not already own. Thus, it is safest for producers to either provide necessary materials themselves, or limit their activity suggestions to materials that the target audience is likely to already have close at hand. After all, if users do not have access to the materials, they cannot be expected to engage children in the activities.

In summary, all of the factors discussed here carry a common theme: To be effective, television-based outreach programs must make adults' lives easier and not harder. Like broadcast television, television-based outreach materials must be appealing to children and educationally rich. However, whereas that is a necessary condition, it is not sufficient. Because such projects typically require the involvement of an adult, the materials must meet the needs of their adult users as well. If the materials succeed on both levels—for adults and for children—then they can serve as valuable tools in both formal and informal education.

II

THEORETICAL
APPROACHES

10

Comprehension of Educational Content: The Capacity Model[1]

How can Elmo find out more about bicycles?
Oh! Elmo can watch the Bicycle Channel!

—Elmo, *Sesame Street*

The numerous studies reviewed throughout this volume provide ample evidence that children can—and do—learn from educational television. Although all of these studies show that children learn from television, however, they do little to explain *how* this learning occurs. A few theoretical approaches have been proposed to describe aspects of the processing that allows viewers to understand televised narratives (notably the models proposed by Anderson & Bryant, 1983; Collins and his colleagues, e.g., Collins, 1983; and Lang, 2000), but almost no mechanisms have been proposed to explain how children extract and comprehend educational content from television. Perhaps the theory that has come closest to addressing this question is the model presented in a brief but thoughtful discussion by Clifford et al. (1995). Yet, although the Clifford et al. model touches on some of the concepts that are discussed here, it draws only a broad distinction between "drama" and "factual" (i.e., educational) television programs. This presents a limitation for the Clifford et al. model, because many educational programs (e.g., *Sesame Street*, *Ghostwriter*) are narrative-based themselves, thus requiring both types of processing simultaneously.

Although narrative and educational content may be intertwined in educational television programs, they are, in fact, two different things. Stated simply, this chapter uses the term *narrative* to refer to the story presented in the program—the sequence of events, the goals set and achieved

---

[1]This chapter is adapted and updated from Fisch (2000).

by its characters, and so on. By contrast, *educational content* refers to the underlying educational concepts or messages that the program is intended to convey, which can include aspects of both declarative knowledge, such as historical facts, and procedural knowledge, such as problem-solving strategies. (This differentiation between narrative and educational content is akin to Bruner's [1985] distinction between narrative and paradigmatic modes of thought.)

To illustrate the distinction between narrative and educational content (and to see how both can be embedded in a single television program), consider an example taken from the science and technology series *Cro* (see chap. 6, this volume). In one episode of *Cro*, the lead character wanted to learn how to play a musical instrument so that he could join a band; in the course of learning about different kinds of instruments, he learned that sound and music are caused by vibration, and that various kinds of instruments (i.e., string, wind, reed, percussion) vibrate in different ways. In this case, the narrative content of the episode revolved around the character's wanting to join a band and the events that led up to his learning how to play an instrument. The educational content of the episode, on the other hand, centered on sound and vibration.

This chapter represents a first attempt at a systematic model to explain how children extract and comprehend educational content from television. The model has its roots in the study of information processing (e.g., Kahnemann, 1973; Shiffrin & Schneider, 1977; Thomas, 1992). In particular, it grows out of the notion that much of the processing of complex stimuli takes place in working memory, but that the limited capacity of working memory places constraints on the amount and depth of processing that can occur simultaneously. Other aspects of information processing, such as the initial encoding of the complex stimuli presented by educational television, are also undoubtedly critical, but are beyond the scope of the present discussion.

THE MODEL

It is widely accepted that working memory plays a fundamental role in thinking and higher-order cognition, among both children and adults. Working memory has been seen to be associated with performance in a wide variety of cognitive tasks, such as text comprehension, solving arithmetic problems, and logical reasoning (e.g., Demetriou, Christou, Spanoudis, & Platsidou, 2002; Engle, 2002). Yet, the limited capacity of working memory constrains the amount and depth of processing that can take place at any given time. For material to be processed effectively, the demands of the task (often referred to as *cognitive load*) cannot exceed the resources available in working memory (e.g., Gopher & Donchin, 1986; Hart, 1986).

Several studies have demonstrated that, as in the case of other complex cognitive tasks, viewers' comprehension of television involves processing that draws on the limited capacity of working memory. This draw on the capacity of working memory is reflected in longer response times and/or poorer performance in secondary tasks that are concurrent with viewing (Armstrong & Greenberg, 1990; Beentjes & van der Voort, 1993; Lang, Geiger, Strickwerda, & Sumner, 1993; Lorch & Castle, 1997; Meadowcroft & Reeves, 1989; Thorson, Reeves, & Schleuder, 1985). The demands of processing material on broadcast television are compounded by the very nature of the medium; unlike reading, a viewer's experience of television encompasses both visual and auditory information simultaneously, and it is not self-paced (Eckhardt, Wood, & Jacobvitz, 1991). Viewers of broadcast television cannot control the speed of the incoming information or review material that they have difficulty understanding (as is typically done in reading; cf. Pace, 1980, 1981). Instead, the processing that underlies their comprehension must be employed in such a way as to fit the pace of the television program.

If the demands of processing a television program exceed the capacity of working memory, then comprehension is impaired; encoding, storage, and (ultimately) retrieval of the information all suffer (Lang, 2000). Given the potential scale of the processing demands involved, it is not surprising that Salomon (e.g., 1983, 1984) has posited—and demonstrated—that children's comprehension of print and audiovisual media is associated with their amount of invested mental effort (AIME), a construct that is clearly related to (if not synonymous with) the amount of working memory resources devoted to comprehension. When viewers expend greater AIME, according to Salomon, they process the televised information more deeply, and comprehension is enhanced.

However, although the amount of mental effort may be important, it is not a complete explanation when dealing with educational television. Because comprehension of educational television programs requires viewers to process both narrative and educational content simultaneously, we must consider not only the *amount* of cognitive resources involved, but also the *allocation* of those resources among the two parallel processes. This point provides a central motivation for the model proposed here.

Specifically, the model (henceforth referred to as the *capacity model*) revolves around the notion that a critical issue in the comprehension of educational television is the degree to which working memory resources are devoted to comprehension of narrative versus embedded educational content. The model is comprised of a theoretical construct and a set of governing principles that guide the allocation of resources among the components of that construct.

Theoretical Construct

Under the model, demands on capacity are seen to stem from three basic elements: processing of narrative, processing of educational content, and the distance (d) between the two—that is, the degree to which the educational content is integral or tangential to the narrative (Fig. 10.1). In broad terms, the model argues that similar kinds of processing (e.g., accessing prior knowledge, drawing inferences) are employed, essentially simultaneously, in understanding both narrative and educational content on television. When the educational content is tangential to the central narrative of a television program, the two parallel processes of comprehension compete for limited resources in working memory. The result is that the educational content cannot be processed as deeply as it might otherwise be, and comprehension of the educational content (though perhaps not the narrative, as is discussed later in the "Governing Principles" section) is likely to be impaired. On the other hand, when the distance between narrative and educational content is small (i.e., when the educa-

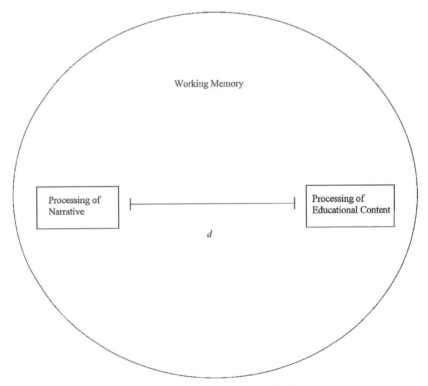

FIG. 10.1. Theoretical construct described by the capacity model (unelaborated version).

tional content is woven tightly into the narrative), then the two parallel processes become complementary rather than competitive, and comprehension is likely to be strengthened.

When the processing of narrative and educational content compete for resources in working memory, the scope of the competition depends on the level of the demands that each type of processing places on those resources—that is, the amount of resources each requires. In general, the literature on information processing has shown that a greater amount of prior knowledge allows information to be integrated in larger chunks, and that familiar, well-practiced tasks can be performed more automatically, reducing the demands on working memory resources and allowing for more efficient use of parallel processes (e.g., Norman & Bobrow, 1976; Shiffrin & Schneider, 1977). Following from this tradition, the capacity model predicts that factors that allow for more efficient processing of either televised narrative or educational content (e.g., prior knowledge) will reduce the demands of processing that type of information.[2] Thus, competition is reduced, and the result is more efficient—and effective—parallel processing of narrative and educational content.

Let us consider each of the three components of the model in more detail, along with the contributing factors that determine its demands on working memory and empirical data that support them.

Processing of Narrative.   The presence of narrative is self-evident in the many educational television programs that employ fictional (or even factual) stories and characters. However, I argue that *all* televised presentations of educational content also involve some form of narrative. This

---

[2]It should be noted that, contrary to this general prediction, Lorch and Castle (1997) found that engagement of cognitive capacity was *greater* while viewing comprehensible segments of *Sesame Street* than when scenes were edited randomly or the audio track was made incomprehensible. However, the two positions can be reconciled easily. Lorch and Castle's comparison between material that is comprehensible or impossible to comprehend seems very different from a comparison between material that is merely easier or more difficult to comprehend. Based on the work of Allport (1989), Lang et al. (1993) drew a distinction between several different types of capacity limitations in watching television: those related to perceptual systems, attention or selection of stimuli to which viewers attend, and controlled processing (i.e., the ability to thoughtfully process and store information). The latter type of limitation is most relevant to the kinds of processing addressed by the capacity model, but the effects found by Lorch and Castle may rest in lower-level processing. Alternately, even if the same types of processing are involved, it may be that the relationship between comprehensibility and working memory resources is actually curvilinear, with viewers devoting minimal resources when material is incomprehensible (because they quickly give up), the greatest amount of resources when material is comprehensible but difficult to understand, and a relatively smaller amount of resources when material is familiar or easy to understand.

point is not limited only to the case of story-based educational television, such as the example from *Cro* discussed earlier, but applies to any program that portrays a series of events. To take an extreme example, even a televised lecture can be conceived of as containing some level of narrative, albeit a simple and rudimentary one (e.g., "First, he welcomed us and thanked us for watching. Then, while he talked, he drew some diagrams on the blackboard to show the structure of the atom. Then, he told us that next week, he'll talk about molecules, and that was the end.").

Of all of the components of the model, the processing of narrative is the one that has received the greatest attention in past literature and, thus, is the one about which we know the most. Both theory and empirical research have painted a picture of television viewers as actively constructing their understanding of televised narratives through many of the same processes used in reading, such as accessing prior knowledge and drawing inferences (e.g., Anderson & Bryant, 1983; Collins, 1983; Huston & Wright, 1997; Palmer & MacNeil, 1991; Pearl, Bouthilet, & Lazar, 1982). Much, if not all, of this processing would be presumed to take place in working memory, and therefore, would place demands on its limited resources.

The demands that narrative places on working memory resources are far from constant. Numerous factors have been shown to affect comprehension of televised narrative and, presumably, the demands of the processing that leads to that comprehension as well. These factors include characteristics of both the television program and the viewer (Fig. 10.2).

One important viewer characteristic that affects the demands of processing narrative is viewers' prior knowledge of the subject matter around which the narrative revolves; Newcomb and Collins (1979) found that children's comprehension of a televised narrative was enhanced when their ethnic and social class background matched that of the characters and situations portrayed in the program. Often, discussions of prior knowledge are framed in terms of the scripts and schemata stored in viewers' memories before they come to the program. The presence of elaborate schemata has been found to aid comprehension of narratives in text (e.g., Bower, 1978), and it is reasonable to expect that the same holds true for television. For example, it is probably easier for a viewer who knows a great deal about baseball (e.g., the rules of the game, the typical sequence of events in a game) to understand a television drama about a baseball game than it is for a viewer who has never seen a baseball game before. (Indeed, a text comprehension study by Spilich, Vesonder, Chiesi, & Voss, 1979, found that baseball fans were better able to recall central information from a story about a baseball game than non-fans were.) The existence of prior knowledge allows the narrative to be assimilated into memory more easily, thus reducing the demands of processing.

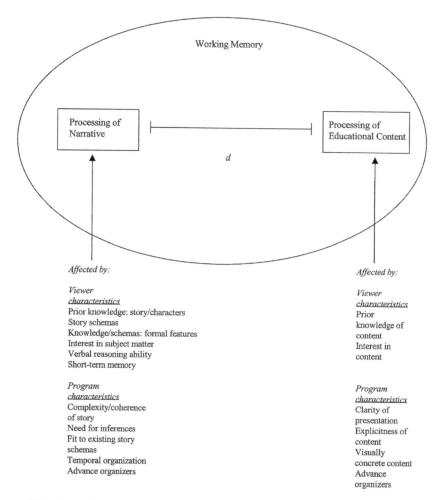

FIG. 10.2. Theoretical construct described by the capacity model, with factors that determine the resource demands for comprehending narrative and educational content.

A related viewer characteristic that can also reduce the demands of processing narrative is viewers' more general schemas regarding the structure of stories themselves. Research on text comprehension has shown that story schemas (i.e., an understanding of the basic structure of stories as a hierarchical series of events) aid in comprehension and recall of narratives (e.g., Thorndyke, 1977; cf. Mandler & Johnson, 1977). Within the context of television, a study by Meadowcroft and Reeves (1989) provided empirical evidence that advanced story schema skills are related to reduced processing effort, increased memory for narrative, and greater flexibility in the allocation of working memory resources across concurrent tasks.

Just as demands can be lessened by viewers' knowledge of the structure of stories, demands can also be lessened by knowledge of the conventions of television. Television conventions include "formal features" such as cuts, fades, and montage that convey narrative information in and of themselves. Facility in understanding these conventions allows viewers to more easily comprehend televised narratives (e.g., Huston & Wright, 1983; Smith, Anderson, & Fischer, 1985).

The demands of processing narrative can also be lessened by viewers' more general cognitive abilities. Verbal ability and visual short-term memory have been shown to contribute to viewers' comprehension of television, with some researchers hypothesizing that these benefits are due to more efficient use of resources within working memory (Eckhardt et al., 1991; Jacobvitz, Wood, & Albin, 1991; Pezdek, Simon, Stoeckert, & Kiely, 1987).

All of these factors would be expected to increase comprehension by reducing working memory demands. However, viewer interest in the subject matter of the narrative would be expected to facilitate comprehension through a different means: by increasing the overall pool of resources dedicated to processing the program in general. Because of this greater availability of resources, the expected result would be greater comprehension of the narrative, but also could include greater comprehension of the educational content as well. Indeed, studies involving educational texts (both expository and narrative texts) have shown significant correlations between interest in the topic of the text and either recall or learning (Schiefele, 1998).

In addition to characteristics of the viewer, the demands of processing narrative can also be affected by characteristics of the television program itself. One such characteristic is the complexity of the narrative (often operationalized in terms of the number of events in a story and the connections among them; e.g., Mandler & Johnson, 1977; Rumelhart, 1975). Developmental research in text comprehension has found that young children can use schemas to process stories only when they are structured simply and clearly state causal linkages (Mandler & Johnson, 1977; cf. Meadowcroft & Reeves, 1989). Thus, narratives containing long and/or complex chains of events are likely to place greater demands on working memory resources, both because of the amount and complexity of material to be processed and because of the relative inaccessibility of schemata that might otherwise reduce those demands.

A related program characteristic is the degree to which the narrative conforms to the prototypic structure of story schemas. Just as children's knowledge of story schemas was shown to be related to reduced processing effort (Meadowcroft & Reeves, 1989), it is reasonable to expect that this benefit would emerge only when the narrative conforms to the prototypic structure described by such schemas. Stories that depart greatly from this kind of structure are less likely to benefit from viewers' knowledge of story schemas. Indeed, the schemas might even interfere with comprehension in this case.

Other program characteristics that contribute toward ease of processing include the degree to which narrative information is explicit or needs to be inferred (e.g., Collins, 1983) and the degree to which information is linear and temporally ordered (Collins, Wellman, Keniston, & Westby, 1978). Because inferences draw on working memory capacity, conditions that rely more heavily on inferences (e.g., implicit content, or viewers' attempts to make sense of scenes that are scrambled in time) are likely to require greater resources, so it is not surprising that comprehension would be weaker in these cases.

Finally, the demands of processing narrative are likely to be reduced through the use of advance organizers (i.e., cues presented early in the program to alert viewers as to its subject matter, such as previews of upcoming material). Because advance organizers can help to orient viewers by identifying the type of information that will be central (rather than peripheral) to the narrative, it seems likely that less resources would be needed for viewers to identify and extract this central information when it arises later in the program. As a result, it is not surprising that studies have shown advance organizers to result in greater comprehension of televised narratives (e.g., Calvert, Huston, & Wright, 1987).

Processing of Educational Content.   Because the comprehension of educational content on television has received far less attention than comprehension of narrative in the literature, any discussion of factors that contribute to the demands of processing educational content is necessarily more speculative than the one just presented. Based on the factors that have been shown to contribute to comprehension of narrative, however, several analogous factors seem likely to help determine the demands of processing educational content as well. As in the comprehension of narrative, these factors include characteristics of both viewers and the television programs themselves (Fig. 10.2).

Among the characteristics of viewers, it seems reasonable to expect that just as prior knowledge relevant to the subject matter of a narrative facilitates comprehension of that narrative (Newcomb & Collins, 1979), prior knowledge or existing schemata regarding the educational content of a television program should reduce the demands for processing that educational content and enhance comprehension. Indeed, Eckhardt et al.

(1991) found that adult viewers' delayed recall of the educational content in a televised drama about the Underground Railroad increased as a function of their prior knowledge about this topic. Moreover, this effect was additive to (i.e., independent from) a concurrent effect of viewers' verbal ability. If we imagine that verbal ability might have served to help reduce the demands of processing the narrative in the television program, whereas knowledge of the Underground Railroad helped to reduce processing demands for the educational content, it would make sense for the effects of knowledge and verbal ability to be additive rather than producing a significant interaction.

As discussed earlier, another viewer characteristic that is likely to contribute to the processing of educational content is viewer interest (Schiefele, 1998), which can cause viewers to dedicate a greater pool of resources to processing the program. This interest can be interest in either the subject matter of the narrative (in which case the educational content benefits from a greater pool of resources for the program in general) or in the educational content itself (in which case a greater proportion of those resources also may be allocated to the content). In fact, research on text comprehension may support the notion of these two different mechanisms. One text-based study of children's comprehension of and performance in mathematical word problems found that boys' comprehension of the word problems was enhanced if they were interested in the narrative context in which the problem was embedded (e.g., football); however, interest in the narrative context was not a significant factor in the performance of children who were interested in mathematics (Renninger, 1998). From the standpoint of the model, one might imagine that these data reflect two different mechanisms: Interest in the subject matter of the narrative context resulted in a greater pool of available resources (benefitting both comprehension of the narrative context and mathematical problem solving), whereas interest in mathematics resulted in more resources being allocated to the mathematical content of the problems, regardless of the size of the overall pool.

In addition to viewer characteristics, some of the program characteristics that would be expected to affect the resource demands for processing educational content are also analogous to characteristics that contribute to the demands of processing narrative. Just as the demands of processing narrative are expected to be lower if the complexity of the narrative is low and narrative information is explicit, one would expect the demands of processing educational content to be reduced if the presentation of the educational content is clear (i.e., if it is explained well and on an age-appropriate level) and if the content is made explicit within the program (e.g., by talking about the geometry involved in a basketball player's difficult shot, rather than simply showing the player make the shot without any discussion).

Similarly, empirical studies have suggested that comprehension of educational content is likely to be greater if the content is visually concrete, rather than abstract. This appears to be true of both academic content (e.g., concepts in physics) among school-age children (Goodman et al., 1993; cf. Fisch et al., 1995) and prosocial content (e.g., sharing versus telling the truth) among preschoolers (Fisch, McCann Brown, & Cohen, 2001).

Lastly, in the same way that advance organizers that highlight central narrative information can help viewers identify central content and comprehend the narrative (e.g., Calvert et al., 1987), one would expect that advance organizers focusing on educational content would have a parallel effect on processing demands for educational content. In this case, the advance organizers orient viewers toward the educational content and make it easier to extract this educational content from the narrative in which it is embedded. Thus, the demands of processing educational content would be expected to be reduced, and comprehension of the educational content would increase.

Distance. The notion of distance between the narrative and the educational content of an educational television program is one of the features that is unique to the capacity model. As noted earlier, "distance" refers to the degree to which the educational content is integral or tangential to the narrative, a concept that Sesame Workshop dubbed "content on the plotline" (e.g., Hall & Williams, 1993; see chap. 4, this volume). Adopting the language of researchers who have studied story structure within the domain of text comprehension (e.g., Mandler & Johnson, 1977; Rumelhart, 1975; Thorndyke, 1977; Trabasso, Secco, & van den Broek, 1984), distance can be conceptualized in terms of the role of the educational content in the causal chain or hierarchical structure of story events.[3] Specifically, a small distance between narrative and educational content corresponds to educational content that is embedded in causal-chain events (i.e., events that are causally connected to a large number of subsequent events) or at relatively high levels in the hierarchical structure of the story. A large distance corresponds to educational content that is embedded in dead-end events (i.e., events that do not forward the story) or at lower levels in the hierarchy.

An example of a large distance between narrative and educational content is provided by the episode of *Cro* discussed earlier, in which the narra-

---

[3]I am indebted to Elizabeth Lorch for bringing this point to my attention.

tive concerned learning how to play a musical instrument and the educational content concerned the notion that sound is caused by vibration. Although the narrative and the educational content of this episode were related (particularly as the episode showed the ways in which vibration is manifest in different musical instruments), they were not integral to each other, because knowledge about vibration is not a necessary precursor to learning how to play a musical instrument.

By contrast, an example of a small distance between narrative and educational content can be found in a series of segments produced for the mathematics program *Square One TV*. The narrative in these segments concerned a pair of mathematical detectives who helped a young boy find a hidden treasure by figuring out a series of puzzles and clues, all of which were built around a mathematical sequence of numbers known as the "Fibonacci sequence."[4] Here, the educational content was far more integral to the narrative; without manipulating the mathematical sequence, the characters could not solve the puzzles, and thus could not find the treasure.

It seems reasonable to expect that when the distance between narrative and educational content is large, the two types of content must compete with each other for resources within working memory. Because similar kinds of processing are required to understand both narrative and educational content (e.g., accessing and forming connections to prior knowledge in long-term memory, drawing inferences), and because viewers would employ both types of processing concurrently, interference stemming from viewers' processing of the narrative would make the educational content less likely to be processed as deeply or thoroughly. The probable result would be that comprehension of the educational content would be weaker than it might be otherwise.

When the distance between narrative and educational content is small, however, a very different situation emerges. The intertwining of narrative and educational content in this case means that, rather than competing with each other for limited resources, the parallel processes responsible for comprehending narrative and educational content actually complement each other instead. For example, in the *Square One TV* segments just described, the use of the Fibonacci sequence is essential in characters' movement from setting to attaining goals in the event structure of the narrative. Thus, the processing that allows viewers to understand the Fibonacci sequence while watching the program is not only part of their processing of educational content, but of their processing of the narrative as well.

---

[4]The Fibonacci sequence (1, 1, 2, 3, 5 ...) is derived by adding each two successive numbers to arrive at the next number in the sequence. For example, $1 + 1 = 2$, $1 + 2 = 3$, $2 + 3 = 5$, and so on.

On an empirical level, this construct predicts that (all other things being equal) comprehension of educational content on television will be stronger when the distance between narrative and educational content is small than when it is large. In fact, this prediction was confirmed in a summative study of *Cro* (Goodman et al., 1993; cf. Fisch et al., 1995 and chaps. 4 and 6, this volume). Data from this study showed that children who viewed *Cro* showed a significantly greater understanding of the technological principles presented in some episodes than nonviewers did. However, this difference was not significant for all of the episodes tested, and one of the factors that distinguished between episodes that produced significant effects and episodes that did not was the centrality of the educational content to the narrative plotline. Significant differences emerged only for two episodes in which the educational content was closely tied to the narrative; there was no difference for two other episodes, in which the educational content was more tangential to the narrative. (For similar data in the area of literacy, see Hall & Williams, 1993). Indeed, although no controlled comparison was made to material in which distance was larger, it is also worth noting that a separate study found that after viewing the *Square One TV* material discussed here (in which distance was small), many 8- to 12-year-old children were able to describe and/or explain the Fibonacci sequence as much as 2 weeks later (*Square One TV* Research, 1988).

Governing Principles

To some degree, the allocation of working memory resources between the processing of narrative and educational content is a function of the demands of each. However, the capacity model specifies several broad governing principles that also help to determine the differential allocation of resources among the processing of narrative and educational content.

Narrative Dominance.   The first of these principles is that, as a default, the model posits that priority is given to comprehension of narrative over educational content (a principle I refer to as *narrative dominance*). For this reason, when the processing of narrative and educational content are in competition with each other—when distance is large or the demands of processing narrative and/or educational content are high—a greater proportion of working memory resources are devoted to the narrative than the educational content (although the allocation of resources is also subject to some degree of voluntary control, as discussed next).

There are two chief reasons to believe that this is the case. First, television is primarily an entertainment medium. Although Greenberg (1974) found, when asking children about their reasons for watching television, that approximately 20% of the variance was attributable to social learning, the remainder centered on entertainment functions: relaxation, habit, arousal, forgetting problems, killing time, and alleviating boredom. Given that children's comprehension of television is affected by whether they are watching to learn or to have fun (Salomon & Leigh, 1984), it seems reasonable to think that at least part of this effect is due to the allocation of resources in working memory. Thus, if viewers' primary reason for watching television is entertainment (and as the entertainment value of a program is likely to lie in its narrative), it seems likely that, all other things being equal, the default would be for viewers to devote a greater proportion of working memory resources to processing narrative.

Second, if we think of an educational television program as having "surface" (i.e., explicit) content and "deep" (i.e., more implicit) content, it is likely that the narrative will comprise the surface content whereas the educational content may lie more deeply within the program. Although educational content may be embedded within a narrative (as in the examples from *Cro* and *Square One* that were presented earlier), it is difficult to imagine how one might construct a television program in which the opposite is true (i.e., the narrative is embedded within educational content). Even if the educational content is fairly explicit within the narrative, it is still embedded within the narrative. All other things being equal, then, when only limited resources are available in working memory, it seems reasonable to expect that those resources would be devoted primarily to the surface content of the program—that is, the narrative.

Indeed, although no empirical studies have tested the narrative dominance hypothesis directly, past research may provide some limited support for this principle. As discussed in chapter 5 (this volume), a study of children's comprehension of several *Square One TV* segments found that recall of the characters' problem and solution (the level most closely tied to narrative in the segments) was consistently higher than understanding of underlying mathematical concepts. When children comprehended only one aspect of the segments in this study, it tended to be aspects related to the narrative rather than the underlying educational content (Peel et al., 1987).

Relative Availability of Resources.   In light of the principle of narrative dominance, the second governing principle is that the pool of resources available for processing educational content on television is a function of the amount of resources not already committed to the narrative. A basic concept in research on information processing is that, when parallel processes take place concurrently, less resources are available than if either process takes place in isolation (e.g., Norman & Bobrow, 1976; Shiffrin & Schneider, 1977). When the processing of narrative and educational content compete for resources, the model predicts that any deficit would be most likely to appear in the resources available for processing educational content.

In practice, the amount of resources available for processing educational content depends on both the factors that determine the demands of processing each type of content and the distance between them. When the demands of processing narrative are relatively low (e.g., when the narrative is fairly simple), more resources are available for processing the educational content. Conversely, when the demands of processing educational content are relatively low (e.g., when the presentation of the content is clear), less of the working memory resources are needed, so the residual resources not consumed by processing the narrative may be sufficient. Finally, as discussed earlier, when the distance between the narrative and educational content is small, the processing of the two types of content become intertwined, so the resources devoted to one can also contribute to the processing of the other.

Thus, the strongest comprehension of educational content would be expected to be observed when the demands of processing both narrative and educational content are low, and the distance between them is small. The weakest comprehension would be expected when the demands of both types of processing are high and the distance between them is large.

Voluntary Allocation of Resources. Although narrative dominance may operate as a default, the capacity model also assumes that viewers can choose to allocate resources differentially among the processing of narrative and educational content. This principle, too, has not been tested directly in past research. However, several studies have shown that a number of factors can affect not only the amount of a televised narrative that is recalled, but also the level at which the narrative is understood. One such factor is viewers' reason for watching; studies by Kwaitek and Watkins (1981) and Salomon and Leigh (1984) both found that instruction to view for learning led to greater recall of televised material, including higher levels of abstraction. Another factor is parental commentary during coviewing with their children; a number of studies found such comments to enhance children's comprehension of educational television (see chap. 8, this volume). Indeed, Collins, Sobol, and Westby (1981) found that parental comments during coviewing resulted in greater comprehension of implicit content among children, which suggests that part of the effect of coviewing may stem from parents' orienting children toward embedded content (such as educational content within a narrative). Although one might argue that the facilitation of comprehension found by Collins et al. (1981) could be due to alternate mechanisms (e.g., parents' comments making the implicit content more explicit), it is difficult to imagine an explanation of the Kwaitek and Watkins (1981) or Salomon and Leigh (1984) data that does not assume a differential allocation of working memory resources to the processing of implicit content. Indeed, research on text comprehension has indicated that providing college students with questions before they read a text results in more time spent with (i.e., more resources devoted to) passages related to those questions (Reynolds & Anderson, 1982). The parental comments in the Collins et al. study may have had a similar effect on viewers' allocation of resources.

Just as motivation and commentary affect the level on which narrative is comprehended, one might expect similar factors to lead viewers to allocate a greater proportion of resources to educational content as well. Thus, viewers' motivation to view a program for the purposes of learning, parental commentary, or any other factor that serves to make the educational content more salient in the mind of the viewer is likely to result in a greater proportion of working memory resources being allocated to educational content.

Finally, it is important to note that, although each of these considerations would be expected to increase the proportion of resources allocated to educational content, none of them would be expected to result in viewers' abandoning the processing of narrative altogether. The principle of narrative dominance, coupled with the notion that educational content is embedded more deeply in television programs than narrative is, implies that it would be difficult for viewers to extract and process educational content without also processing the narrative, at least to some extent. Rather, viewers' voluntary allocation of greater resources to educational content would be expected to increase the depth of processing of educational content and perhaps reduce (but not eliminate) the processing of narrative.

DEVELOPMENTAL ASPECTS OF THE MODEL

Many studies have demonstrated that, barring ceiling effects, children's comprehension of both narrative and educational content on television increases with age (see Huston & Wright, 1997 for a review that includes numerous studies demonstrating age differences in comprehension of television). From the standpoint of the capacity model, these developmental trends raise questions as to how the processing described by the model changes with age.

In fact, both the literature on children's comprehension of television and the more general literature on information processing point to developmental trends in several factors that contribute to comprehension under the model. For the purposes of this discussion, these factors can be divided into two broad classes: those that affect the demands of process-

ing narrative and/or educational content, and those that affect the allocation of resources in working memory.

Development and the Demands of Processing

Inasmuch as the model assumes that comprehension of educational
content is affected greatly by the demands of processing both narrative
and educational content, developmental factors that serve to reduce
these processing demands should also contribute to better comprehension of educational content. Several such factors have been identified
in past literature.

Prior Knowledge. Perhaps the most obvious developmental factor
relevant to the capacity model is children's acquisition of increasing
amounts of world knowledge as they get older. As previously discussed, a
greater amount of existing knowledge or more elaborate schemata for a
particular topic allows new information to be assimilated more easily.
Thus, as children gradually accumulate knowledge with age, this greater
knowledge base would be expected to reduce the demands of processing
new information. This would hold true for the processing of both narrative and educational content; prior knowledge or schemata relevant to a
particular story would reduce the demands of understanding narrative,
whereas prior knowledge relevant to the underlying educational content
would reduce the demands of processing educational content.

Inferences. Another way in which prior knowledge plays a role is in fa-
cilitating the generation of inferences to aid in comprehension. Children's
ability to draw inferences regarding televised narrative increases with age
(Collins, 1983), and research on parallel effects outside the realm of television has suggested that this trend is due primarily to older children's
having a greater knowledge base on which they can draw (Omanson, Warren, & Trabasso, 1978). Although the use of inferences has been investigated primarily with regard to comprehension of narrative, it seems likely
that knowledge relevant to the educational content of a television program would lead to a similar facilitation of inferences regarding that content. Despite the fact that the process of drawing such inferences itself
requires working memory resources, the ability that it provides to anticipate information and fill in gaps seems likely to make the processing of
both narrative and educational content more efficient on the whole.
(And, indeed, children's ability to draw such inferences is likely to become
more automatic and draw less on working memory resources as they get
older, as discussed later.)

Formal Features.   In addition to knowledge about the subject matter of the narrative and about the educational content, knowledge about the conventions of television itself may also be relevant. Research has shown that children's understanding of the formal features of television increases with age (e.g., Huston & Wright, 1983). Because, as discussed earlier, a greater knowledge of formal features is associated with greater comprehension of televised narrative (e.g., Smith et al., 1985), this factor, too, may reduce the demands of processing narrative as children grow older. As children are able to devote less effort and resources to making sense of the conventions of television (e.g., uniting successive scenes), more attention can be given to the story—and, perhaps, the educational content—itself.

Automaticity.   A long line of information processing research has indicated that, as cognitive tasks become more practiced, they also become more automatic and draw less on the resources of working memory (e.g., Shiffrin & Schneider, 1977). Given that American children spend a tremendous amount of time watching television—estimated between 11 and 28 hours per week across studies (e.g., Anderson et al., 1985; Huston et al., 1987, 1989; Roberts et al., 1999)—this represents time spent practicing all of the skills needed to understand televised narratives, such as decoding formal features, engaging in semantic and syntactic analyses, drawing inferences, and so on. Thus, one would expect that children's extensive experience in watching (and understanding) television programs would lead to a better and more automatic processing of televised narrative as they get older. If we add to this body of experience the time children spend reading and listening to stories that are not on television, the likelihood that their processing of narrative becomes more automatic with age increases exponentially.

At the same time, children's vast experience with educational content in both formal (i.e., school) and informal settings makes it likely that the processing of educational content, too, becomes increasingly automatic with age. Together, the greater automaticity of processing both narrative and educational content reduces the demands of each kind of processing, thus allowing for an easier management of resources across the two.

Development and the Allocation of Resources

Apart from the preceding factors, which reduce the demands of processing narrative and/or educational content as children grow older, research has also pointed to aspects of working memory itself that develop with age. Even assuming a constant level of demands for the dual processing of narrative and educational content, these aspects of development would contribute to more efficient management of those parallel processes, and thus, greater comprehension of educational content (and, perhaps, narrative as well).

Speed of Processing.   Developmental research has shown that, as children mature, they can hold increasing amounts of information in working memory (Dempster, 1981; Gathercole & Baddeley, 1993). Studies by Kail (1992; Kail & Park, 1994), Fry and Hale (1996), and Demetriou et al. (2002) have suggested that this improvement is due not to an increase in the capacity of working memory itself, but to a developmental increase in the speed of information processing within working memory. Faster information processing allows for more efficient use of the limited resources available in working memory.

Particularly within the realm of television, where (unlike reading) the input of information is not self-paced, an increase in processing speed clearly would provide a great advantage. Such an increase would allow for more efficient and effective management of the parallel processing of nar-

TABLE 10.1

Predictions of the Capacity Model: Program Characteristics That Result in Greater Comprehension of Educational Content

Increase in:	*Underlying mechanism*
Conformity to story schemas	Decreased demands for processing narrative
Temporal ordering	Decreased demands for processing narrative
Advance organizers re: narrative	Decreased demands for processing narrative
Clarity of educational content	Decreased demands for processing educational content
Explicitness of educational content	Decreased demands for processing educational content
Advance organizers re: content	Decreased demands for processing educational content
Decrease in:	*Underlying mechanism*
Complexity of narrative	Decreased demands for processing narrative
Need for inferences in narrative	Decreased demands for processing narrative
Distance	Reduced competition between narrative & educational content

TABLE 10.2
Predictions of the Capacity Model: Viewer Characteristics That Result in Greater Comprehension of Educational Content

Increase in:	*Underlying mechanism*
Prior knowledge: story/characters	Decreased demands for processing narrative
Story schemas	Decreased demands for processing narrative
Knowledge of television conventions	Decreased demands for processing narrative
Verbal ability/ Verbal reasoning ability	Decreased demands for processing narrative and/or educational content
Short-term memory	Decreased demands for processing narrative and/or educational content
Prior knowledge: educational content	Decreased demands for processing educational content
Motivation to learn	Greater allocation of resources to educational content
Adult commentary re: educational content	Greater allocation of resources to educational content
Speed of processing	More efficient management of resources
Ability to manage multiple goals	More efficient management of resources
Interest in subject matter of narrative	Greater allocation of resources (in general)

rative and educational content, and potentially, for deeper processing of each while viewing.

Management of Multiple Goals. A related factor may concern developmental changes in children's ability to manage multiple goals in working memory. Lawson and Kirby (1981) demonstrated that the skill of managing multiple problem-solving goals in working memory can be taught, suggesting that this ability may increase with age and experience. (Consistent with this idea, Wickens [1974] found evidence of a developmental shift from "single channel" processing, in which children attend to only one thing at a time, to parallel processing, in which they can coordinate attention to multiple sources of information at the same time.)

If this ability does increase with age, then one benefit under the capacity model could be an increased ability to allocate working memory resources effectively, making it easier to process narrative and educational content concurrently. Indeed, because the skill of managing multiple goals in working memory can be taught, it is even possible that, within the realm of educational television, the ability to balance resources among processing of narrative and educational content would improve with practice. In other words, as children watch increasing amounts of educational television, their cumulative experience in processing narrative and educational content simultaneously could make it easier for them to balance these two types of processing when watching other educational television programs in the future. (Alternately, of course, it is also possible that such an effect might only be obtained with explicit training analogous to that used by Lawson & Kirby, 1981.)

ISSUES RAISED AND LESSONS LEARNED

Naturally, the capacity model raises numerous issues regarding theory and research on children's comprehension of television. In addition, it also raises implications for the production of effective educational television programs.

Implications for Research

First and foremost, the implications of the capacity model lie in helping us understand how children extract and comprehend educational content from television programs. To summarize, the capacity model revolves around three basic components:

- Processing of narrative
- Processing of educational content
- Distance

The processing demands for comprehending narrative and educational content are affected by numerous factors, including: prior knowledge (of information relevant to the story and the educational content, as well as the formal features of television); the ability to engage in top-down processing and identify central information in the narrative; the complexity of the story; the need for inferences; the use of advance organizers; and the clarity of the presentation of educational content.

Allocation of working memory resources among the processing of narrative and educational content is determined by three governing principles:

1. As a default, priority is given to narrative over educational content (*narrative dominance*).
2. High demands of processing narrative leave less resources available for educational content, whereas low demands of narrative leave more resources available. A small distance between narrative and educational content reduces the degree to which they must compete for limited resources.
3. Resources also can be allocated voluntarily, depending on a variety of factors (e.g., reason for viewing, parental commentary during coviewing), but processing of narrative is never abandoned entirely in favor of educational content.

Based on these components and governing principles, there are five ways in which comprehension of educational content can be increased: (a) by increasing the total amount of working memory resources devoted to understanding the television program as a whole (akin to Salomon's [1983] theory of AIME); (b) by reducing the demands of processing narrative, so that more resources are available for processing educational content; (c) by reducing the demands of processing educational content, so that a smaller amount of resources is needed; (d) by minimizing the distance between narrative and educational content in the program (i.e., by making the educational content integral to the narrative) so that the two parallel sets of processing complement each other, rather than compete; and (e) via viewers' voluntary allocation of a greater proportion of working memory resources to the processing of educational content (e.g., because of a motivation to learn).

More specifically, the model gives rise to numerous empirical predictions regarding the conditions under which comprehension of educational content will be strongest. These conditions are summarized in Tables 10.1 and 10.2, and include characteristics of the program (Table 10.1) and of the viewer (Table 10.2). Some of these predictions are already supported by existing studies in the research literature (as noted throughout this chapter), and further research will be needed to test others.

Implications for Production

Apart from its implications on a theoretical level, the model also holds more practical implications for the creation of effective educational television programs. Because comprehension depends in part on features of the program (as in Table 10.2), the effectiveness of an educational television program can be enhanced through the inclusion of these features in the program.

In other words, by incorporating appropriate program characteristics, such as advance organizers or a small distance between narrative and educational content, into the design of material for educational television, producers may be able to maximize comprehension and impact of that material among its target audience. Indeed, several of these factors are already recognized and used by some television producers, with positive results (e.g., Connell & Palmer, 1971; Fisch & Truglio, 2001a; Hall & Williams, 1993).

Hopefully, through the efforts of researchers in this field, these features will be incorporated more widely into the design of educational television programs. If they are implemented successfully, the benefits for the viewing audience can be made even more powerful.

11

Transfer of Learning From Educational Television: When and Why Does It Occur?

Let's play "What Do We Know?"

—George Frankly, *Square One TV*

As seen throughout this volume, numerous studies have shown that viewing educational television results in significant gains in preschool and school-age children's academic knowledge or skills. However, the evidence is less consistent regarding transfer of learning. *Transfer of learning* or *learning transfer* refers to the application of knowledge or skills learned in one context (in this case, a story in an educational television program) to a new problem or situation that differs from the one that was encountered previously.

Consider, for example, one of the findings from summative research on the science and technology series *Cro* (see chap. 6, this volume). After watching an episode of *Cro* about airplanes and flight, viewers of *Cro* showed significantly greater comprehension of the educational content in the episode than children who had not viewed the episode. When shown pictures of failed attempts at flying machines that were taken from the episode, significantly more *Cro* viewers than nonviewers explained the failures in terms of underlying principles (i.e., the size, shape, and sturdiness of the wings), rather than surface features (e.g., saying that the devices did not look like airplanes). Yet, when the children were presented with an analogous new problem in which they could apply the same underlying principles, viewers did not differ significantly from nonviewers. In other words, the data indicated that viewers had comprehended the relevant principles, but failed to transfer them to a new problem (Goodman et al., 1993; cf. Fisch et al., 1995).

Similarly, an early summative study of the mathematics series *Square One TV* assessed comprehension of the mathematical content in several mathematical problem-solving segments on three levels: recall of the

164

problem and solution shown, understanding of the underlying mathematical content, and extension (i.e., transfer) to new problems. Although comprehension varied somewhat across the 10 segments used in the study, a general trend emerged, with the greatest performance found on the level of recall, followed by understanding, which was followed in turn by extension. Thus, some of the children in the study showed evidence of understanding the mathematical content without transferring it to new problems (Peel et al., 1987; see chap. 5, this volume). A comparable transfer failure was reported by Hodapp (1977), who found that 5- and 6-year-old children could reproduce the problem-solving strategies modeled in a segment from *Sesame Street* but not apply the same strategies to a new problem—even though other studies have found long-term effects of exposure to *Sesame Street* that endure between 1 and 10 years (Anderson et al., 1998, 2001; Huston et al., 2001; Wright et al., 2001; Zill, 2001; see chap. 2, this volume).

Several explanations could be offered for these patterns of results. One approach might grow out of developmental differences; perhaps the thinking of the children in these studies was simply too literal and concrete to allow them to abstract the knowledge gained from the programs to novel problems. A second could concern the limitations of television as a medium; perhaps the two-dimensional, presentational format of television does not encourage transfer in the same way that hands-on experience might. Indeed, in comparing learning from two-dimensional paper diagrams versus hands-on experience, Ferguson and Hegarty (1995) found that the two treatments produced equal improvement on a learning task, but that the hands-on learners were better able to solve application problems; they attributed this difference, in part, to the fact that children in the hands-on condition could interact with the materials whereas those in the diagram condition could not. A third, less sweeping approach might stem from characteristics of the specific television programs and problems used in the study; perhaps there were aspects of the programs that inhibited the conditions necessary for transfer, either during the initial acquisition of the information from the television programs or during the children's attempts to solve the subsequent transfer problems that were presented to them.

Of these three approaches, the literature suggests that the last approach is the most reasonable. Although no significant transfer was found in the study on *Cro*, other studies have provided ample evidence of instances of significant learning transfer from educational television. For example, Hall, Esty, et al. (1990; cf. Hall, Fisch, et al., 1990) found that extended viewing of *Square One TV* resulted in significant improvement in fifth graders' subsequent performance on mathematical problem-solving tasks that were not shown in the series. Similar transfer effects were found in problem solving among preschoolers and science experimentation among school-age children (Bryant et al., 1999; Mulliken & Bryant, 1999; Rockman Et Al., 1996; see chaps. 3, 5, and 6, this volume). Thus, a conception of television as incapable of producing transfer is not supported by the literature. In addition, because some of these studies found significant transfer from preschool television programs, it does not appear that lack of transfer can be explained solely through age differences either. Rather, the most likely scenario is that the occurrence of transfer from educational television is contingent upon several complementary factors: characteristics of the television program, the viewer, and the novel problem that is subsequently encountered in the transfer situation.

In fact, just as transfer effects have emerged inconsistently with regard to educational television, research outside the realm of television has shown transfer to be an elusive phenomenon as well. Many studies in the broader fields of education and cognition failed to find evidence of transfer—so many that Detterman (1993) concluded that transfer is probably rare and accounts for little human behavior. Other researchers have been far less pessimistic about the existence of transfer, but nonetheless acknowledge the difficulty inherent in eliciting transfer in experimental settings (e.g., Bransford & Schwartz, 1999; Sternberg & Frensch, 1993).

The inconsistent appearance of transfer in education and cognitive tasks has given rise to a variety of theoretical approaches that attempt to explain the successes and failures of learning transfer in domains such as reasoning, mathematics, problem solving, and vocational training, among others (e.g., Gentner, 1983; Gott, Hall, Pokorny, Dibble, & Glaser, 1993; Greeno, Moore, & Smith, 1993; Holyoak, 1985; Reed, 1993; Salomon & Perkins, 1989). The mechanisms proposed in these theories run the gamut from schema-based cognitive theories to approaches grounded in pragmatic knowledge to theories that treat knowledge as situated so that they focus on characteristics of situations rather than mental representations.

This chapter takes several factors that are common across many of the existing theories of transfer and applies them to the context of educational television. By synthesizing the literature on transfer with empirical research on educational television (as well as the *capacity model* described in chap. 10), the chapter represents a first attempt to provide a theoretical basis for transfer from educational television and to describe factors that can be built into educational television programs to maximize the possibility of transfer.

Before proceeding to the theoretical discussion, it is helpful to define our terms. Prior researchers have drawn numerous distinctions among different types of transfer: near versus far transfer, forward versus backward, high-road versus low-road, direct application versus preparation for future learning, and so on. Indeed, Haskell (2001) distinguished among as many as 14 different classes of transfer. The focus of this chapter is on the type of transfer investigated most often in studies of educational television. This sort of transfer falls into the categories of direct application (Bransford & Schwartz, 1999) and high-road transfer (Salomon & Perkins, 1989), although the transfer might be conceived as either near or far and either forward or backward. In other words, the transfer discussed in this chapter entails direct application of knowledge acquired from a television program to a new problem or situation, through a process that relies on mindful abstraction of the material beyond the context shown in the television program. However, the novel problem may be either similar or dissimilar to the one seen on television, and the bulk of the cognitive "work" in the transfer process may take place either during viewing or when trying to solve the subsequent problem.

THEORETICAL APPROACH

Stated simply, the finding that significant comprehension of educational television can occur in the absence of transfer can be explained by the fact that transfer requires more than just comprehension of educational content. When all of the necessary prerequisites are met, transfer is likely to occur. Conversely, transfer can be prevented by a failure in any of these areas.

This chapter focuses on three pieces of the puzzle that have been seen as critical to aspects of transfer of learning (see, e.g., reviews by Bransford, Brown, & Cocking [1999] and Haskell [2001]):

- The viewer's *initial learning or comprehension* of the educational content in a television program
- The nature of the viewer's *mental representation* of that content
- The *transfer situation*—that is, the novel problem or solution to which the content is subsequently applied

Each of these is considered in turn, within the context of educational television.

Initial Learning/Comprehension

In some ways, the most obvious prerequisite for transfer from educational television is sufficient comprehension or learning of the material being transferred. After all, if viewers have not fully understood the material presented in the program, they can hardly be expected to apply it in other contexts. As Singley and Anderson (1989) noted, failures to transfer are often simply failures to learn the material in the first place.

Numerous researchers have pointed to the importance of a firm knowledge base as a prerequisite for transfer, with particular attention paid to "local knowledge" about the subject at hand (e.g., Bassok & Holyoak, 1993; Bereiter, 1995; Bransford & Schwartz, 1999; Ceci & Ruiz, 1993, Gott et al., 1993; Haskell, 2001; Perkins & Salomon, 1994). Bransford et al. (1999) noted that this knowledge base must include an elaborated understanding of the material learned, rather than simply rote memorization (e.g., understanding the reasoning that underlies a mathematical formula, not just memorizing the formula itself).

Drawing from a wide body of empirical research, the capacity model specifies a number of factors that contribute to children's comprehension of educational television, as detailed in chapter 10 (this volume). To recap briefly, the model posits that comprehension of the educational content in a television program is likely to be stronger under three conditions: (a) when the distance between narrative and educational content is small (i.e., when the content is integral, rather than tangential, to the narrative), (b) when the processing demands of the narrative are relatively small (e.g., because few inferences are needed to understand the story or the viewer's language skills are sufficiently sophisticated to follow the narrative easily), or (c) when the processing demands of the educational content are small (e.g., because it is presented clearly or the viewer has some knowledge of the subject already). Lists of factors that contribute to these processing demands can be found in Fig. 10.2 in chapter 10.

Because comprehension can be seen a prerequisite for transfer, each of these conditions would also be expected to promote transfer by enhancing comprehension. However, the point about distance between narrative and educational content poses particular issues for transfer, as will be discussed shortly.

Mental Representation

Researchers such as Hoijer (1990) have suggested that viewers' comprehension of educational content on television involves their using some sort of mental representation to make sense of that content. If the content is thoroughly unfamiliar, then one might imagine that a new representation would be formed. If, as is probably more often the case, the content bears some relation to material already stored in memory, then viewers would be more likely to retrieve an existing representation that is already stored in memory and use it to make sense of the new information from the television program. In Piagetian terms, the content of the program would be assimilated into a preexisting mental representation (and interpreted in a manner consistent with the representation), or the mental representation itself would be modified to accommodate the information acquired from the program.

With few exceptions (e.g., Greeno et al., 1993), most theories of transfer assign a central role to the learner's mental representation of the material learned (e.g., Gentner, 1983; Gick & Holyoak, 1983; Salomon & Perkins, 1989; Singley & Anderson, 1989). For learned material to lend itself to transfer, its mental representation must be abstracted beyond the initial context in which it was encountered so that it can be applied in other situations. Some researchers have seen this abstraction as a conscious process, as in Salomon and Perkins' (1989) discussion of "mindful abstraction" or Haskell's (2001) discussion of "reflective practice." Although concrete examples can be helpful in promoting initial comprehension of educational content, overly contextualized content can actually impede transfer if the content is too closely tied to its original context (e.g., Bransford & Schwartz, 1999; Eich, 1985; Gott et al., 1993).

From the standpoint of the capacity model, the notion that transfer requires both strong comprehension and a mental representation that is not overly contextualized might appear to produce an inherent contradiction. The model posits that one of the key characteristics that can promote comprehension is a small distance between narrative and educational content, which occurs when the educational content is highly contextualized in the narrative presented in the program. From the standpoint of theoretical models of transfer, however, deep contextualization could actually impede, rather than enhance, transfer.

How, then, can this seeming contradiction be resolved? The answer may lie in presenting the same educational concept more than once. For television, the optimal solution may lie in tying educational content and narrative together closely, but also addressing the same educational content multiple times in different contexts (as in television series such as *Sesame Street*, where the letter *C* might be presented in the context of several different words, such as *cow, car*, and *cookie*, in the space of a single episode). Such exposure could help children generalize the content beyond any one of the contexts presented and see it as applicable in a broad range of situations. (However, it is worth noting the caveat that, as Truglio and I have argued, viewers need to recognize the link among these multiple presentations for such a strategy to be effective [Fisch & Truglio, 2001b]).

In fact, this proposal is supported by theory and research outside the realm of television, which has suggested that transfer is promoted by the use of *varied practice*—that is, the use of multiple examples and/or repeated practice set in a variety of different contexts (e.g., Gick & Holyoak, 1983; Salomon & Perkins, 1989; Singley & Anderson, 1989). Through this sort of experience, the mental representation of the underlying content is forced to adapt in subtle ways to each new context, yielding a representation that gradually becomes more detached from the specific contexts presented, so that it can be applied more easily in new situations as they are encountered. Indeed, Butterworth, Slocum, and Nelson (1993) went so far as to argue that presenting only one example provides no basis for generalization and transfer.

Adopting this approach can help us to understand the successes and failures of transfer discussed at the beginning of this chapter. Series such as *Sesame Street* and *Square One TV*, which have been successful in eliciting transfer, have employed magazine formats in which a single episode is made up of a number of short segments. This format provides ample opportunities for reinforcement and varied treatment of the same educational content in multiple narrative contexts. For example, in *Square One TV*, the use of probability was modeled in a variety of segments and contexts, such as a segment in which characters figure out what makes a rigged carnival game unfair, a music video in which a character has to select the right key to escape a haunted house, and a game show in which strategic play requires considering the probability of different numbers coming up on a spinner. Each of these segments employed a small distance between narrative and educational content, but the cumulative effect of exposure to all of these segments may have contributed to a more abstract, decontextualized representation of probability. By contrast, although the *Cro* episode on flight also employed a small distance between narrative and educational content, the content was presented in the context of only one story. As a result, it was successful in producing effects on comprehension, but the underlying mental representation may have been less likely to be abstracted beyond the specific context shown in the program.

The Transfer Situation

To this point, this discussion has dealt primarily with the "front end" of the process of transfer, focusing on children's initial comprehension of an educational television program and their mental representations of its content. However, to fully understand transfer, we also must understand the processing that takes place later, when children encounter a problem to which the content might be applied (referred to in the literature as the *transfer situation*)—that is, the processing that allows them to retrieve the appropriate information from memory and apply it to the problem at hand.

Transfer effects do not occur in a vacuum, and the material learned from an educational television program is not the only information that is stored in children's memory as they approach a potential transfer situation. Rather, children come to such situations with a repertoire of strategies and information that may be more or less applicable to the particular situation at hand (e.g., Anderson, 1983; Siegler, 1989). The probability with which the content acquired from a television program will be applied is a function of the associative strength of that content relative to all of the other competing material that is stored in memory. This principle is akin to literature on the effects of mental set in problem solving, such as Luchins' (1942) and Duncker's (1945) classic experiments on functional fixedness, in which subjects' preconceptions of the functions of familiar objects prevented them from using the objects in novel ways to solve a problem.

As Hall, Fisch, et al. (1990) postulated in explaining effects of *Square One TV* on children's use of problem-solving heuristics to solve mathematical problems, such effects can arise because children have added new problem-solving heuristics to their repertoire, because they come to see heuristics that already exist in their repertoires as more applicable to a broad range of mathematical problems (the point most relevant to the present discussion), or to increased motivation during problem solving.

From this perspective, to find significant effects of transfer from educational television, it is not sufficient for the material to have been comprehended and for an appropriate mental representation to have been stored in memory. The child must also see the educational content of the program as applicable to the present situation (e.g., Bassok & Holyoak, 1993; Salomon & Perkins, 1989) and select it from among all of the other knowledge stored in memory as the piece that will be applied in the transfer situation. Indeed, if a child holds a particularly strong misconception related to the transfer situation (e.g., a naive theory about a scientific principle that is actually invalid), the child could wind up applying a strategy that is not only different from the one presented in the educational television program, but completely incorrect (e.g., Butterworth et al., 1993; Haskell, 2001).

How do children choose among all of the material in their repertoire to select the particular approach that will be used in the transfer situation? As in the case of initial learning of the material, most theorists posit that children create a mental representation of the problem presented in the transfer situation. Beginning with Thorndike's (1913; Thorndike & Woodworth, 1901) work a century ago, a lengthy tradition suggests that the mental representation of the problem is compared to the existing representation of the material learned earlier (in this case, the educational content of the television program) to evaluate the degree to which they share similar elements. If they are seen as sufficiently similar, then the material is applied and transfer occurs (e.g., Singley & Anderson, 1989). However, the similarity must not only exist but also be recognized by the child; if the similarities are not noticed, then the appropriate material is less likely to be applied (e.g., Ceci & Ruiz, 1993).

This state of affairs is complicated by the fact that there is more than one way in which the representations might be similar, and the type of similarity to which the child attends can hold implications for its effectiveness in producing transfer. Several researchers have drawn a distinction between surface structure similarity and deep structure similarity (e.g., Holyoak & Koh, 1987; Medin & Ortony, 1989; Novick, 1988), a distinction that is consonant with the capacity model's differentiation between narrative and educational content. *Surface structure similarity* refers to similarity between the story contexts of the initial learning situation and the transfer situation (e.g., whether they both concern baseball), and *deep structure similarity* reflects common underlying principles (i.e., whether they are isomorphic problems; see also Bassok & Holyoak's [1993] similar distinction between pragmatically relevant and irrelevant aspects of problems and Reed's [1993] distinction among equivalent, similar, and isomorphic problems).

Just as the capacity model predicts that, under some conditions, television viewers will comprehend the narrative content of a program without understanding its underlying educational content, researchers in the area of transfer have noted that learners may attend to surface structure similarity rather than deep structure similarity when searching memory for material to be applied in a transfer situation. Often, this type of search, too, may aid performance, as surface and deep structure are typically correlated (that is, in the terms used in the capacity model, distance is small). However, when the two do not go hand-in-hand (i.e., what the capacity model refers to as a large distance), a reliance on surface structure similarity can actually impair performance via negative transfer of inappropriate strategies that seem appropriate to the learner only because of the similar contexts in which they were embedded (e.g., Bassok & Holyoak, 1993; Holyoak & Koh, 1987; Medin & Ortony, 1989; Novick, 1988; Reed, 1993). Thus, an abstract mental representation of the problem encountered in the transfer situation is as necessary for effective transfer as an abstract representation of the initial content learned.

DEVELOPMENTAL CONSIDERATIONS

As noted earlier, transfer of learning from educational television has been found to occur in children as young as preschoolers (Bryant, Mulliken, et al., 1999; Mulliken & Bryant, 1999; cf. research on the long-term impact of *Sesame Street*, which probably reflects a somewhat different type of transfer). However, although transfer of learning does occur among young children, several aspects of development can contribute to make transfer more likely to occur as children grow older.

In comparing comprehension of metaphor among 4- and 5-year-olds, 9- and 10-year-olds, and adults, Gentner (1988) found significant age differences in the degree to which subjects appreciated metaphors on the level of their underlying relational structure, rather than shared surface attributes. Thus, one would expect it to be easier for children to attend to deep structure similarities as they grow older, resulting in a greater tendency toward transfer.

Interestingly, Brown, Kane, and Long (1989) proposed that such differences stem less from limitations on young children's thinking than from the smaller knowledge base that they have available to apply to transfer situations. Within the context of analogical reasoning, these researchers found children's performance to be greater when they possessed the knowledge base that was necessary for understanding the relations used in their analogies. Similarly, in comparing adult experts to novices, researchers such as Novick (1988) found that novices are more likely to attend to surface structure similarities, whereas experts are more likely to attend to deep structure similarities. Inasmuch as knowledge increases naturally with age, one would expect children to attend more easily to deep structure similarities and demonstrate transfer as they grow older.

A similar, but less broad, factor concerns age differences in children's comprehension of television. In the absence of ceiling effects, numerous studies have found comprehension of television to increase with age (see, e.g., the review by Huston & Wright, 1997). If, as argued earlier, comprehension is essential to transfer from educational television, then one would expect the probability of transfer to increase along with comprehension.

Moreover, some age differences in comprehension of television have been shown to stem from older viewers' greater ability to draw inferences about events and characters' motives (e.g., Collins, 1983). This suggests that older viewers are better able to go beyond the information presented on the screen and elaborate it more fully, which could result in more elaborate and abstract mental representations of the content shown. As a result, older viewers might create mental representations that are more abstract; this could be conducive to a greater tendency toward transfer as well.

Finally, age differences may also stem from developmental increases in metacognition. Several theories of transfer have proposed that metacognitive processes such as comprehension monitoring or active monitoring of learning strategies play a critical role in transfer, either in encoding material during initial learning or in guiding the search for relevant stored material while engaged in a transfer situation (e.g., Bransford & Schwartz, 1999; Gick & Holyoak, 1983; Gott et al., 1993; Salomon &

Perkins, 1989; Sternberg & Frensch, 1993). As research has shown that children's facility with metacognitive processes such as comprehension monitoring increases with age (see, e.g., Baker & Brown, 1984 for a review), this greater metacognitive ability could also contribute to developmental increases in transfer.

ISSUES RAISED AND LESSONS LEARNED

Implications for Research

This chapter opened with the question of why educational television programs are sometimes successful in promoting transfer and sometimes not. The various considerations discussed here are by no means a comprehensive list of all of the determining factors in transfer (see reviews by Bransford et al., 1999; Haskell, 2001; Perkins & Salomon, 1994). However, these considerations can help us to understand the pattern of effects regarding transfer that has emerged from literature on the impact of educational television.

For significant transfer effects to appear, several conditions must be satisfied: Viewers must comprehend and/or learn the educational content presented in the program. They must create a mental representation of the content that is abstracted beyond the narrative context of the program. They must create a similarly abstract representation of the problem encountered in the transfer situation. They must retrieve the representation of the television program's educational content from memory. They must see the stored content as applicable to the new problem, perhaps by mapping similar elements (particularly deep structure elements) of the two representations onto each other. And they must take action by applying the stored content in the transfer situation. A failure at any of these stages can impede or even prevent transfer entirely.

The likelihood with which transfer will occur is a function of both viewer and program characteristics, as well as characteristics of the transfer situation. The previous section on developmental differences lists some of the characteristics of viewers that can contribute to transfer. To this list, we can add other viewer characteristics that may be less integrally tied to development, such as viewers' motivation or their orientation toward encoding for transfer (e.g., Bransford et al., 1999; Haskell, 2001; Sternberg & Frensch, 1993), as well as the various viewer characteristics that contribute to viewers' initial comprehension of the educational content in the television program (see chap. 10, this volume).

Program characteristics, too, include those characteristics that contribute to initial comprehension of the program (see chap. 10, this volume), as well as characteristics that pertain more directly to transfer itself. In particular, issues arise concerning the role of the distance between the narrative and educational contents in the program. On one hand, the distance between narrative and educational content should be kept small to enhance comprehension. On the other hand, if the educational content is tied too closely to the narrative, then it may not lend itself to a sufficiently abstract mental representation to produce transfer. As argued earlier, then, the optimal solution may be to present the same educational content repeatedly but embedded in different narrative contexts. It is noteworthy that when Peel et al. (1987) presented children with a single *Square One TV* segment on a given mathematical topic, they found stronger performance on understanding of the mathematical content than on extension to new problems. Yet, Hall, Esty, et al. (1990; cf. Hall, Fisch, et al., 1990) found significant evidence of transfer after presenting children with multiple segments (many of which employed similar mathematics content in different contexts) from the same television series. Similarly, Hodapp (1977) failed to find transfer effects from a single *Sesame Street* segment, but several studies found long-term effects of more prolonged exposure to *Sesame Street* (Anderson et al., 1998, 2001; Huston et al., 2001; Wright et al., 2001; Zill, 2001). And one of the tasks on which Bryant, Mulliken, et al. (1999) found significant transfer effects from *Blue's Clues* employed a format that was strikingly similar to the type of problem presented at the end of every episode (i.e., a riddle task that involved guessing an object from three clues/attributes).

Factors inherent in the transfer situation include the relative strength of the approaches that viewers have acquired from sources other than the television program, which compete with the educational content of the program during retrieval. Naturally, this is not to say that the competing approaches are necessarily wrong; they may also be applicable to the problem at hand, but would reflect transfer from something other than the television program. Thus, transfer from an educational television program would be more likely to occur in the absence of either a well-practiced, appropriate but competing strategy (which could also produce a correct response in the transfer situation) or a deeply held naive theory or misconception (which would be more likely to produce an incorrect response). I return to this notion of repertoires and misconceptions in chapter 12 (this volume).

Consistent with the key role that the capacity model assigns to distance in comprehension, another factor relevant to the transfer situation is the relationship between the surface structure (i.e., narrative) and deep structure (i.e., underlying educational content) at work in the transfer situation. When the surface structure and deep structure map closely onto each other (i.e., when the distance between the two is small), it is more likely that a subsequent memory search via surface structure will result in retrieving useful information. Conversely, when surface structure and deep structure do not coincide, attention to surface structure over deep structure can result in negative transfer effects and the wrong material being applied.

Implications for Production

Although the focus of this chapter is on transfer of learning, it is important to note that transfer is not the only standard by which educational television programs should be measured. After all, if a television program "merely" produces significant growth in children's understanding or interest in its educational content, that program certainly can be deemed successful—even if it fails to promote transfer as well. Indeed, transfer has proven to be difficult to elicit in formal classroom education, too (e.g., Detterman, 1993).

With that said, however, the success of an educational television program is clearly greater if it also succeeds in promoting transfer of its educational content to problems or situations not shown on the screen. To that end, there are features that producers can build into educational television programs to increase their chances of eliciting transfer. Some of these features (discussed in chap. 10) contribute to transfer by maximizing comprehension.

In addition, a feature that pertains more specifically to transfer stems from the notion of varied practice. Often, to avoid "sameness" and a loss of appeal, producers are reluctant to treat the same educational topic more than once over the course of a broadcast season. This is particularly true if the series does not employ a magazine format, so that only one story and one educational topic are presented in each episode. Yet, despite producers' reluctance, research on transfer suggests that the opposite approach may actually be more effective from an educational standpoint. By devoting several segments or episodes to the same topic, but embedding the educational content in a different narrative context each time, the chances of promoting transfer may be improved. At the same time, the fact that each segment or episode employs a different narrative context may make it simpler to avoid issues of "sameness."

A FINAL NOTE

All of this is only the tip of the iceberg regarding transfer from educational television. The factors discussed here are not exhaustive, nor does this discussion pertain to all types of transfer that have been considered in the literature on education and cognitive psychology. In particular, Bransford and Schwartz (1999) have begun to explore a type of transfer that they term *preparation for future learning*, in which transfer effects consist not of applying previously learned material directly to a new problem, but of past learning helping learners to ask the right questions and seek appropriate information to help them in approaching a new problem or situation. Such a construct might be helpful in considering effects such as the long-term impact of *Sesame Street* over a period of years (e.g., Anderson et al., 1998, 2001; Huston et al., 2001; Wright et al., 2001; chap. 2, this volume), the impact of *Dragon Tales* on young children's inclination to pursue challenges (Rust, 2001; chap. 3, this volume), or the impact of *Cro* on children's interest in engaging in science and technology activities (Fay, Teasley, et al., 1995; Fay, Yotive, et al., 1995; chap. 6, this volume).

Clearly, many unanswered questions remain. Yet, although this chapter does not provide an exhaustive theoretical explanation for transfer, it does provide a first step and a starting point for conversation. Hopefully, future theory and research will carry the discussion forward, to yield a richer understanding of learning transfer from educational television.

12

The Social Nature
of Children's Learning
From Educational Television

I learn a lot just by watching you. How else do you think I got so good?

—Sister, *The Berenstain Bears*

As noted in chapter 10 (this volume), presentations of educational content on television typically do not take the form of didactic lectures. Rather, most educational content on television is embedded in some form of narrative: dramatic stories, comedy sketches, and so forth.

One of the implications of this reliance on narrative is that educational content is generally presented in the context of social interactions among characters. Thus, to fully understand the processing that underlies children's comprehension of educational content on television, we must also understand the social factors that are likely to mediate learning from educational television.

The discussion in this chapter is predicated on two base assumptions:

- Children's observation of characters on television resembles their observation of other people in real life. Thus, the processing that children use to understand social interactions on television is likely to be highly similar to (if not the same as) the processing that allows them to understand live social interactions.
- Television (whether educational or non-educational) operates as one source of information among many in children's lives. Thus, effects of television must be considered within the context of all of the other influences that operate on children's knowledge, attitudes, and behavior.

To gain insight into social aspects of children's learning from educational television, this chapter draws on research literature in three areas:

the role of narrative in learning, effects of television on social behavior, and children's learning from educational television.

NARRATIVE AND LEARNING

The idea of using narrative to convey educational content is by no means new. Over the course of millennia, many cultures have used storytelling as a means of passing accumulated wisdom from one generation to the next. Indeed, Schank and Abelson (1995) went so far as to assert the radical view that *all* knowledge stored in long-term memory is represented in the form of stories. Although a position this extreme is probably an overstatement (see, e.g., the accompanying chapters in Wyer, 1995), it is widely accepted that information is processed differently when it is presented in a narrative than when it is not.

On one level, comprehension of educational content embedded in a narrative depends on the *way* in which it is embedded. The capacity model (chap. 10, this volume) predicts that, because of the limited resources in working memory, children's comprehension of the educational content is determined in part by three factors: the demands of processing the educational content, the demands of processing the narrative, and the degree to which the educational content is well-integrated or tangential to the narrative.

Assuming that educational content is integrated well into a narrative, several features of narrative may make it a particularly conducive medium for learning. Narrative has an inherent structure that can help a learner organize information to promote better recall (Bower & Clark, 1969; Nelson, 1996). A meaningful narrative may activate related information in memory to support richer comprehension of new information (e.g., Newcomb & Collins, 1979). The sequencing of events in a narrative parallels the way events unfold in real life, which may make it easier to generate a mental representation in narrative than propositional form (Baumeister & Newman, 1995). Information might also carry more weight when presented in narrative form, as Bruner (1985, 1986) has drawn a distinction between narrative modes of thought (e.g., as in a story) and paradigmatic modes of thought (e.g., as in a logical argument). In paradigmatic modes of thought, material is judged as acceptable based on its truth or falsity, but in narrative modes of thought, material is judged for versimillitude and believability.

Another distinctive characteristic of narrative—and one that provides the central motivation for this chapter—lies in its portrayal of social interaction among characters.

SOCIAL ASPECTS OF EDUCATIONAL TELEVISION

As Read and Miller (1995) have pointed out, social interaction plays a central role in human existence, and stories (whether factual or fictional) are fundamentally about social interaction. Stories on television are no different, and a great deal of research indicates that children are sensitive to the social aspects of television programs. Wilson and Smith (1998) argued that, because of its extensive portrayals of emotion and interaction, television provides children with a rich source of learning about emotions. Children attribute personality traits to television characters along the same dimensions that they use for real people, and they sometimes fantasize about interacting with favorite characters (Giles, 2002; Reeves & Greenberg, 1977; Reeves & Nass, 1996). Moreover, children learn social behavior from television, whether for good or ill (e.g., Mares & Woodard, 2001; Paik & Comstock, 1994).

Various theories have proposed that viewers' learning of social behavior arises through their observing the behavior of on-screen characters and listening to their conversations (e.g., Bandura, 1971, 1986, 2002; Berkowitz, 1984; Berkowitz & Rogers, 1986; Huesmann, 1986). A moment's consideration makes it apparent that these same means are often used to convey academic content in educational television programs, as well. Viewers watch characters engage in processes of scientific experimentation or rewrite passages as they compose a letter in a literacy program. They listen as characters explain concepts to each other or figure out a problem in the course of a conversation. For example, consider the following exchange from a *Square One TV* parody of the film *Casablanca*, in which a French airline inspector computes the passengers' weight to make sure the airplane will not be overloaded:

HUMPHREY BOGART:	If that plane leaves the ground and you're not on it, you'll regret it. Maybe not today, maybe not tomorrow, but soon—and for the rest of your life. Look, I'm not good at being noble, but ...
INSPECTOR:	Madame Novak, your papers are in order. And now, your weight please?
INGRID BERGMAN:	That's rather personal, isn't it?
INSPECTOR:	Alas, yes, it is. But my lips are sealed, and the audience will keep it a secret.
BERGMAN:	Very well ... (*thinks*) Umm ... 118 ... pounds.
INSPECTOR:	(*wagging a finger*) Uh, uh, uh, Madame ...

BERGMAN: Must you make a scene? (*pause*) 123.
INSPECTOR: Hmm. We'll round that up to 130.
BERGMAN: (*melodramatic*) Why round *up* to 130?! Why not round *down* to 120? Why, why make things heavier than they really are?
INSPECTOR: To be on the safe side. We are concerned that the plane might be overloaded, so we are rounding the numbers up. Better safe than crunch-ed.
BERGMAN: Viva la calorie.

In the course of this sketch, the characters employ a variety of mathematical ideas—rounding (including rationales for rounding up versus rounding down), arithmetic, and aspects of mathematical problem solving—embedded in the context of a meaningful narrative.[1] The educational content emerges out of the interaction among the characters, where it is intertwined with social and emotional relationships: the reluctant farewell between the Humphrey Bogart and Ingrid Bergman characters, the inspector's soft-spoken but firm insistence on learning each passenger's weight, the hesitation that each character shows before divulging his or her true weight, and so on. From the standpoint of a viewer, then, the educational content is not merely stated on screen, but socially constructed among the characters.

Discussions of the social construction of academic knowledge usually concern sociocultural approaches to education (e.g., Gauvain, 2001) or guided participation and scaffolding (e.g., Rogoff, 1990; Vygotsky, 1978; Wood & Middleton, 1975). Typically, these discussions concern situations in which a child gains knowledge through collaboration with an adult or more experienced peer in a hands-on task—a different experience from watching characters interact on television. However, although joint hands-on activities may be the prototypic instances of such learning, even these theoretical approaches do not view hands-on interaction as always necessary to the process. Researchers such as Rogoff (1990), Lave and Wenger (1991), and Brownell and Carriger (1991) also discussed similar types of learning that arise through children's actively observing adults or peers who are engaged in an activity. Bandura's social cognitive theory places an even greater emphasis on observation; Bandura (1986) argued that, like social learning, academic learning is also the result of observation and modeling.

---

[1] In fact, this sketch was inspired by the real-life experience of one of the members of the *Square One TV* production team, who went through a similar process before boarding a small commercial airplane.

These perspectives, coupled with the inherently social nature of educational television programs, invite the question of how the mechanisms by which viewers learn social and academic content from television might overlap. Assuming that the conditions are favorable for learning from educational television (as described by the capacity model), how might theories of social learning from television be applied to help explain the learning of academic content?

Naturally, this attention to social processes should not be taken as implying that more strictly "cognitive" processing is unimportant. Considerable research in the field of social cognition illustrates that cognitive processing is necessary, not only for learning academic content, but even in the course of social interaction itself (e.g., Flavell & Ross, 1981; Shantz, 1975). In light of the inherently social nature of educational television programs, it is likely that "cognitive" and "social" processing work in tandem to contribute to learning.

SOCIAL INFLUENCES ON LEARNING FROM EDUCATIONAL TELEVISION

The following discussion draws on several theoretical models that have been used to explain social learning from television, to see whether they might also play a role in children's initial learning, storage, and retrieval of academic content presented in educational television. It represents not a conclusive and comprehensive explanation, but a first exploration of the influence of social factors on learning from educational television.

Initial Learning: Emotion and Identification

For educational content to be learned from television, viewers must first attend to and encode it. These processes are subject to a variety of influences stemming from characteristics of the program, the viewer, and the context in which the program is viewed. Let us consider two factors that have received a fair amount of attention in the literature on television and social behavior: emotion and identification.

Emotion. It is generally accepted that television programs not only evoke emotional responses in viewers, but that such responses are an integral part of the viewing experience (e.g., Cantor, 1998; Tannenbaum, 1980; Wilson & Smith, 1998). Apart from whatever role these responses might play in children's short-term or long-term emotional development, emotional responses during educational programs also hold implications for children's processing of educational content.

As Miron, Bryant, and Zillmann (2001) showed, viewers exhibit greater levels of sustained attention (or "vigilance") to television when the program causes them to feel either positive or negative emotions, such as enjoyment or fear. Numerous studies have shown enhanced memory for narrative and/or educational content in television programs that contain humor or elicit emotional responses (e.g., Lang, Dhillon, & Dong, 1995; Reeves, Newhagen, Mailbach, Basil, & Kurtz, 1991; Thorson & Friestad, 1989; Zillmann, Williams, Bryant, Boynton, & Wolf, 1980).[2]

However, this benefit can disappear—or even be replaced by a deficit—if the emotional response is too strong. Brosius (1993) found that emotional visuals served to narrow viewers' attention to specific parts of a television news item; as a result, recall of the item was based on reconstruction rather than simple retrieval from memory. (By the same token, the capacity model predicts that, unless educational content is integral to the narrative in an educational television program, viewers will focus on an emotionally compelling story at the expense of attending to its educational content.) Bruner (1986) argued that a certain level of emotional involvement is necessary to keep a learner on task, but that too much emotion can lead to "narrowness" or "singlemindedness." Strong emotional states cause less time to be devoted to information processing, so the depth of processing is diminished. Consistent with this point, Miron et al. (2001) suggested that television programs that elicit mild levels of emotion are conducive to poor short-term memory but good long-term memory; the opposite is true for programs that elicit strong emotions among viewers.

Thus, we can imagine the relationship between emotional content and learning from educational television as an inverse U-shaped curve (Fig. 12.1). All other things being equal, a program that elicits moderate emotional responses from viewers (e.g., via humor) is likely to promote better comprehension and learning. However, if the program elicits responses that are too strong (e.g., via side-splitting humor), learning may be impaired.[3]

---

[2]An important caveat here is that it is important to consider not only the emotional response itself, but also the nature of the material that elicits it. For example, Zillmann et al. (1984) found that some types of humor promoted learning, but humor that distorted the educational content (e.g., irony, exaggeration) produced misconceptions among viewers.

[3]Naturally, definitions of "moderate" and "strong" levels of emotion are likely to vary across individual viewers, as are the types of television programs that elicit these responses. Nevertheless, the same principle should hold true across viewers, even if the specific thresholds for designating a particular level of emotional arousal as "weak," "moderate," or "strong" are subject to individual differences.

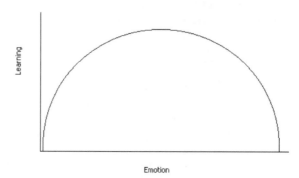

FIG. 12.1. Hypothetical relationship between emotion elicited by an educational television program and learning.

Identification. A central component of Bandura's social cognitive theory is modeling, that is, the observation and acquisition of behavior or knowledge from another person. Children can learn from models on television as well as real life, as seen in the long history of research on the modeling of aggressive behavior on television (Bandura, 1986, 2002).

However, not all television characters serve equally well as models. Children find some characters more appealing than others, and they attend more to some than others. As a child develops a preference toward a particular character—and especially as he or she identifies with that character—the child is likely to attend more to that character and assign more weight to the things the character says or does. Identification with a character (i.e., mentally comparing oneself to and imagining oneself like the character) increases emotional involvement with a television program and contributes toward the perceived reality of the program (Harris, 1999). Not surprisingly, then, a meta-analysis by Paik and Comstock (1994) found that violent programs had a greater effect on viewer behavior when they featured characters with whom the viewers identified. By the same token, it is also reasonable to assume that a viewer will learn educational content more effectively if it is presented by a character with whom he or she identifies.

The degree to which viewers identify with characters is influenced by several features of the character. One such feature is the degree to which the character is appealing or attractive to the audience. Children attend more and are more influenced by models whom they find appealing (e.g., Bandura, 1986). A variety of factors can contribute to a character's appeal, including both their physical attractiveness and their behavior—children tend to like characters whom they perceive to be smart and helpful (e.g., Fisch, in press-a).

Character appeal and identification are also likely to be greater if the character serves as the protagonist in the story. To some degree, the greater weight given to protagonists may stem from the fact that many protagonists in children's television programs are heroes who exhibit the kinds of behaviors and attitudes that contribute to character appeal, as just described. Indeed, Liss, Reinhardt, and Friedriksen (1983) found that children were more likely to model aggressive behavior from a violent cartoon if the cartoon featured a superhero. Yet, even if a program does not feature a clear "hero" or "villain," the protagonist may still hold an advantage for identification. Abelson (1975) proposed that, in listening to stories, people tend to adopt the visual point of view of the protagonist. In fact, even Bandura's earliest research on observational learning may suggest a preference for protagonists as models. Bandura (1965) found that children were *less* likely to hit an inflatable Bobo doll if they watched a film in which an adult model was punished for doing so—despite the fact that part of the model's punishment was a spanking from another character. Clearly, the subjects in their study were modeling the behavior of the character who hit the doll, rather than the character who subsequently spanked the aggressor. This selective modeling is easily explained if we imagine that children were identifying with the first character because the story was told from his perspective.

A third factor in identification is similarity between the character and the viewer. Children do not show exclusive preferences for television characters who are "like themselves," but research has shown that similarity can contribute to character preferences and identification. Fisch et al. (1994) reported that children's choices of favorite characters in the television series *Ghostwriter* frequently matched the children's own gender and ethnicity (although the favorite character among all children was the invisible ghost Ghostwriter). Similarly, research on television violence has shown that boys are more likely to imitate male perpetrators, whereas girls respond more to female characters (Bandura, Ross, & Ross, 1963). With regard to ethnicity, Greenberg (1972) found that more African-American children than White children identified with African-American characters in a television program (although a significant number of White children did so as well). Finally, similarity of age may also be a factor; children enjoy seeing other children on television, particularly if the child characters are slightly older than themselves (presumably for aspirational reasons; Fisch, in press-a).

Taken together, the literature on identification implies that, on one hand, children can learn from any television character (just as, for example, Greenberg [1972] found that some White children identified with African-American characters). However, it also suggests that the efficacy of educational content on television may be mediated by the character who delivers it. If viewers identify with the character—because the character is either appealing, heroic, the protagonist, or similar to the viewers—then viewers may attend more to the character's words or actions. Moreover, viewers may also be more likely to project themselves into the story and imagine engaging in on-screen activities alongside (or in place of) the character. All of these outcomes would be expected to result in viewers' processing the educational content more fully.

Storage and Retrieval: Repertoires

In attempting to explain the effects of violent television on social behavior, Huesmann (1986) and Berkowitz (1984; Berkowitz & Rogers, 1986) both employed concepts such as behavioral repertoires, activation, and motivation. Berkowitz proposed that effects reflect the activation of a network of aggressive thoughts that are already stored in long-term memory, whereas Huesmann hypothesized that violent television leads viewers to add new scripts for aggressive behavior to their existing repertoires of social behavior.

Interestingly, these approaches are very consistent with the potential explanations that Hall, Esty, et al. (1990) and Hall, Fisch, et al. (1990) offered for the effects of *Square One TV* on children's use of mathematical problem-solving heuristics: that they either might add new problem-solving heuristics to their repertoires, come to see existing heuristics as applicable to a wider array of problems, or grow more motivated to use them. (See chaps. 5 and 11, this volume.)

Indeed, one might imagine a common mechanism at work in the storage of both social and academic content (at least in the case of procedural knowledge, such as problem-solving heuristics, literacy strategies, or scientific experimentation). According to this approach, children can be seen as possessing repertoires of behavior within various domains: ways to decode a difficult text, ways to catch a ball, ways to deal with a conflict over a favorite toy, and so on. These repertoires are built up over the course of children's lives, as they engage in daily activities, interact with others, and observe other people's behavior. When children subsequently attempt to retrieve something from memory, entries that are stored in the repertoire compete for selection to determine which will be applied (e.g., which of several possible strategies will be used to solve a mathematical problem or to resolve an interpersonal conflict).

Naturally, much of the selection of a strategy depends on which strategy provides the most appropriate fit to the demands of the situation. However, not all of the entries in the repertoire receive equal consideration. At any given time, some of the entries will be stronger than others—because, for example, they have been practiced or observed more often, because they have proven to be more successful than others, be-cause they have been activated temporarily by recent exposure to related information or observations, and so on. This view of memory is consis-tent with the finding that memory for televised material is greater if the same segment or program is viewed repeatedly (e.g., Lesser, 1974) or if the material in the program is related to prior knowledge (e.g., Bandura, 1986; cf. Newcomb & Collins, 1979). In these cases, memory would be strengthened by rehearsal and/or a richer network of associations.

Conversely, as mentioned in chapter 11 (this volume), one would ex-pect children to be less likely to recall or apply educational content from a television program when the content conflicts with a strong misconcep-tion or social stereotype that is also stored in the repertoire. In this case, the information presented in the television program might simply be out-weighed by other, more heavily weighted entries in the repertoire. Exam-ples of this phenomenon in both academic and social domains can be found in Truglio, Lovelace, Seguí, and Scheiner's (2001) review of forma-tive research in the production of *Sesame Street*. Preschoolers' common misconception that trees are not alive (because they do not move on their own) posed challenges for children's comprehension of *Sesame Street* sci-ence segments on the topic of "What's Alive?" Similarly, although race re-lations segments were effective in promoting recall of the activities in which on-screen children engaged, the effects were limited by children's perceptions that their mothers would be less happy about their having playmates of other ethnicities. Within Bandura's (1986, 2002) frame-work, one might imagine such constraints mediating either retention pro-cesses (e.g., weaker entries in the repertoire might decay over time), production processes (e.g., weaker entries could fail to be retrieved), or motivational processes (e.g., children could choose to suppress a particu-lar behavior because of the likelihood that their parents would disap-prove). Thus, learning from educational television is a function not only of the material in the television program itself, but also of all of the other material stored in a child's memory as well.

DEVELOPMENTAL CONSIDERATIONS

Barring ceiling effects, children's comprehension of educational television typically increases with age. In chapter 10 (this volume), several aspects of cognitive development were proposed as contributing to this phenome-non: increases in prior knowledge, skill in drawing inferences, under-standing of the formal features of television, processing speed, automaticity, and the management of multiple goals. These factors are just as applicable to the social aspects of children's learning as they are to the more strictly cognitive aspects. For example, the advantages provided

by developmental changes in prior knowledge can refer just as easily to social knowledge as they can to world knowledge or prior knowledge about a
given academic subject. In each case, prior knowledge would be expected
to increase with age and thus contribute to better comprehension of the
educational content in a television program.

In addition to these factors, several aspects of development relate
more specifically to the kinds of processing discussed in this chapter.
These, too, would be expected to impact on children's learning from educational television.

Emotional Stimuli

First, consider developmental changes in children's emotional responses
to television. If humor can promote vigilance and, thus, learning from
television (e.g., Miron et al., 2001), then it is important to recognize
that children appreciate different types of humor at different ages. Early
formative research for *Sesame Street* found that preschool children consistently responded to certain types of humor (e.g., incongruity and surprise, slapstick, adult errors, silly wordplay), but not more sophisticated
forms of humor such as puns that required viewers to appreciate the double meanings of words (Lesser, 1974). Whereas puns might be expected
to promote vigilance among older children, they are less likely to have
any effect on younger children's attention, simply because they would
fail to get the joke.

As children grow, they also become more sophisticated in responding
to other emotional cues on television. For example, at different ages,
children find different types of televised stimuli frightening. Preschoolers' fear frequently stems from characters' appearance, whereas
older children's fear is more often caused by portrayals of realistic
threats (Cantor, 1998). Thus, data on both humor and fear demonstrate
that, as we consider the role of emotion in mediating learning, we must
note that the same emotion is likely to be elicited by different types of
stimuli at different ages.

Emotional Regulation

Children's ability to regulate their emotions also increases with age (e.g.,
Fox, 1994). As children grow older (particularly in the early years), their
expressions of emotion become more controlled, and less intense and ex-
aggerated. To the degree that strong emotional responses interfere with
learning, it would be expected that greater control over one's emotions
would facilitate learning from educational television.

Identification

Developmental changes can also be expected to affect children's selective identification with characters in an educational television program. On the most basic level, children must attend to characters if they are to learn from them, and young children's attentional skills have been found to increase with age (e.g., Anderson, 1999; Bandura, 1986). Older children can sustain attention for longer periods of time, and they become more selective in paying attention. Both of these abilities would contribute to more effective learning from models.

Moreover, children's understanding of the behavior, attitudes, and motivation exhibited by television characters is also likely to become more sophisticated as they grow older. Social cognition has been found to increase with age, and research on "theory of mind" has pointed to developmental changes in children's accuracy in attributing thoughts and beliefs to other people (e.g., Astington, 1993; Flavell & Miller, 1998; Overton, 1983). Presumably, older children's greater sophistication in these areas would allow them to construct a richer understanding of the behavior and attitudes they observe on television. Therefore, although younger and older children might watch the same character engage in the same behavior in the same television program, their mental representations of that behavior might actually be significantly different from each other.

Repertoire

Last, it is probably self-evident to note that, as children grow older, their repertoires of knowledge and behavioral strategies change. Over time, repertoires are likely to differ in both quantity and quality. More material is stored in memory, a more elaborate network of connections is likely to emerge, and children's experiences may cause the strength of each entry to increase or decrease.

To the degree that the educational content of a television program is consistent with or supported by other material in a child's repertoire, comprehension and learning should be facilitated. Thus, in general, older children's more extensive and elaborate repertoires should contribute to greater comprehension among older children. However, in contrast to the other developmental factors discussed in this section, the notion of repertoires also implies that there is one case in which older children actually might be expected to perform *less* well than their younger counterparts: namely, if their greater experience has led them to acquire and rehearse misconceptions or contrary messages that interfere with the material from the program or inhibit the responses that would otherwise follow.

ISSUES RAISED AND LESSONS LEARNED

Clearly, the intersection of social and cognitive processing of television presents rich fodder for investigation, and this chapter represents only the beginning of a full exploration of the topic. Yet, even at this preliminary stage, this discussion suggests a number of implications regarding research on children's learning from educational television, data on academic versus social effects of television, and the role of television as a socializing agent.

Implications for Research

Let us begin by summarizing the preceding discussion: Because of the inherently social nature of narrative, this approach sees social interaction among characters as a vehicle for delivering educational content on television. As a result, the social interaction among characters (and viewers' processing of that interaction) serves as a mediating variable in children's learning from educational television. The processing that viewers use to make sense of social interactions on television greatly resembles the processing that they employ in real life.[4]

Comprehension and learning are expected to be stronger when the program elicits a mild level of emotional involvement on the part of viewers. However, the opposite may be true if viewers' emotional response is too strong. Comprehension and learning of educational content should also be enhanced if the content is delivered by a character with whom a viewer identifies (because the character is either appealing, the protagonist, or similar to the viewers). This is not to say that educational content cannot be understood if it is emotionally neutral or delivered by a different character. However, the educational content is likely to be more effective when these conditions hold true.

Turning to storage and retrieval, this approach assumes the existence of repertoires of knowledge, behavior, attitudes, and strategies within viewers' long-term memory. As a child views an educational television program, the educational content in the program may be added to the child's repertoire, reinforce and elaborate upon content that has already been stored, or activate the previously stored content, thus making it more likely to be retrieved and applied in a given situation.

---

[4]In fact, this assertion may even be an understatement. Research by Reeves and Nass (1996) indicated that, in many ways, users' behavior toward inanimate electronic media is governed by the same sorts of social rules as their interactions with other people (e.g., politeness).

At the time of retrieval, the educational content acquired from the program competes with other material stored in the repertoire, and the strongest, most applicable options are retrieved. Even once the material is retrieved, though, the child may choose to apply it or not, depending on situational cues in his or her environment (e.g., the reaction that he or she anticipates from other people). In this way, children's learning from educational television is not only a function of children's television viewing in the here-and-now. Rather, it is also affected by the prior experiences that have contributed to children's repertoires, and by their awareness of subsequent real-life constraints that may encourage or inhibit a demonstration of their learning.

Academic Versus Social Effects

The preceding discussion emphasizes the similarities between children's processing of academic and social content on television. Yet, it is also true that, in general, effects on academic outcomes have often emerged more strongly and consistently than effects on prosocial behavior (see chap. 8, this volume). To some degree, of course, this might be attributed to the greater difficulty of measuring change in social behavior than in academic performance. Or it may be that the prosocial programs used in these studies simply were not as effective as the academic educational programs.

However, if we conceive of both academic and prosocial effects as involving repertoires in memory, another possibility also presents itself: The existence of such repertoires might make social behavior more difficult to change. Children acquire social behavior not only from television, but from a host of real-life experiences that are likely to carry more weight than a single exposure (or even prolonged exposure) to a television program. Thus, competing material in a child's repertoire might inhibit his or her learning from or imitating the prosocial content modeled in the program. Recall, for instance, that the effectiveness of *Sesame Street* in negating stereotypes was limited by children's perceptions of their parents' attitudes (Truglio et al., 2001).

These sorts of conflicting, inhibitory effects may be less likely to occur with regard to academic effects. Often, academic effects entail adding new knowledge or skills where none existed before, as opposed to countering misconceptions that children already hold. Indeed, series such as *Square One TV* and *3-2-1 Contact* were specifically designed to target children *before* they reached the age at which attitudes toward mathematics and science typically decline. Moreover, as discussed in chapter 2 (this volume), the *early learning model* posits that long-term academic effects of educational television (e.g., associations between preschool viewing and subsequent success in high school) can be attributed to a cascading effect in which preschool television viewing contributes to early success in school, which then promotes further academic successes (Anderson et al., 2001; Huston et al., 2001). If the early learning model is correct, then influences other than television (e.g., teachers, family) would be seen to complement the effects of educational television programs rather than work against them.

Television as a Socializing Agent

Speaking more broadly, all of the points raised in this chapter feed into a conception of television as an agent for children's socialization. Sociocultural views of education have pointed out that education serves not only to convey knowledge, but also to show children what it is important to think *about* (e.g., Gauvain, 2001). Just as violent television has been shown to contribute toward attitudes regarding real-life violence (e.g., Drabman & Thomas, 1974; Linz, Donnerstein, & Penrod, 1984, 1988), exposure to educational television can affect children's attitudes toward academic subjects and the value that they assign to these subjects.

By presenting educational content through appealing characters who are comfortable and competent in working with the content, who employ the content as a useful tool to achieve their goals, and who enjoy it, educational television programs simultaneously show viewers that this knowledge is valued and useful in our society. As Fisch and Truglio (2001b) suggested, when (for example) an African-American character is shown using scientific experimentation to discover something new, the lesson for viewers is not merely the science lesson itself. Because the activity has been driven by an African-American, it also shows viewers that African-Americans can be confident and successful in pursuing scientific activities.

Seeing television as a socializing agent means seeing it as one agent among many, alongside other (probably more powerful) factors such as family, school, and peers—all of which can mediate, facilitate, or negate the effects of educational television programs. From this perspective, the effects of educational television should not be seen as a simple path from viewing to knowledge or behavior. Television viewing does not take place in a vacuum, and its effects do not occur in a vacuum either. A complete explication of children's learning from educational television will require not only an understanding of children's interaction with television, but also an understanding of the ways in which television interacts with the myriad other influences in children's lives.

III

THE FUTURE

13

Looking to the Future: Convergence and Educational Television

We are all interested in the future, for that is where you and I will spend the rest of our lives.

—Criswell, *Plan 9 from Outer Space*

As noted in chapter 1, children spend vast amounts of time with electronic media. In recent years, those media have been evolving with meteoric speed, as seen in the rapid growth of technology such as computers, cell phones, interactive toys, and handheld devices. Yet, despite children's use of various media, research shows that television remains their medium of choice. A 1999 survey sponsored by the Kaiser Family Foundation found that American children spent an average of 2 hours and 46 minutes per day watching television—considerably more time than they spent with computers (21 minutes per day), video games (20 minutes), or the Internet (8 minutes; Roberts et al., 1999). The same trend was confirmed one year later in a national survey conducted at the University of Pennsylvania (Woodard, 2000).

However, even if television maintains its dominance in years to come, the nature of television itself is likely to change. Since the early 1990s, much has been written about *convergence*—that is, the availability of multiple media through a single device or delivery system. One prominent example of convergent media is often referred to as either *enhanced* or *interactive television* (a subcategory of *digital television*; e.g., Ducey, 1999; Tarpley, 2001).

Enhanced television holds the potential to extend the impact of educational television programs by coupling them with simultaneous data streams that can be accessed during viewing, all through the same television receiver device. In the future, these data streams could carry supplemental information for further learning, or interactive games and activities in which viewers can engage.

195

At present, the development and dissemination of enhanced television has proceeded far more slowly than projected, so the technology remains very much in its infancy. Part of the delay can be attributed to the financial depression of the online industry. Another part stems from the fact that, although various producers and broadcasters have begun to experiment with possible formats for enhanced television experiences, none of these experiments has yet uncovered "the" approach that will prove most effective. To date, most applications of enhanced television in the United States have been fairly limited, such as clickable television program listings or options to buy clothes that on-screen characters are wearing via e-commerce (e.g., Mundorf & Laird, 2002; Tarpley, 2001). In place of enhanced television, far more American television series simply display a URL at the end of a program (or, in some cases, during the program) that viewers can access via a computer if they want to search for related information or activities once the program is over.

Some slightly more sophisticated applications of enhanced television have begun to appear in Europe. These include applications that allow viewers to change camera angles on a sports event, place bets on horse races electronically, watch 24-hour live webcasts from the site of a reality television series, or predict the winner of a game show. An example of an existing educational application can be found in the broadcast of the British documentary series *Walking with Beasts*, which was accompanied by extra facts about evolution at the bottom of the screen. Those viewers who had the appropriate input device were given the option to explore these topics in greater detail by pressing buttons on their remote controls (Lee, 2001). These experiments—and many others (e.g., WebTV)—represent useful first steps in moving toward true enhanced television. Nevertheless, it is still difficult to know what the ultimate form of the medium will be.

FORMS OF ENHANCED TELEVISION

Even if we cannot know which technologies will endure and proliferate, there is value in considering the educational potential of enhanced television now, as opposed to trying to catch up to the technology later on. In particular, consider four possible directions that have been predicted for enhanced television: video on demand, links to existing web resources, specially produced educational games, and branching television stories.

Each of these forms of enhanced television poses its own opportunities beyond those of traditional broadcast television. Broadband access may provide video on demand, in which, rather than a network broadcasting a single program at a time, individual viewers can order programming that meets their personal interests or needs at any given time.

Links to existing Web resources might bear the closest resemblance to current efforts, in which television viewers can access additional information or activities by visiting the Web sites related to specific television series. With enhanced television, however, access to the Web site would take place through the television set (perhaps even during the program, via a pop-up window), rather than requiring viewers to turn their attention away from the television to log onto their computers.

Taking that concept one step further, enhanced television programs might also provide children with interactive games that are specially designed to map onto the educational content of the television program. Such games could either accompany the program as optional ancillary activities, or (analogous to some current CD-ROM and online games) they might arise in the course of the program, requiring the viewer to help characters solve a puzzle before the television program can continue.

Finally, the multiple data streams delivered through digital television could even make it possible for television programs themselves to become interactive through the use of branching stories. Under this scenario, at certain points during the program, the viewer would choose among several options to determine how the story will proceed.

By using these four possible directions to chart out a broad landscape of possible options, we can anticipate some of the issues that are likely to arise in applying enhanced television toward educational ends. In particular, let us consider some of the potential benefits, challenges, and design issues that may come with the advent of enhanced educational television.

BENEFITS

The educational impact of interactive media has been tested far less extensively than the impact of educational television. Where studies have been conducted, however, they suggest that educational computer games can contribute to children's learning in areas as disparate as estimation skills and self-management of asthma (e.g., Greenfield, 1984; Lieberman, 1999). Papert (e.g., 1998) argued that such materials are most effective when they provide "hard fun"—that is, activities that are sufficiently difficult and interesting to challenge children to achieve.

Yet, even if interactive technology can promote learning, the question remains as to whether combining television with interactivity would yield benefits beyond those that traditional educational television already provides. As seen throughout this volume, there is ample evidence that traditional (i.e., non-interactive) educational television programs can produce significant, long-lasting increases in children's knowledge and attitudes regarding a variety of academic subjects. Indeed, traditional television programs such as *Blue's Clues* or *Square One TV* have even been found to elicit some degree of interaction in the form of viewer participation (Anderson et al., 2000; Fisch & McCann, 1993). Given such effects, a natural question is whether any increased benefit would be provided by adding an interactive layer to traditional educational television.

To my knowledge, no studies to date have compared children's learning from the same educational program when it is enhanced and when it is not. However, based on data on the impact of traditional educational television and studies of television-based outreach materials (chap. 9, this volume), I believe that there are several reasons to expect that the benefits of enhanced educational television could be incremental to those of television alone.

Matching Programs to Needs

As noted in chapter 9, one of the limitations of educational television is that, because television is a mass medium, educational programs cannot be personalized to fit the needs, prior knowledge, or developmental level of an individual viewer. The same program is seen by children in advanced and remedial classes, and by children of various demographic backgrounds.

New opportunities present themselves, however, with the introduction of video on demand. Personalization becomes far more feasible if viewers have the ability to choose the programs they would like to watch at any given time, instead of being limited to whatever is being broadcast at the moment. Under these conditions, the same programs would not necessarily be seen by children of diverse backgrounds or abilities. Such access would make it possible for a parent or teacher (or even children themselves) to select segments or episodes of an educational television series that map onto the skill level of an individual child, or to supply material on a specific topic that the child is having trouble grasping in school.

A Springboard for Learning

Chapter 9 reviewed an assortment of outreach projects that use educational television to introduce concepts and motivate children, then extend the learning via hands-on activities and/or live discussion. Many forms of enhanced television have the potential to deliver similar opportunities by pairing a television program with links to supplementary information or interactive games regarding the same educational content. Viewers would have the option either to view the television program without further elaboration or to pursue topics further via supplementary information, games and activities, and/or links to outside Web sites. For example, an engaging educational television program that dramatizes the Battle of Lexington and Concord might be linked to background information that delves into greater detail, images of real documents or artifacts (e.g., a letter written by someone who fought in the battle), or interactive games that challenge users to replicate the military strategies that were used.

This sort of strategy could serve several purposes. By providing access to informational resources beyond the television program, it could promote a richer understanding of the subject matter than children would obtain from the television program alone. Interactive games could provide children with the opportunity not only to watch characters apply knowledge and heuristics, but also apply the same concepts themselves.[1] Thus, ancillary activities such as these could reinforce and extend the educational content of the television program, with the potential to produce better learning.

Individualized Feedback

Interactive games resemble participatory television programs (e.g., *Blue's Clues*) in that both provide viewers with opportunities to become actively involved with the relevant educational content (see chap. 3, this volume). However, a significant difference between the two lies in the fact that, although television characters can create the illusion of having seen or heard the viewer's response (e.g., "What did you say?... Oh! Good idea!"), the character's replies cannot truly take the viewer into account. The situation is very different in the case of interactive games, where feedback is genuinely contingent on users' input. This contingency allows feedback to be far more specific in an interactive game. In addition, children can be given the opportunity to make multiple attempts to solve the same problem if a puzzle proves difficult, and software can be programmed to select different games to match the level of expertise that a child has demonstrated in prior games that involve the same content.

In some ways, the benefits provided by contingent feedback resemble opportunities for individualized instruction that are provided by parents, teachers, or child-care providers in television-based outreach (chap. 9, this volume). Certainly, the opportunities provided in a game are far less extensive than what children receive in face-to-face interaction with a live partner, and game feedback is much less flexible. Conversely, however,

---

[1] Alternately, a similar benefit might be provided by presenting the television program as a branching story, in which viewers' choice of a military strategy takes the narrative in different directions. Either a game or a branching story could succeed in prompting children to think critically about the subject matter. (Of course, great care would be necessary in allowing choices in a history program, so as not to inadvertently leave viewers with misconceptions about how the events truly occurred. Branching stories could be applied in a more straightforward manner for subjects such as science or mathematics.)

convergent media can provide such support on a mass scale, rather than requiring the involvement of a live adult for every viewer.

Promoting Transfer

A third possible benefit lies in the potential for convergent media to provide a foundation for transfer of learning—that is, children's ability to apply the material learned from an educational television program in new contexts or situations. The discussion of transfer in chapter 11 (this volume) proposed that transfer is more likely to occur when the same educational content is embedded in several different contexts (e.g., *Square One TV* segments that deal with probability in the context of figuring out a rigged carnival game, choosing the right key to escape a haunted house, and planning effective strategy in a game show). This sort of *varied practice* is seen as contributing to a more generalized mental representation of the content, which can be applied more easily to new situations.

If designed properly, convergent media could provide fertile ground for varied practice. A television segment on a topic such as probability could be linked to other television segments, interactive games, or supplementary resources that deal with the same content in different contexts. Thus, instead of gaining varied practice from sustained viewing over multiple episodes of a television series, viewers could reap similar benefits in the course of a single session.

Involvement

The potential for viewers to take an active role in enhanced television could encourage them to become more involved in an educational program. This greater involvement could arise in several ways. Consider two possible routes toward heightened involvement: flow and personal responsibility.

Flow. Funk (2002) proposed that immersion in interactive games can produce a "flow state" of psychological absorption that can enhance learning (cf. Csikszentmihalyi & Csikszentmihalyi, 1988). Psychological absorption is also commonly found in engagement with compelling stories, including those shown on television. It is interesting to speculate, then, on how flow states might operate in the context of convergent media.

Several possibilities present themselves. On one hand, one might imagine that flow states would be disturbed when viewers switch back and forth between a television program and an associated interactive game. Alternately, absorption might cause a child to engage with only one medium, and inhibit his or her inclination to explore the other material that accompanies it (e.g., just play a game or watch a television program without doing both). A third possibility is that children might enter a series of flow states if they explore the different media consecutively (e.g., first become absorbed in the television program and then, once the program ends, become absorbed in playing a related game).

Yet another possibility arises if the game and the narrative of the television program are actually one and the same. For example, if the characters in a television program encounter a problem or puzzle, and viewers must help them solve it to advance the story, then the television and interactive components might fold in naturally to operate more seamlessly within a single state of flow. This might be all the more likely if the experience has the appearance of taking place within a single medium (as opposed to "television plus video game"), as in the case of the interactive, branching stories described earlier. As convergent media evolve, empirical research will be needed to determine which of these possible effects (if any) holds true.

Responsibility.   Vorderer (2000) offered another reason why branching stories might be expected to promote greater involvement on the part of viewers. Using the example of a suspenseful, interactive television program in which a character needs to defuse a bomb and viewers decide which wire to cut, Vorderer argued that viewers' ability to interfere in the narrative produces a sense of responsibility that causes viewers to feel more involved in the program.

Whatever the cause (flow or personal responsibility), greater involvement in a convergent television experience would be expected to produce increased learning from educational television. Greater involvement could contribute to deeper processing of educational content, stronger identification with characters, and/or a greater readiness to accept information uncritically—all of which would serve to bolster the effectiveness of the program.[2]

Authoring

To this point, our discussion has revolved around interactive activities and online resources that are fairly well defined and closed-ended. Apart from such materials, enhanced television also has the potential to deliver appli-

---

[2]Naturally, in keeping with the capacity model (chap. 10, this volume), this assumes that the interactive games or choice points in a branching story are designed to tie directly to the educational content of the television program. If they do not, then the interactivity would be expected to draw children's attention away from the educational content and hinder learning.

cations that provide more open-ended *authoring tools*—that is, tools children can use for their own personal expression via writing, drawing, and so on (like the tools that are currently available online or in some CD-ROMs).

In addition to encouraging children's creativity, the convergent use of authoring tools with educational television provides unique opportunities for extending the educational effectiveness of the television program. For example, consider some of the benefits that could arise from using such tools in conjunction with a television program about literacy: Prompts within the television program could direct children to engage in the same sorts of activities as on-screen characters (e.g., composing rap lyrics), to write their own stories about the characters, or to share their work with family or friends. By giving children only a small amount of additional direction (to ensure that their efforts focus on the relevant subject matter), such tools could be applied to other subject areas as well.

CHALLENGES

To achieve these benefits, producers of enhanced television will have to overcome a number of significant challenges. Not the least of these is financial: The production of enhanced television is necessarily more expensive than the production of traditional broadcast television. This is due largely to the cost of producing the supplementary material that "enhances" the television program, whether that consists of ancillary material, interactive games, or the additional television footage that would be necessary to produce all of the potential branches in a branching story. A discussion of business models for enhanced television is beyond the scope of this chapter. However, it is important to note that, whatever direction enhanced television ultimately takes, the choice is likely to be determined at least as much by financial considerations as by creative choices.

Apart from these sorts of financial issues, the challenges that face enhanced television can be conceptualized as falling into two broad categories: challenges of use and challenges of design.

Challenges of Use

Challenges of use reflect issues that operate on a relatively macro-level. These include access to the necessary hardware, families' decisions to obtain and use the technology, and constraints on use during family viewing.

Access.   First and foremost, enhanced television cannot have its desired impact unless children have access to the hardware that is necessary for its use. Much has been written about the "digital divide"—that is, the overrepresentation of computer technology among Whites and those of higher SES, as compared to the concomitant lack of access among minorities and lower SES populations (e.g., Cakim, 1999; National Center for Educational Statistics, 1998). Thankfully, efforts to place computers and Internet access in schools and libraries that serve low-SES and minority populations appear to have borne fruit. Data from the U.S. Census and NAEP indicate that school access to computers no longer differs significantly across demographic lines; nearly 90% of 6- to 17-year-olds had used computers at either home or school in the year 2000 (Newburger, 2001; Wenglinsky, 1999).[3]

Although great strides have been made in bridging the digital divide, it is likely that the same issues will surface yet again in the context of enhanced television. Because platform devices for new media typically debut with significant price tags attached, it seems safe to assume that the same patterns of trickle-down penetration that emerged for computers and the Internet (or, several decades ago, television) are likely to hold true for enhanced television as well. Just as poor and minority children are seen as disadvantaged by their relative lack of access to computer-based educational materials today, this same pattern of catch-up is likely to continue as new generations of media appear.

Adoption.   Even if enhanced television can be designed to be both commercially and educationally viable, the question will remain as to whether consumers will want to use it. In fact, despite the promise of the medium, there are reasons to think that they might not. As Arthur Orduna (vice president of marketing for an enhanced television production company) admitted, "No one in the U.S. has ever stood up and said, 'I want interactive television'" (quoted in Lee, 2001).

Part of the problem may lie simply in the public's not knowing what the medium is, or what it can do. That is certainly understandable as, at the time of this writing, even those in the industry are not certain themselves. Once enhanced television becomes a reality, this issue may be overcome with nothing more than an effective marketing campaign to promote public awareness.

However, a deeper issue stems from people's reasons for using media. Several studies have found that one of viewers' primary reasons for watching television is relaxation (e.g., Greenberg, 1974; Vorderer, 2000), which raises questions as to whether viewers will want to engage actively while

---

[3]This is not to say that the problem has been solved completely. Although physical access and use is now more equal, disparities continue to exist. In particular, teachers in higher SES schools continue to be better trained in technology, and they use computers more effectively to promote higher-order thinking (Wenglinsky, 1999).

viewing, as opposed to simply sitting back and watching the television program. Indeed, Stipp (1998) pointed out that most people look to television for relaxation and entertainment, whereas computers are seen as sources of information. Thus, at any given time, people may be inclined to pursue one of these goals or the other, as opposed to using convergent media to perform both functions in tandem.

To develop a form of enhanced television that consumers will genuinely want and use, producers might be best served by taking the needs of their audience, rather than the capabilities of the technology, as their starting point. From this standpoint, the success of enhanced television very well may lie in a two-step process. The first step will be to identify the types of enhancements that the majority of users want and need. The second will be to find ways to make those convergent enhancements available to users who are motivated to use them without requiring their use by those who would rather just watch television or surf the Web instead. Orduna used a similar point to explain why enhanced television has already achieved wider use in Europe than in the United States: "Here, we were focused on building a better mousetrap ... In Europe they were figuring out what the mouse really wanted to eat" (quoted in Lee, 2001).

Family Use.   Even if enhanced television is made accessible and designed in ways that make consumers want to use it, children's use of enhanced television will also be affected by the constraints of the setting in which it is being used. In particular, consider the nature of home viewing of television and its implications for enhanced television.

Computer-based applications are often designed for use by a single user, who controls the input device (e.g., mouse, keyboard). Existing enhanced television devices (e.g., WebTV) are designed in similar ways. Frequently, though, television viewing is not a solitary activity; children coview television with friends, siblings, parents, and others. Viewing of enhanced television is likely to be no different.

For this reason, joint viewing of enhanced television raises issues as to interaction among viewers and the design of input devices and interfaces. Research on the use of standard remote controls during family coviewing indicates that fathers are most likely to hold and dominate remote control devices, followed by sons. Mothers and daughters are far less likely to maintain control of the devices (Walker & Bellamy, 2001). It is reasonable to expect that similar patterns would emerge for input devices that control enhanced television, and to expect that older siblings would dominate these devices more than younger siblings. Even if one viewer physically holds the input device, it is possible that coviewing children might collaborate in choosing the course of a branching story, or playing a game, or choosing to follow links. But it is equally possible that, in at least some

cases, one child might gain the benefits of using the interactive enhancements, whereas a coviewing friend or sibling would wind up doing little
more than watching the screen.

One possible way to avoid this situation would be to develop input devices and interfaces that can be controlled by multiple users at the same
time. Such devices would be a natural fit to enhancements that involve interactive games, in the same way that video game systems typically allow
multiple players to take turns or play the game simultaneously. However,
it will probably be more challenging to design systems that allow multiple
users to participate in accessing information, ordering video on demand,
or making choices in branching stories—particularly if the users disagree.

Challenges of Design

Challenges of design refer, on a more micro-level, to issues of usability as
reflected in the design of input devices and interfaces. This class of challenges stems from constraints posed by the medium and by the cognitive
level of its users. These challenges include hardware and interface issues,
the integration of educational content, relationships among the various
components (i.e., the television program, games, etc.), and issues of pace
and cognitive load.

Input Devices and Interfaces.   Children (particularly young children)
can only take advantage of the opportunities offered by enhanced television if their manual dexterity is sufficient to operate the hardware that
controls it, and if they understand how to use the interface. Usability research with computers has shown that not all types of input devices are
equally easy for young children to use. For example, one series of studies
compared preschool children's ability to operate several different input
devices: keyboard arrow keys, touch screen, light pen, joystick, trackball,
and mouse. Together, these studies found that the devices that young children used most easily were the touch screen, light pen, and trackball (although only the trackball was included in all three studies); the input
device that proved most difficult was the keyboard arrow keys (Revelle,
Strommen, & Medoff, 2001).

These findings hold implications for enhanced television, because existing enhanced television systems such as WebTV rely on arrow keys (on
either a keyboard or remote control) and drop-down menus for navigation. As a result, such systems may pose difficulties for use by young children. Indeed, subsequent research by Revelle and Medoff (2002)
examined the usability of a controller for Sony's Playstation 2, a convergent video game system that also provides online access to Web-based
games. Like the previous research, results showed arrow keys to be diffi-

cult for preschool children. They were more successful in using keys that were coded by color and shape, as long as the color and orientation of on-screen icons matched those of the keys on the controller.

As these examples illustrate, the development of both input devices and on-screen interfaces will require substantial care. Ongoing usability testing will be essential in informing this development, so that the final product will fit the needs and abilities of the audience.

Integration of Educational Content. The discussion of the capacity model in chapter 10 (this volume) stressed the role of *distance*—that is, the degree to which educational content is integral or tangential to the narrative in a television program. This point applies equally strongly to the other components of enhanced television. For an interactive game to succeed in delivering educational content, it is probably best if the educational content is integral to the task that the user must perform in the game (e.g., completing a mathematical pattern to open a locked gate). Similarly, if viewers' psychological involvement can be heightened by making choices in branching stories (per Vorderer, 2000), learning is likely to be strongest if the relevant educational content is integral to the decision that is made at a choice point.

In both of these cases, by maintaining a small distance between the educational content and either the game or choice point, viewers' participation in the activity requires them to think about and apply the educational content. The result would likely be deeper and more elaborate processing of the content, as well as an opportunity to practice applying it. On the other hand, if distance is greater (e.g., if the educational content in a branching story is not integral to the choice points), then children's heightened involvement with the game or choice points might cause them to devote less processing to the educational content—perhaps even less than in a traditional, non-interactive television program.

Complementarity Among Components. Just as it is important to consider the integration of educational content within a single component of enhanced television (e.g., the television program alone), it is equally important to consider the manner in which the various components are integrated with each other. For example, Mickel (1998; cf. Fisch, 2003) tested the usability of a prototype for an enhanced WebTV version of *Sesame Street*, in which viewers could click away from *Sesame Street* television segments about the letter *Z* and the number *6* to play interactive games that involved the same letter or number. The results of the study made it apparent that the design of the prototype had inadvertently set the television program and interactive game in an either–or relationship. Use of the games occurred in real time, so clicking over to one experience meant missing the other. To play the games, children had to miss part of the television program (which potentially included moments that were key to comprehending its educational content). Conversely, watching the program uninterrupted meant not playing the games.

It is likely that, as technologies converge, this issue may be circumvented through the same technology that is now currently being used in digital video recorders (e.g., TiVo, Replay TV). Unlike videocassette recorders, the buffers in these devices make it possible for users to time-shift television programs by continuing to record the program "live" even as they watch a portion of the same program that aired several minutes earlier. Combining enhanced television with such technology could allow viewers to watch part of an educational television program, switch over to play a game, and then return to the television program—not in real time, but from the precise point at which they stopped.

Aside from technological solutions, though, this issue also may be overcome by designing convergent media such that their components complement, rather than compete with, each other. For example, branching stories provide opportunities for viewers to apply educational content and solve puzzles alongside characters at designated choice points—all in real time, without requiring digital video recorder technology to store any part of the program in a buffer. In this way, the television program and the interactive application become one and the same thing, rather than two potentially competing activities that must be coordinated.

Cognitive Load.   One of the key concepts in the capacity model (chap. 10, this volume) is the notion that the limitations of working memory constrain the resources that are available for viewers to process televised narrative and educational content simultaneously. One would expect cognitive load to be even greater when narrative and educational content are simultaneously accompanied by additional layers of material, such as interactivity in the form of a game or multiple options at the choice point in a branching story.

In fact, this proposal draws some support from research on viewers' enjoyment of enhanced television (Vorderer, 2000; Vorderer, Knobloch, & Schramm, 2001). These studies found that viewers' enjoyment of enhanced television depended on their cognitive capacity; those adult viewers who had greater cognitive capacity enjoyed TV movies more when they believed that they determined the course of the story, but viewers with smaller cognitive capacity preferred the movies when they were not interactive.

Although Vorderer and his colleagues measured appeal rather than comprehension or learning, it seems reasonable to expect that analogous results would be found for these variables as well. In other words, viewers with greater cognitive capacity would be expected to learn more when television is enhanced, whereas viewers with smaller cognitive capacity would be expected to learn more from traditional television. In this way, individual and developmental differences in cognitive capacity would be expected to make enhanced television more beneficial for some viewers than others.

Naturally, cognitive capacity is not the only factor that will determine whether a viewer is able to process an enhanced television program sufficiently to achieve comprehension or learning. The capacity model specifies a number of viewer characteristics and program characteristics that contribute to the demands of processing traditional educational programs (see chap. 10, this volume), and all of these are applicable to enhanced television as well. Indeed, factors that contribute to cognitive load in processing traditional educational television programs are likely to become all the more important in the context of the greater cognitive demands posed by enhanced television.

CONCLUSION

Perhaps the broadest conclusion to be drawn from this volume is that educational television works. Thoughtfully crafted television programs can hold significant benefits for preschoolers and school-age children in a wide range of subject areas. Moreover, these benefits can result in effects that last for years.

This is not to say, of course, that all television programs are beneficial for child viewers, any more than it would be reasonable to claim that all television is bad for children. Indeed, Wright, Huston, Scantlin, et al.'s (2001) 3-year longitudinal study of the impact of *Sesame Street* found not only that viewing *Sesame Street* was associated with subsequent positive effects on literacy and school readiness, but also that preschool viewing of commercial entertainment cartoons sometimes had significant negative effects on the same outcome measures. Clearly, the critical factor here is not the medium itself, but the content it carries.

As television moves into the future and evolves into new forms of convergent media, technological advances will bring new opportunities for education, but new challenges as well. By bringing expertise in education, child development, and empirical research to bear on the process of production, we will be able to maximize the educational strengths presented by each new medium. In this way, we can ensure that television—in all of its possible forms—will continue to educate children for generations to come.

References

Abelson, R. P. (1975). Does a story understander need a point of view? In B. Nash-Webber & R. Schank (Eds.), *Theoretical issues in natural language processing* (pp. 140–143). Cambridge, MA: Bolt, Beranek, & Newman.

Acord, K., & Romontio, N. (1995). *An evaluation of* Sesame Street *PEP trainings and program utilization by Bay area child care providers, 1994–1995: A final report submitted to the California Department of Education, Child Development Division.* San Francisco: KQED Center for Education and Lifelong Learning.

Action Team on School Readiness. (1992). *Every child ready for school.* Washington, DC: National Governor's Association.

Aidman, A. J. (1993). *Television as activity system:* Mr. Rogers' Neighborhood *and the development of polite behavior routines in preschoolers.* Unpublished doctoral thesis, University of Illinois, Urbana-Champaign, IL.

Allport, A. (1989). Visual attention. In M. Posner (Ed.), *Foundations of cognitive science* (pp. 631–682). Cambridge, MA: MIT Press.

American Academy of Pediatrics. (1997). *Media Matters: A national media education campaign.* Elk Grove Village, IL: Author.

American Academy of Pediatrics. (2001). Children, adolescents, and television. *Pediatrics, 107,* 423–426.

American Association for the Advancement of Science. (1993). *Benchmarks for science literacy.* Washington, DC: Author.

Anderson, D. R. (1999, April). Toward a theory of sustained attention to television. In Fisch, S.M. (Chair), *Theoretical perspectives on children's processing of television.* Symposium presented at the 63rd annual meeting of the Society for Research in Child Development, Albuquerque, NM.

Anderson, D. R., & Bryant, J. (1983). Research on children's television viewing: The state of the art. In J. Bryant & D. R. Anderson (Eds.), *Children's understanding of television: Research on attention and comprehension* (pp. 331–354). New York: Academic Press.

Anderson, D. R., Bryant, J., Wilder, A., Santomero, A., Williams, M., & Crawley, A. M. (2000). Researching *Blue's Clues*: Viewing behavior and impact. *Media Psychology, 2,* 179–194.

Anderson, D. R., & Burns, J. (1991). Paying attention to television. In J. Bryant & D. Zillmann (Eds.), *Responding to the screen: Reception and reaction processes* (pp. 3–25). Hillsdale, NJ: Lawrence Erlbaum Associates.

Anderson, D. R., Field, D. E., Collins, P. A., Lorch, E. P., & Nathan, J. G. (1985). Estimates of young children's time with television: A methodological comparison of parent reports with time-lapse video home observation. *Child Development, 56,* 1345–1357.

Anderson, D. R., Huston, A. C., Schmitt, K. L., Linebarger, D. L., & Wright, J. C. (2001). Early childhood television viewing and adolescent behavior. *Monographs of the Society for Research in Child Development, 66,* 1.

Anderson, D. R., Huston, A. C., Wright, J. C., & Collins, P. A. (1998). *Sesame Street* and educational television for children. In R. G. Noll & M. E. Price (Eds.), *A communications cornucopia: Markle Foundation essays on information policy* (pp. 279–296). Washington, DC: Brookings Institution Press.

Anderson, D. R., Lorch, E. P., Field, D. E., & Sanders, J. (1981). The effects of TV program comprehensibility on preschool children's visual attention to television. *Child Development, 52,* 151–157.

Anderson, J. R. (1983). *The architecture of cognition.* Cambridge, MA: Harvard University Press.

ARC Consulting LLC. (1995). *Research findings:* The Magic School Bus *(Vol. 1, Executive summary, & Vol. 2, Comprehensive report).* New York: Author.

Armstrong, G. B., & Greenberg, B. S. (1990). Background television as an inhibitor of cognitive processing. *Human Communication Research, 16,* 355–386.

Astington, J. W. (1993). *The child's discovery of the mind.* Cambridge, MA: Harvard University Press.

Atkin, C. K. (1978). Broadcast news programming and the child audience. *Journal of Broadcasting, 22,* 47–61.

Atkin, C. K., & Gantz, W. (1978). Television news and the child audience. *Public Opinion Quarterly, 42,* 183–198.

Bachen, C. M. (1998). *Channel One* and the education of American youths. *Annals of the American Academy of Political and Social Science, 557,* 132–146.

Baker, L., & Brown, A. L. (1984). Metacognitive skills in reading. In D. P. Pearson, M. Kail, R. Barr, & P. Mosenthal (Eds.), *Handbook of reading research* (pp. 353–394). New York: Longman.

Ball, S., & Bogatz, G. A. (1970). *The first year of* Sesame Street: *An evaluation.* Princeton, NJ: Educational Testing Service.

Ball, S., & Bogatz, G. A. (1973). *Reading with television: An evaluation of* The Electric Company. Princeton, NJ: Educational Testing Service.

Ball, S., Bogatz, G. A., Karazow, K. M., & Rubin, D. B. (1974). *Reading with television: A follow-up evaluation of* The Electric Company. Princeton, NJ: Educational Testing Service.

Bandura, A. (1965). Influence of models' reinforcement contingencies on the acquisition of imitative responses. *Journal of Personality and Social Psychology, 1,* 589–595.

Bandura, A. (1971). *Social learning theory.* New York, NY: General Learning Press.

Bandura, A. (1986). *Social foundations of thought and action: A social cognitive theory.* Englewood Cliffs, NJ: Prentice-Hall.

Bandura, A. (2002). Social cognitive theory of mass communication. In J. Bryant & D. Zillmann (Eds.), *Media effects: Advances in theory and research* (2nd ed., pp. 121–154). Mahwah, NJ: Lawrence Erlbaum Associates.

Bandura, A., Ross, D., & Ross, S. A. (1963). Imitation of film-mediated aggressive models. *Journal of Abnormal and Social Psychology, 66,* 3–11.

Barnett, W. S. (1995). Long-term effects of early childhood programs on cognitive and school outcomes. *The Future of Children, 5*(3), 25–50.

Barr, R., & Hayne, H. (1999). Developmental changes in imitation from television during infancy. *Child Development, 70,* 1067–1081.

Barton, P. E. (1997). *Raising achievement and reducing gaps: Reporting progress toward goals for academic achievement in mathematics* (report to the National Education Goals Panel). Washington, DC: National Education Goals Panel.

Bassok, M., & Holyoak, K. J. (1993). Pragmatic knowledge and conceptual structure: Determinants of transfer across quantitative domains. In D. K. Detterman & R. J. Sternberg (Eds.), *Transfer on trial: Intelligence, cognition, and instruction* (pp. 68–98). Norwood, NJ: Ablex.

Baumeister, R. F., & Newman, L. F. (1995). The primacy of stories, the primacy of roles, and the polarizing effects of interpretive motives: Some propositions about narratives. In R. S. Wyer (Ed.), *Knowledge and memory: The real story* (pp. 97–108). Hillsdale, NJ: Lawrence Erlbaum Associates.

Beentjes, J. W. J., & van der Voort, T. H. A. (1993). Television viewing versus reading: Mental effort, retention, and inferential learning. *Communication Education, 42,* 191–205.

Bennett, W. J. (1988). *American education: Making it work.* Washington, DC: U.S. Department of Education.

Bereiter, C. (1995). A dispositional review of transfer. In A. McKeough, J. Lupart, & A. Marini (Eds.), *Teaching for transfer: Fostering generalization in learning* (pp. 21–34). Mahwah, NJ: Lawrence Erlbaum Associates.

Bereiter, C., & Engelman, S. I. (1966). *Teaching disadvantaged children in preschool.* Englewood Cliffs, NJ: Prentice-Hall.

Berkowitz, L. (1984). Some effects of thoughts on anti- and prosocial influences of media events: A cognitive neoassociation analysis. *Psychological Bulletin, 95,* 410–427.

Berkowitz, L., & Rogers, K. H. (1986). A priming effect analysis of media influences. In J. Bryant & D. Zillmann (Eds.), *Perspectives on media effects* (pp. 57–82). Hillsdale, NJ: Lawrence Erlbaum Associates.

Bernstein, L. J. (2000). Sesame Bridge: Peace building in the Middle East through television for children. In P. Senge, N. Cambron-McCabe, T. Lucas, B. Smith, J. Dutton, & A. Kleiner, (Eds.), *Schools that learn: A Fifth Discipline fieldbook for educators, parents, and everyone who cares about education* (pp. 519–526). New York: Doubleday.

Big Bag Research. (1997). *Participation.* Unpublished research report. New York: Children's Television Workshop.

Binkley, M. R. (1988). *Becoming a nation of readers: What parents can do.* Washington, DC: Office of Educational Research and Improvement, U.S. Department of Education.

Block, C., Guth, J. A., & Austin, S. (1993). *Galaxy Classroom evaluation: Language arts, grades 3–5, final report: Executive summary.* San Francisco, CA: Far West Laboratory for Educational Research and Development.

Bloom, B. S. (1964). *Stability and change in human characteristics.* New York: Wiley.

Bogatz, G. A., & Ball, S. (1971). *The second year of Sesame Street: A continuing evaluation.* Princeton, NJ: Educational Testing Service.

Bower, G. H. (1978). Experiments on story comprehension and recall. *Discourse Processes, 1,* 211–231.

Bower, G. H., & Clark. M. C. (1969). Narrative stories as a mediator for serial learning. *Psychonomic Science, 14,* 181–182.

Boyer, E. (1992). *Readiness to learn: A mandate for the nation.* Princeton, NJ: Carnegie Council for the Advancement of Teaching.

Brand, J. E., & Greenberg, B. S. (1994). Commercials in the classroom: The impact of *Channel One* advertising. *Journal of Advertising Research, 34,* 18–27.

Bransford, J. D., Brown, A. L., & Cocking, R. R. (Eds.). (1999). *How people learn: Brain, mind, experience, and school.* Washington, DC: National Academy Press.

Bransford, J. D., Hasselbring, T., Barron, B., Kulewicz, S., Littlefield, J., & Goin, L. (1988). The use of macro contexts to stimulate mathematical thinking. In R. Charles & E. Silver (Eds.), *The teaching and assessing of mathematical problem solving* (pp. 125–147). Hillsdale, NJ: Lawrence Erlbaum Associates.

Bransford, J. D., & Schwartz, D. L. (1999). Rethinking transfer: A simple proposal with multiple implications. *Review of Research in Education, 24,* 61–100.

Bredekamp, S., & Copple, C. (Eds.). (1997). *Developmentally appropriate practice in early childhood programs* (Rev. ed.). Washington, DC: National Association for the Education of Young Children.

Brederode-Santos, M. E. (1993). *Learning with television: The secret of Rua Sésamo.* (English translation of Portuguese, M. E. Brederode-Santos, Trans., 1991, *Com a Televiso o Segredo da Rua Sésamo.* Lison: TV Guia Editora) Unpublished research report.

Brosius, H. (1993). The effects of emotional pictures in television news. *Communication Research, 20,* 105–124.

Brown, A. L., Kane, M. I., & Long, C. (1989). Analogical transfer in young children: Analogies as tools for communication and exposition. *Applied Cognitive Psychology, 3,* 275–293.

Browne, K. (1978). Comparisons of factual recall from film and print stimuli. *Journalism Quarterly, 55,* 350–353.

Brownell, C. A., & Carriger, M. S. (1991). Collaborations among toddler peers: Individual contributions to social contexts. In L. B. Resnick, J. M. Levine, & S. D. Teasley (Eds.), *Perspectives on socially shared cognition* (pp. 365–383). Washington, DC: American Psychological Association.

Bruner, J. (1985). Narrative and paradigmatic modes of thought. In E. Eisner (Ed.), *Learning and teaching the ways of knowing: Eighty-fourth yearbook of the National Society for the Study of Education, Part 2* (pp. 97–115). Chicago, IL: University of Chicago Press.

Bruner, J. (1986). *Actual minds, possible worlds.* Cambridge, MA: Harvard University Press.

Bryant, J., Cho, J. Y., Maxwell, M., & Raney, A. A. (1999, March). *Relationship between Integrated Science and Stanford Achievement Test science scores* (Report submitted to the Center for Communication and Educational Technology). Tuscaloosa, AL: Institute for Communication Research.

Bryant, J., Maxwell, M., Stuart, Y., Ralstin, L., & Rainey, A. A. (1999). *Longitudinal effects of PBS Ready to Learn outreach initiative.* Tuscaloosa, AL: Institute for Communications Research, University of Alabama.

Bryant, J., McCollum, J., Ralstin, L., Raney, A., McGavin, L., Miron, D., Maxwell, M., Venugopalan, G., Thompson, S., DeWitt, D., & Lewis, K. (1997). *Effects of two years' viewing of Allegra's Window and Gullah Gullah Island.* Tuscaloosa, AL: Institute for Communication Research, University of Alabama.

Bryant, J., Mulliken, L., Maxwell, M., Mundorf, N., Mundorf, J., Wilson, B., Smith, S., McCollum, J., & Owens, J. W. (1999). *Effects of two years' viewing of Blue's Clues.* Tuscaloosa, AL: Institute for Communication Research, University of Alabama.

Bryant, J., Stuart, Y., & Maxwell, M. (1999). *A compendium of research on Ready to Learn.* Tuscaloosa, AL: Institute for Communications Research, University of Alabama.

Bryant, J., Zillmann, D., & Brown, D. (1983). Entertainment features in children's educational television: Effects on attention and information acquisition. In J. Bryant & D. R. Anderson (Eds.), *Children's understanding of television: Research on attention and comprehension* (pp. 221–240). New York: Academic Press.

Bryant, J. A., Bryant, J., Mulliken, L., McCollum, J. F., & Love, C. C. (2001). Curriculum-based preschool television programming and the American family: Historical development, impact of public policy, and social and educational effects. In J. Bryant & J. A. Bryant (Eds.), *Television and the American family* (2nd ed., pp. 415–434). Mahwah, NJ: Lawrence Erlbaum Associates.

Buerkel-Rothfuss, N. L., & Buerkel, R. A. (2001). Family mediation. In J. Bryant & J. A. Bryant (Eds.), *Television and the American family* (2nd ed., pp. 355–376). Mahwah, NJ: Lawrence Erlbaum Associates.

Butterworth, E. C., Slocum, T. A., & Nelson, G. N. (1993). Cognitive and behavioral analyses of teaching and transfer: Are they different? In D. K. Detterman & R. J. Sternberg (Eds.), *Transfer on trial: Intelligence, cognition, and instruction* (pp. 192–254). Norwood, NJ: Ablex.

Cairns, E. (1984). Television news as a source of knowledge about the violence for children in Ireland: A test of the knowledge-gap hypothesis. *Current Psychological Research and Reviews, 3,* 32–38.

Cairns, E., Hunter, D., & Herring, L. (1980). Young children's awareness of violence in Northern Ireland: The influence of Northern Irish television in Scotland and Northern Ireland. *British Journal of Social and Clinical Psychology, 19,* 3–6.

Cakim, I. (1999, April 12). Analyst insight: Old racial issues in a new medium. *Industry Standard, 46.*

Calvert, S. (1999). *Children's journeys through the information age.* Boston: McGraw-Hill.

Calvert, S. L. (1995). *Impact of televised songs on children's and young adults' memory of verbally-presented content.* Unpublished manuscript, Georgetown University, Washington, DC.

Calvert, S. L. (2001). Impact of televised songs on children's and young adults' memory of verbally-presented content. *Media Psychology, 3,* 325–342.

Calvert, S. L., Huston, A. C., Watkins, B. A., & Wright, J. C. (1982). The relation between selective attention to television forms and children's comprehension of content. *Child Development, 53,* 601–610.

Calvert, S. L., Huston, A. C., & Wright, J. C. (1987). Effects of television prepay formats on children's attention and story comprehension. *Journal of Applied Developmental Psychology, 8,* 329–342.

Calvert, S. L., & Pfordresher, P. Q. (1994, August). *Impact of a televised song on students' memory of information.* Poster presented at the annual meeting of the American Psychological Association, Los Angeles, CA.

Calvert, S. L., Rigaud, E., & Mazella, J. (1991). *Presentational features for students' recall of televised educational content.* Poster presented at the biennial meeting of the Society for Research in Child Development, Seattle, WA.

Calvert, S. L., & Tart, M. (1993). Song versus verbal forms for very-long-term, long-term, and short-term verbatim recall. *Journal of Applied Developmental Psychology, 14,* 245–260.

Cambre, M. A., & Fernie, D. (1985). *Formative evaluation of Season IV, 3-2-1 Contact: Assessing the appeal of four weeks of educational television programs and their influence on children's science comprehension and science interest.* New York: Children's Television Workshop.

Cantor, J. (1998). *"Mommy, I'm scared": How TV and movies frighten children and what we can do to protect them.* San Diego, CA: Harcourt Brace.

Carnegie Task Force on Learning in the Primary Grades (1996). *Years of promise: A comprehensive learning strategy for America's children.* New York, NY: Carnegie Corporation of New York.

Carpenter, C. J., Huston, A. C., & Spera, L. (1989). Children's use of time in their everyday activities during middle childhood. In M. Bloch & A. Pellegrini (Ed.), *The ecological context of children's play* (pp. 165–190). Norwood, NJ: Ablex.

Ceci, S. J., & Ruiz, A. (1993). Transfer, abstractness, and intelligence. In D. K. Detterman & R. J. Sternberg (Eds.), *Transfer on trial: Intelligence, cognition, and instruction* (pp. 161–198). Norwood, NJ: Ablex.

Chen, M. (1994a). Television and informal science education: Assessing the past, present, and future of research. In V. Crane, H. Nicholson, M. Chen, & S. Bitgood (Eds.), *Informal science learning: What the research says about television, science museums, and community-based projects* (pp. 15–60). Ephrata, PA: Science Press.

Chen, M. (1994b). *The smart parent's guide to kids' TV.* San Francisco, CA: KQED Books.

Children Now. (1994). *Tuned in or tuned out?: America's children speak out on the news media.* Oakland, CA: Author.

Children's Defense Fund. (2000). *The state of America's children yearbook 2000.* Washington, DC: Author.

Children's Television Workshop. (1981). 3-2-1 Contact *resource manual.* New York: Author.

Children's Television Workshop. (1987). Square One *TV teacher's guide.* New York: Author.

Children's Television Workshop. (1994). *Learning from* Ghostwriter*: Strategies and outcomes.* New York: Author.

Children's Television Workshop Research Division. (1989). Sesame Street *research bibliography.* New York: Author.

Choat, E. (1988). Children, television, and learning in nursery and infants' schools. *Educational Studies, 14,* 9–21.

Christenson, P. G., & Roberts, D. F. (1983). The role of television in the formation of children's social attitudes. In M. J. A. Howe (Ed.), *Learning from television: Psychological and educational research* (pp. 79–99). London: Academic Press.

Chugani, H. T. (1996). Neuroimaging of developmental non-linearity and developmental pathologies. In R. W. Thatcher, G. R. Lyon, J. Rumsey, & N. Krasnegor (Eds.), *Developmental neuroimaging: Mapping the development of brain and behavior* (pp. 187–195). San Diego: Academic Press.

Clifford, B. R., Gunter, B., & McAleer, J. (1995). *Television and children: Program evaluation, comprehension, and impact.* Hillsdale, NJ: Lawrence Erlbaum Associates.

Coates, B., Pusser, H. E., & Goodman, I. (1976). The influence of *Sesame Street* and *Mister Rogers' Neighborhood* on children's social behavior in the preschool. *Child Development, 47,* 138–144.

Cognition and Technology Group at Vanderbilt, The. (1997). *The Jasper Project: Lessons in curriculum, instruction, assessment, and professional development.* Mahwah, NJ: Lawrence Erlbaum Associates.

Cole, C. F., Richman, B. A., & McCann Brown, S. K. (2001). The world of *Sesame Street* research. In S. M. Fisch & R. T. Truglio (Eds.), *"G" is for "growing": Thirty years of research on children and Sesame Street* (pp. 147–179). Mahwah, NJ: Lawrence Erlbaum Associates.

Collins, W. A. (1983). Interpretation and inference in children's television viewing. In J. Bryant & D. R. Anderson (Eds.), *Children's understanding of television: Research on attention and comprehension* (pp. 125–150). New York: Academic Press.

Collins, W. A., Sobol, B. L., & Westby, S. (1981). Effects of adult commentary on children's comprehension and inferences about a televised aggressive portrayal. *Child Development, 52,* 158–163.

Collins, W. A., Wellman, H., Keniston, A. H., & Westby, S. D. (1978). Age-related aspects of comprehension and inference from a televised dramatic narrative. *Child Development, 49,* 389–399.

Common Ground Productions, Search for Common Ground in Macedonia, & Sesame Workshop. (2000). *Lessons from Nashe Maalo: A research report on what ethnic Albanian, Macedonian, Roma, and Turkish youth learned from watching Nashe Maalo.* Washington, DC: Author.

Comstock, G. (1989). *The evolution of American television.* Newbury Park, CA: Sage.

Comstock, G., & Paik, H. (1991). *Television and the American child.* New York: Academic Press.

Condry, J., Scheibe, C., Bahrt, A., & Potts, K. (1993, March). *Children's television before and after the Children's Television Act of 1990.* Poster presented at the Society for Research in Child Development, New Orleans, LA.

Connell, D. D., & Palmer, E. L. (1971). *Sesame Street*: A case study. In J. D. Halloran & M. Gurevitch (Eds.), *Broadcaster/researcher cooperation in mass communication research* (pp. 64–85). Leeds, England: Kavanagh & Sons.

Cook, T. D., Appleton, H., Conner, R. F., Shaffer, A., Tamkin, G., & Weber, S. (1975). Sesame Street *revisited.* New York: Russell Sage Foundation.

Cooney, J. G. (1966). *The potential uses of television in preschool education: A report to the Carnegie Corporation of New York.* New York: Carnegie Corporation.

Corder-Bolz, C. R. (1980). Mediation: The role of significant others. *Journal of Communication, 30,* 106–118.

Corteen, R. S., & Williams, T.M. (1986). Television and reading skills. In T.M. Williams (Ed.), *The impact of television: A natural experiment in three communities* (pp. 39–85). Orlando, FL: Academic Press.

Craik, F. I. M., & Lockhart, R. S. (1972). Levels of processing: A framework for memory research. *Journal of Verbal Learning and Verbal Behavior, 12,* 599–607.

Crawley, A. M., Anderson, D. R., Santomero, A., Wilder, A., Williams, M., Evans, M. K., & Bryant, J. (2002). Do children learn how to watch television? The impact of extensive experience with *Blue's Clues* on preschool children's television viewing behavior. *Journal of Communication, 52,* 264–280.

Crawley, A. M., Anderson, D. R., Wilder, A., Williams, M., & Santomero, A. (1999). Effects of repeated exposures to a single episode of the television program *Blue's Clues* on the viewing behaviors and comprehension of preschool children. *Journal of Educational Psychology, 91,* 630–637.

Csikszentmihalyi, M., & Csikszentmihalyi, I. S. (1988). *Optimal experience: Psychological studies of flow in consciousness.* Cambridge, UK: Cambridge University Press.

Davis, E. P., Friedman, G. I., & Martin, L. (1990). Community education and child-care programs. *Educational Technology Research and Development, 38*(4), 45–54.

DeFleur, M. L., Davenport, L., Cronin, M., & DeFleur, M. (1992). Audience recall of news stories presented by newspaper, computer, television, and radio. *Journalism Quarterly, 69,* 1010–1022.

Demetriou, A., Christou, C., Spanoudis, G., & Platsidou, M. (2002). The development of mental processing: Efficiency, working memory, and thinking. *Monographs of the Society for Research in Child Development, 67,* 1 (Whole No. 268).

Dempster, F. N. (1981). Memory span: Sources of individual and developmental differences. *Psychological Bulletin, 89,* 63–100.

Detterman, D. K. (1993). The case for the prosecution: Transfer as an epiphenomenon. In D. K. Detterman & R. J. Sternberg (Eds.), *Transfer on trial: Intelligence, cognition, and instruction* (pp. 1–24). Norwood, NJ: Ablex.

Deutsch, M. (1965). Race and social class as separate factors related to social environment. *American Journal of Sociology, 70,* 474.

Diaz-Guerrero, R., & Holtzman, W. H. (1974). Learning by televised *Plaza Sésamo* in Mexico. *Journal of Educational Psychology, 66*(5), 632–643.

Drabman, R. S., & Thomas, M. H. (1974). Does media violence increase children's tolerance of real-life aggression? *Developmental Psychology, 10,* 418–421.

Drew, D. G., & Reese, S. D. (1984). Children's learning from a television newscast. *Journalism Quarterly, 61,* 83–88.

Drew, D. G., & Reeves, B. B. (1978). Children and television news. *Journalism Quarterly, 57,* 45–54, 114.

Drew, D. G., & Reeves, B. B. (1980). Learning from a television news story. *Communication Research, 7,* 121–135.

Druin, A., Bederson, B., Boltman, A., Miura, A., Knotts-Callahan, D., & Platt, M. (1999). Children as our technology design partners. In A. Druin (Ed.), *The design of children's technology* (pp. 51–72). San Francisco, CA: Morgan Kaufman.

Ducey, R. V. (1999). *Internet + DTV broadcasting = UN-TV.* Washington, DC: National Association of Broadcasters. Available: www.nab.org/Research/Reports/DTV-Internet.asp

Dudko, M. A., & Larsen, M. (1993). Barney & Friends: *Watch, play, and learn.* Allen, TX: The Lyons Group.

Duncker, K. (1945). On problem solving. *Psychological Monographs, 58* (Whole No. 270).

Dunn, G. (1977). *The box in the corner: Television and the under-fives.* London: Macmillan.

Eckenrod, J., & Rockman, S. (1988). Connections between television and the social studies curriculum. *Social Education, 52,* 357–362.

Eckhardt, B. B., Wood, M. R., & Jacobvitz, R. S. (1991). Verbal ability and prior knowledge: Contributions to adults' comprehension of television. *Communication Research, 18,* 636–649.

Egan, L. M. (1978). Children's viewing pattern for television news. *Journalism Quarterly, 55,* 337–342.

Ehman, L. (1995, April). *A case study of* Channel One *in the instruction and curriculum of a middle school.* Paper presented at the annual meeting of the American Education Research Association, San Francisco, CA.

Eich, E. (1985). Context, memory, and integrated item/context imagery. *Journal of Experimental Psychology: Learning, Memory, and Cognition, 11,* 764–770.

Einzig, R., Cappella, E., & Michaelis, B. (1996). *Sesame Street Fire Safety Station: Third edition fire safety materials, Phase II research report.* Unpublished research report. New York: Children's Television Workshop.

Elias, M. J. (1983). Improving coping skills of emotionally disturbed boys through television-based social problem solving. *American Journal of Orthopsychiatry, 53,* 61–72.

Engle, R. W. (2002). Working memory capacity as executive attention. *Current Directions in Psychological Science, 11,* 19–23.

Entwistle, D. R., Alexander, K. L., & Olson, L. S. (1997). *Children, schools, and inequality.* Boulder, CO: Westview Press.

Eron, L. D., Walder, L. L., & Lefkowitz, M. M. (1971). *The learning of aggression in children.* Boston: Little, Brown, & Co.

Esty, E. T., Hall, E. R., & Fisch, S. M. (1990). *Children's problem-solving behavior and their attitudes toward mathematics: A study of the effects of* Square One TV *(Vol 2. The effects of* Square One TV *on children's problem solving).* New York: Children's Television Workshop.

Faccoro, L. B., & DeFleur, M. L. (1993). A cross-cultural experiment on how well audiences remember news stories from newspaper, computer, television, and radio. *Journalism Quarterly, 70,* 585–601.

Falk, J. H., Donovan, E., & Woods, R. (Eds.). (2001). *Free-choice science education: How we learn science outside of school (Ways of knowing in science and mathematics).* New York: Teachers College Press.

Family Communications, Inc. (1998). *Mister Rogers' plan and play book* (5th ed.). Pittsburgh, PA: Author.

Fay, A. L., Teasley, S. D., Cheng, B. H., Bachman, K. M., & Schnakenberg, J. H. (1995). *Children's interest in and their understanding of science and technology: A study of the effects of* Cro. Pittsburgh, PA: University of Pittsburgh and New York: Children's Television Workshop.

Fay, A. L., Yotive, W. M., Fisch, S. M., Teasley, S. D., McCann, S. K., Garner, M. S., Ozaeta, M., Chen, L., & Lambert, M. H. (1995, August). The impact of *Cro* on children's interest in and understanding of technology. In S. M. Fisch (Chair), *Science on Saturday morning: The Children's Television Act and the role of* Cro. Symposium presented at the annual meeting of the American Psychological Association, New York, NY.

Federal Communications Commission (1991, April). Report and order: In the matter of policies and rules concerning children's television programming. *FCC Record, 6,* 2111–2127.

Federal Communications Commission (1993, March). *FCC notice of inquiry.* FCC 93–123.

Federal Communications Commission (1995, April). *FCC notice of proposed rule making.* FCC 95–143.

Federal Interagency Forum on Child and Family Statistics (2001). *America's children: Key national indicators of well-being 2001.* Washington, DC: U.S. Government Printing Office.

Ferguson, E. L. & Hegarty, M. (1995). Learning with real machines or diagrams: Application of knowledge to real-world problems. *Cognition and Instruction, 13*(1), 129–160.

Fetler, M. (1984). Television viewing and school achievement. *Journal of Communication, 34, 4*(2), 104–118.

Fisch, S. M. (1998). The Children's Television Workshop: The experiment continues. In R. G. Noll & M. E. Price (Eds.), *A communications cornucopia: Markle Foundation essays on information policy* (pp. 297–337). Washington, DC: Brookings Institution Press.

Fisch, S. M. (2000). A capacity model of children's comprehension of educational content on television. *Media Psychology, 2*(1), 63–91.

Fisch, S. M. (2003). Challenges for the future of educational media. In E. L. Palmer (Ed.), *Faces of televisual media: Teaching, violence, selling to children* (pp. 125–139). Mahwah, NJ: Lawrence Erlbaum Associates.

Fisch, S. M. (in press-a). Characteristics of effective materials for informal education: A cross-media comparison of television, magazines, and interactive media. In M. Rabinowitz, F. C. Blumberg, & E. Everson (Eds.), *The impact of media and technology on instruction.* Mahwah, NJ: Lawrence Erlbaum Associates.

Fisch, S. M. (in press-b). Using television to promote respect and understanding: Impact of past projects and implications for the future. In C. Cole & G. S. Lesser (Eds.), *Begin with the children.* Mahwah, NJ: Lawrence Erlbaum Associates.

Fisch, S. M., & Bernstein, L. (2001). Formative research revealed: Methodological and process issues in formative research. In S. M. Fisch & R. T. Truglio (Eds.), *"G" is for "growing": Thirty years of research on children and* Sesame Street (pp. 39–60). Mahwah, NJ: Lawrence Erlbaum Associates.

Fisch, S. M., Goodman, I. F., McCann, S. K., Rylander, K., & Ross, S. (1995, April). *The impact of informal science education:* Cro *and children's understanding of technology.* Poster presented at the 61st annual meeting of the Society for Research in Child Development, Indianapolis, IN.

Fisch, S. M., & Hall, E. R. (1991, April). Back to square one: Interrelationships among problem solving, attitude, and *Square One TV.* In E. R. Hall & S. M. Fisch (Chairs), *Problem solving, attitudes, and television: A summative study of* Square One TV. Symposium presented at the biennial meeting of the Society for Research in Child Development, Seattle, WA.

Fisch, S. M., & McCann, S. K. (1993). Making broadcast television participative: Eliciting mathematical behavior through *Square One TV. Educational Technology Research and Development, 41,* 3, 103–109.

Fisch, S. M., McCann Brown, S. K., & Cohen, D .I. (2001). Young children's comprehension of television: The role of visual information and intonation. *Media Psychology, 3,* 365–378.

Fisch, S. M., Mendelsohn, S., Wilder, G., Williams, M., Lovelace, V., & Hall, E. (1994). *Reaching specific audiences through mass media: Diversity and the Children's Television Workshop.* Symposium presented at the annual meeting of the International Communication Association, Sydney, Australia.

Fisch, S. M., Shulman, J. S., Akerman, A., & Levin, G. A. (2002). Reading between the pixels: Parent-child interaction while reading online storybooks. *Early Education and Development, 13,* 435–451.

Fisch, S. M., & Truglio, R. T. (Eds.). (2001a). *"G" is for "growing": Thirty years of research on children and* Sesame Street. Mahwah, NJ: Lawrence Erlbaum Associates.

Fisch, S. M., & Truglio, R. T. (2001b). Why children learn from *Sesame Street*. In S. M. Fisch & R. T. Truglio (Eds.), *"G" is for "growing": Thirty years of research on children and* Sesame Street (pp. 233–244). Mahwah, NJ: Lawrence Erlbaum Associates.

Fisch, S. M., Truglio, R. T., & Cole, C. F. (1999). The impact of *Sesame Street* on preschool children: A review and synthesis of thirty years' research. *Media Psychology, 1,* 165–190.

Fisch, S. M., Yotive, W. M., McCann, S. K., Cohen, D. I., & Chen, L. (1996, April). *The many faces of science on children's television:* 3-2-1 Contact *and* Cro. Roundtable discussion presented at the annual meeting of the American Educational Research Association, New York, NY.

Fisch, S. M., Yotive, W. M., McCann, S. K., Garner, M. S., & Chen, L. (1997). Science on Saturday morning: Children's perceptions of science in educational and non-educational cartoons. *Journal of Educational Media, 23,* 157–167.

Flagg, B. N. (1994). Learning science from children's radio: Summative evaluation of *Kinetic City Super Crew. Educational Research and Development, 42*(3), 29–43.

Flavell, J. H., & Miller, P. H. (1998). Social cognition. In W. Damon, D. Kuhn, & R. S. Siegler (Eds.), *Handbook of child psychology: Vol. 2. Cognition, perception, and language* (pp. 851–898). New York: Wiley.

Flavell, J. H., & Ross. L. (Eds.). (1981). *Social and cognitive development.* New York, NY: Cambridge University Press.

Forsslund, T. (1990). Contributions to school children—an overview: Factors that influence the use and impact of educational television in school. In C.E. Tidhar (Ed.), *ETV broadcasting research in the Nineties: Readings from the Tel Aviv research seminar 1990* (pp. 127–149). Tel Aviv, Israel: Israel Educational Television & European Broadcasting Union.

Foundation for Advancements in Science and Education. (1997). *Classroom television: A useful resource for mathematics and science education* (FASE Research Report). Los Angeles, CA: Author.

Fox, N. A. (Ed.). (1994). The development of emotion regulation and dysregulation: Biological and behavioral aspects. *Monographs of the Society for Research in Child Development, 59,* 1.

Frenette, M. (1991). Television as a source of informal science learning for pre-adolescents: Design considerations. *Canadian Journal of Educational Communication, 20*(1), 17–35.

Friedrich, L. K., & Stein, A. H. (1973). Aggressive and prosocial television programs and the natural behavior of preschool children. *Monographs of the Society for Research in Child Development, 38,* 4.

Friedrich, L. K., & Stein, A. H. (1975). Prosocial television and young children: The effects of verbal labeling and role playing on learning and behavior. *Child Development, 46,* 27–38.

Fry, A. F., & Hale, S. (1996). Processing speed, working memory, and fluid intelligence: Evidence for a developmental cascade. *Psychological Science, 7,* 237–241.

Funk, J. B. (2002). Video games grow up: Electronic games in the 21st century. In V. Strasburger & B. J. Wilson, (Eds.), *Children, adolescents, and the media* (pp. 117–144). Thousand Oaks, CA: Sage.

Furnham, A., & Gunter, B. (1985). Sex, presentation mode, and memory for violent and non-violent news. *Journal of Educational Television, 11,* 99–105.

Gagne, R., & Burkman, E. (1982). *Promoting science literacy in adults through television: Final report to the NSF.* Tallahassee, FL: Florida State University. (ERIC Document Reproduction Service No. ED 229 234)

Gathercole, S. E., & Baddeley, A. (1993). *Working memory and language.* Hillsdale, NJ: Lawrence Erlbaum Associates.

Gauvain, M. (2001). *The social context of cognitive development.* New York, NY: The Guilford Press.

Gemark (1993). *Plaza Sésamo IV* formative research: Set evaluation. Unpublished research report.

Gentner, D. (1983). Structure-mapping: A theoretical framework for analogy. *Cognitive Science, 7,* 155–170.

Gentner, D. (1988). Metaphor as structure mapping: The relational shift. *Child Development, 59,* 47–59.

Gettas, G. J. (1990). The globalization of *Sesame Street*: A producer's perspective. *Educational Technology Research and Development, 38*(4), 55–63.

Gibbon, S. Y., Palmer, E. L., & Fowles, B. R. (1975). *Sesame Street, The Electric Company*, and reading. In J. Carrol & J. Chall (Eds.), *Toward a literate society* (pp. 215–256). New York: McGraw Hill.

Gibbons, J., Anderson, D. R., Smith, R., Field, D. E., & Fischer, C. (1986). Young children's recall and reconstruction of audio and audiovisual material. *Child Development, 57,* 1014–1023.

Gick, M. L., & Holyoak, K. J. (1983). Schema induction and analogical transfer. *Cognitive Psychology, 15,* 1–38.

Giles, D. C. (2002). Parasocial interaction: A review of the literature and a model for future research. *Media Psychology, 4,* 279–304.

Goldberg, M. E., & Gorn, G. J. (1979). Television's influence on children's preferences of non-white playmates: Canadian "Sesame Street" inserts. *Journal of Broadcasting, 23,* 27–32.

Goodman, I. F., Rylander, K., & Ross, S. (1993). *Cro Season I summative evaluation.* Cambridge, MA: Sierra Research Associates.

Goodman, K. S. (1989). Whole-language research: Foundations and developments. *The Elementary School Journal, 90,* 205–219.

Gopher, D., & Donchin, E. (1986). Workload: An examination of the concept. In K. R. Boff, L. Kaufman, & J. E. Thomas (Eds.), *Handbook of perception and human performance* (pp. 41-1–41-48). New York: Wiley.

Gorn, G. J. Goldberg, M. E., & Kanungo, R. N. (1976). The role of educational television in changing the intergroup attitudes of children. *Child Development, 42,* 277–280.

Gott, S. P., Hall, E. P., Pokorny, R. A., Dibble, E., & Glaser, R. (1993). A naturalistic study of transfer: Adaptive expertise in technical domains. In D. K. Detterman & R. J. Sternberg (Eds.), *Transfer on trial: Intelligence, cognition, and instruction* (pp. 258–288). Norwood, NJ: Ablex.

Gotthelf, C., & Peel, T. (1990). The Children's Television Workshop goes to school. *Educational Technology Research and Development, 38*(4), 25–33.

Graves, S. (1993). Television, the portrayal of African Americans, and the development of children's attitudes. In G. L. Berry & J. K. Asamen (Eds.), *Children and television: Images in a changing sociocultural world* (pp. 179–190). Newbury Park, CA: Sage.

Graves, S. B. (1975). *Racial diversity in children's television: Its impact on racial attitudes and stated program preferences.* Unpublished doctoral dissertation, Harvard University, Cambridge, MA.

Greenberg, B. S. (1972). Children's reactions to TV Blacks. *Journalism Quarterly, 49,* 5–14.

Greenberg, B. S. (1974). Gratifications of television viewing and their correlates for British children. In J. G. Blumler & E. Katz, (Eds.), *The uses of mass communication* (pp. 71–92). Newbury Park, CA: Sage.

Greenberg, B. S., & Brand, J. E. (1993a). Television news and advertising in school: The "Channel One" controversy. *Journal of Communication, 43,* 143–151.

Greenberg, B. S., & Brand, J. E. (1993b). Cultural diversity on Saturday morning television. In G. L. Berry & J. K. Asamen (Eds.), *Children and television: Images in a changing sociocultural world* (pp. 132–142). Newbury Park, CA: Sage.

Greenberg, B. S., & Gantz, W. (1976). Public television and taboo topics: The impact of *VD Blues. Public Telecommunications Review, 4*(1), 56–59.

Greenfield, P. M. (1984). *Mind and media: The effects of television, video games, and computers.* Cambridge, MA: Harvard University Press.

Greeno, J. G., Moore, J. L., & Smith, D. R. (1993). Transfer of situated knowledge. In D. K. Detterman & R. J. Sternberg (Eds.), *Transfer on trial: Intelligence, cognition, and instruction* (pp. 99–167). Norwood, NJ: Ablex.

Groebel, J. (1999). Media access and media use among 12-year-olds in the world. In C. von Fellitzen & U. Carlsson (Eds.), *Children and media: Image, education, participation* (pp. 61–68). Göteborg, Sweden: UNESCO.

Gunter, B. (1987). *Poor reception: Misunderstanding and forgetting television news.* Hillsdale, NJ: Lawrence Erlbaum Associates.

Gunter, B., Furnham, A., & Gietson, G. (1984). Memory for the news as a function of the channel of communication. *Human Learning, 3,* 265–271.

Gunter, B., Furnham, A., & Griffiths, S. (2000). Children's memory for news: A comparison of three presentation media. *Media Psychology, 2,* 93–118.

Gunter, B., Sancho-Aldridge, J., & Winstone, P. (1994). *Television: The public's view—1993.* London: John Libbey

Guth, J. A., Austin, S., DeLong, B., & Pasta, D. J. (1995). *Evaluation of Galaxy Classroom for grades K–2, final report: Executive summary.* San Francisco, CA: Far West Laboratory for Educational Research and Development.

Guth, J. A., Austin, S., DeLong, B., Pasta, D. J., & Block, C. (1995). *Galaxy Classroom science evaluation for grades 3–5, final report: Executive summary.* San Francisco, CA: Far West Laboratory for Educational Research and Development.

Haeffner, M. J., & Wartella, E. A. (1987). Effects of sibling coviewing on children's interpretation of television programs. *Journal of Broadcasting and Electronic Media, 31,* 153–168.

Hall, E. R., Esty, E. T., & Fisch, S. M. (1990). Television and children's problem-solving behavior: A synopsis of an evaluation of the effects of *Square One TV. Journal of Mathematical Behavior, 9,* 161–174.

Hall, E. R., Fisch, S. M., Esty, E. T., Debold, E., Miller, B.A., Bennett, D. T., & Solan, S. V. (1990). *Children's problem-solving behavior and their attitudes toward mathematics: A study of the effects of* Square One TV (Vols. 1–5). New York: Children's Television Workshop.

Hall, E. R., Miller, B. A., & Fisch, S. M. (1990). *Children's problem-solving behavior and their attitudes toward mathematics: A study of the effects of* Square One TV *(Vol 4. The* Square One TV *interview: Children's reactions to the series).* New York: Children's Television Workshop.

Hall, E. R., & Williams, M. E. (1993, May). *Ghostwriter* research meets literacy on the plot-line. In B. J. Wilson (Chair), *Formative research and the CTW model: An interdisciplinary approach to television production.* Symposium presented at the annual meeting of the International Communication Association, Washington, DC.

Harris, R. J. (1999). *A cognitive psychology of mass communication* (3rd ed.). Mahwah, NJ: Lawrence Erlbaum Associates.

Harrison, L. F., & Williams, T. M. (1986). Television and cognitive development. In T.M. Williams (Ed.), *The impact of television: A natural experiment in three communities* (pp. 87–138). Orlando, FL: Academic Press.

Hart, S. G. (1986). Theory and measurement of human workload. In J. Zeidner (Ed.), *Human productivity enhancement* (pp. 396–455). New York: Praeger.

Harvey, F. A., Quiroga, B., Crane, V., & Bottoms, C. L. (1976). *Evaluation of eight* Infinity Factory *programs.* Newton, MA: Education Development Center.

Haskell, R. E. (2001). *Transfer of learning: Cognition, instruction, and reasoning.* San Diego: Academic Press.

Hayes, D. S., & Birnbaum, D. W. (1980). Preschoolers' retention of televised events: Is a picture worth a thousand words? *Developmental Psychology, 16,* 410–416.

Healy, J. M. (1990). *Endangered minds: Why our children don't think.* New York: Simon & Schuster.

Hearold, S. (1986). A synthesis of 1043 effects of television on social behavior. In G. Comstock (Ed.), *Public communication and behavior* (Vol. 1, pp. 65–133). New York: Academic Press.

Hendershot, H. (1998). *Saturday morning censors: Television regulation before the v-chip.* Durham, NC: Duke University Press.

Hendershot, H. (1999). *Sesame Street*: Cognition and communications imperialism. In M. Kinder (Ed.), *Kids' media culture.* Durham, NC: Duke University Press.

Herbert, D. (1988). Behind the scenes of *Mr. Wizard.* In M. Druger (Ed.), *Science for the fun of it: A guide to informal science education* (pp. 51–56). Washington, DC: National Science Teachers Association.

Himmelweit, H., Oppenheim, A. N., & Vince, P. (1958). *Television and the child: An empirical study of the effects of television on the young.* London: Oxford University Press.

Hodapp, T. V. (1977). Children's ability to learn problem-solving strategies from television. *The Alberta Journal of Educational Research, 23*(3), 171–177.

Hoijer, B. (1990). Learning from television: Viewers' reception of informative television discourse. In C. E. Tidhar (Ed.), *ETV broadcasting research in the nineties: Readings from the Tel Aviv research seminar, 1990* (pp. 161–176). Tel Aviv: Israel Educational Television and European Broadcasting Union.

Höller, C., & Müller, S. (1999, December). "Eh-oh—it's Teletubby time": The results of a qualitative study in Germany. *Telvizion*, 47–48.

Holyoak, K. J. (1985). The pragmatics of analogical transfer. In G. H. Bower (Ed.), *The psychology of learning and motivation* (pp. 59–87). New York: Academic Press.

Holyoak, K. J. & Koh, K. (1987). Surface and structural similarity in analogical transfer. *Memory and Cognition, 4,* 332–340.

Howard, S., & Roberts, S. (1999, December). "Teletubbies" down under: The Australian experience. *Telvizion,* 19–25.

Huesmann, L. R. (1986). Psychological processes promoting the relation between exposure to media violence and aggressive behavior by the viewer. *Journal of Social Issues, 42*(3), 125–140.

Huston, A. C., Anderson, D. R., Wright, J. C., Linebarger, D. L., & Schmitt, K. L. (2001). *Sesame Street* viewers as adolescents: The recontact study. In S. M. Fisch & R. T. Truglio (Eds.), *"G" is for "growing": Thirty years of research on children and* Sesame Street (pp. 131–144). Mahwah, NJ: Lawrence Erlbaum Associates.

Huston, A. C., Watkins, B. A., & Kunkel, D. (1989). Public policy and children's television. *American Psychologist, 44,* 424–433.

Huston, A. C., & Wright, J. C. (1983). Children's processing of television: The informative functions of formal features. In J. Bryant & D. R. Anderson (Eds.), *Children's understanding of television: Research on attention and comprehension* (pp. 35–68). New York: Academic Press.

Huston, A. C., & Wright, J. C. (1997). Mass media and children's development. In W. Damon, I. Sigel, & K. A. Renninger (Eds.), *Handbook of child psychology* (Vol. 4, pp. 999–1058). New York: John Wiley.

Huston, A. C., Wright, J. C., Rice, M. L., Kerkman, D., & St. Peters, M. (1987, April). *The development of television viewing patterns in early childhood: A longitudinal investigation.* Paper presented at the Society for Research in Child Development, Baltimore, MD.

Inhelder, B., & Piaget, J. (1964). *The early growth of logic in the child.* London: Routledge & Kegan Paul.

Jacobvitz, R. S., Wood, M. R., & Albin, K. (1991). Cognitive skills and young children's comprehension of television. *Journal of Applied Developmental Psychology, 12,* 219–235.

Johnston, J. (1980). *An exploratory study of the effects of viewing the first season of* 3-2-1 Contact. New York: Children's Television Workshop.

Johnston, J., & Brzezinski, E. (1992). *Taking the measure of* Channel One: *The first year.* Ann Arbor, MI: Institute for Social Research, University of Michigan.

Johnston, J., & Brzezinski, E. (1994). *Executive summary,* Channel One: *A three year perspective.* Ann Arbor, MI: Institute for Social Research, University of Michigan.

Johnston, J., Brzezinski, E., & Anderman, E. (1994). *Taking the measure of* Channel One: *A three year perspective.* Ann Arbor, MI: Institute for Social Research, University of Michigan.

Johnston, J., & Ettema, J. S. (1982). *Positive images: Breaking stereotypes with children's television.* Beverly Hills, CA: Sage.

Johnston, J., & Luker, R. (1983). *The "Eriksson Study": An exploratory study of viewing two weeks of the second season of* 3-2-1 Contact. New York: Children's Television Workshop.

Jones, L. R., Mullis, I. V. S., Raizen, S. A., Weiss, I. R., & Weston, E. A. (1992). *The 1990 science report card: NAEP's assessment of fourth, eighth, and twelfth graders.* Washington, DC: U.S. Department of Education, Office of Educational Research and Improvement.

Jordan, A. B. (2000). *Is the three-hour rule living up to its potential?: An analysis of educational television for children in the 1999/2000 broadcast season* (Rep. No. 34). Philadelphia, PA: Annenberg Public Policy Center, University of Pennsylvania.

Jordan, A. B., & Woodard, E. H. (2001). Electronic childhood: The availability and use of household media by 2– to 3–year-olds. *Zero to Three, 22*(2), 4–9.

Kahnemann, D. (1973). *Attention and effort.* Englewood Cliffs, NJ: Prentice-Hall.

Kail, R. (1992). Processing speed, speech rate, and memory: *Developmental Psychology, 28,* 899–904.

Kail, R., & Park, Y.-S. (1994). Processing time, articulation time, and memory span. *Journal of Experimental Child Psychology, 57,* 281–291.

Katz, P. (Ed.; 2001). *Community connections for science education: Vol. 2. History and theory you can use.* Arlington, VA: National Science Teachers Association.

KCET. (1997). Storytime *connections: A literacy resource guide.* Newark, DE: International Reading Association.

Kirwil, L. (1996a). Study on the reception of the set designed for the Polish version of *Sesame Street* (English trans. of Polish). Unpublished research report.

Kirwil, L. (1996b). *Ulica Sezamkowa* formative character study: Executive summary (English trans. of Polish). Unpublished research report.

Knupfer, N., & Hayes, P. (1994). The effects of the *Channel One* broadcast on students' knowledge of current events. In A. DeVaney (Ed.), *Watching* Channel One: *The convergence of students, technology, and private business.* Albany, NY: State University of New York Press.

Kodaira, S. I. (1990). Lessons from research on creating programs for young children: What works and why, in different countries and cultural contexts. In C. E. Tidhar (Ed.), *ETV broadcasting research in the nineties: Readings from the Tel Aviv research seminar 1990* (pp. 83–124). Tel Aviv, Israel: Israel Educational Television & European Broadcasting Union.

Kodaira, S. I. (2001, March). *What NHK research on children and media tells us and where it could lead.* Paper presented at the 3rd World Summit on Media for Children, Thessaloniki, Greece.

KRC Research & Consulting. (1994). *An evaluative assessment of the* Ghostwriter project. New York: Author.

Kunkel, D. (1998). Policy battles over defining children's educational television. *Annals of the American Academy of Political and Social Sciences, 557,* 39–53.

Kunkel, D. (2001). Children and television advertising. In D. G. Singer & J. L. Singer (Eds.), *Handbook of children and the media* (pp. 375–393). Thousand Oaks, CA: Sage.

Kunkel, D., & Canepa, J. (1995). Broadcasters' license renewal claims regarding children's educational programming. *Journal of Broadcasting and Electronic Media, 38*(4), 397–416.

Kunkel, D., & Wilcox, B. (2001). Children and media policy. In D. G. Singer & J. L. Singer (Eds.), *Handbook of children and the media* (pp. 589–604). Thousand Oaks, CA: Sage.

Kwaitek, K., & Watkins, B. (1981). *The systematic viewer: An inquiry into the grammar of television* (First annual report to the Spenser Foundation). Ann Arbor, MI: Children's Media Project, University of Michigan.

Lampert, M. (1985). Mathematics learning in context: *The Voyage of the Mimi. Journal of Mathematical Behavior, 4,* 157–167.

Lancit Media Productions. (1995). *Teacher's guide: Science comes alive with* Reading Rainbow. Lincoln, NE: Great Plains Northern.

Land, H. W. (1972). *The Children's Television Workshop: How and why it works.* Jericho, NY: Nassau Board of Cooperative Educational Services.

Lang, A. (2000). The limited capacity model of mediated message processing. *Journal of Communication, 50,* 46–70.

Lang, A., Dhillon, P., & Dong, Q. (1995). Arousal, emotion, and memory for television messages. *Journal of Broadcasting and Electronic Media, 39,* 313–327.

Lang, A., Geiger, S., Strickwerda, M., & Sumner, J. (1993). The effects of related and unrelated cuts on television viewers' attention, processing capacity, and memory. *Communication Research, 20,* 4–29.

Larson, R.W. (2001). How U.S. children and adolescents spend time: What it does (and doesn't) tell us about their development. *Current Directions in Psychological Science, 10,* 160–164.

Lave, J., & Wenger, E. (1991). *Situated learning: Legitimate peripheral participation.* Cambridge, England: Cambridge University Press.

Lawson, M. J., & Kirby, J. R. (1981). Training in information processing algorithms. *British Journal of Educational Psychology, 51,* 321–355.

Lee, J. B. (2001, December 31). In the U.S., interactive TV still awaits an audience. *New York Times,* C1, C8.

Leitner, R. K. (1991). *Comparing the effects on reading comprehension of educational video, direct experience, and print.* Unpublished doctoral thesis, University of San Francisco, CA.

Lemish, D., & Rice, M. L. (1986). Television as a talking picture book: A prop for language acquisition. *Journal of Child Language, 13,* 251–274.

Lesser, G. S. (1972). Assumptions behind the writing and production methods in *Sesame Street.* In W. Schramm (Ed.), *Quality in instructional television* (pp. 108–164). Honolulu: University Press of Hawaii.

Lesser, G. S. (1974). *Children and television: Lessons from* Sesame Street. New York: Vintage Books/Random House.

Lesser, G. S., & Schneider, J. S. (2001). Creation and evolution of the *Sesame Street* curriculum. In S. M. Fisch & R. T. Truglio (Eds.), *"G" is for "growing": Thirty years of research on children and* Sesame Street (pp. 25–38). Mahwah, NJ: Lawrence Erlbaum Associates.

Levin, S. R., & Anderson, D. R. (1976). The development of attention. *Journal of Communication, 26*(2), 126–135.

Levin, T., Sabar, N., & Libman, Z. (1991). Achievements and attitudinal patterns of boys and girls in science. *Journal of Research in Science Teaching, 28,* 315–328.

Lewit, E. M., & Baker, L. S. (1995). School readiness. *The Future of Children, 5*(2), 128–139.

Lieberman, D. (1999). The researcher's role in the design of children's media and technology. In A. Druin (Ed.), *The design of children's technology* (pp. 73–97). San Francisco, CA: Morgan Kaufman.

Liggett, T. C., & Benfield, C. M. (1994). Reading Rainbow *guide to children's books: The 101 best titles.* New York: Citadel Press.

Linebarger, D. L. (2000). *Summative evaluation of* Between the Lions: *A final report to WGBH Educational Foundation.* Kansas City, KS: Juniper Gardens Children's Project, University of Kansas.

Linebarger, D. L. (2001). *Summative evaluation of* Dora the Explorer, *Part 1: Learning outcomes.* Kansas City, KS: Media & Technology Projects, ABCD Ventures, Inc.

Linz, D., Donnerstein, E., & Penrod, S. (1984). The effects of multiple exposures to filmed violence against women. *Journal of Communication, 34*(3), 130–147.

Linz, D., Donnerstein, E., & Penrod, S. (1988). Effects of long-term exposure to violent and sexually degrading depictions of women. *Journal of Personality and Social Psychology, 55,* 758–768.

Liss, M. B., Reinhardt, L. C., & Friedriksen, S. (1983). TV heroes: The impact of rhetoric and deeds. *Journal of Applied Developmental Psychology, 4,* 175–187.

Livingstone, S., Holden, K. J., & Bovill, M. (1999). Children's changing media environment: Overview of a European comparative study. In C. von Fellitzen & U. Carlsson (Eds.), *Children and media: Image, education, participation* (pp. 39–59). Göteborg, Sweden: UNESCO International Clearinghouse on Children and Violence on the Screen.

Lorch, E. P., Anderson, D. R., & Levin, S. R. (1979). The relationship of visual attention to children's comprehension of television. *Child Development, 50,* 722–727.

Lorch, E. P., & Castle, V. J. (1997). Preschool children's attention to television: Visual attention and probe response times. *Journal of Experimental Child Psychology, 66,* 111–127.

Lovelace, V. O., & Huston, A. C. (1983). Can television teach prosocial behavior? In J. Sprafkin, C. Swift, & R. Hess (Eds.), *Rx television: Enhancing the preventive effects of TV* (pp. 93–106). New York: The Haworth Press.

Luchins, A. S. (1942). Mechanization in problem solving. *Psychological Monographs, 54,* 6 Whole No. 248.

MacBeth, T. M. (1996). Indirect effects of television: Creativity, persistence, school achievement, and participation in other activities. In T. M. MacBeth (Ed.), *Tuning in to young viewers: Social science perspectives on television* (pp. 149–214). Thousand Oaks, CA: Sage.

Maccoby, E. E. (1951). Television: Its impact on school children. *Public Opinion Quarterly, 15,* 421–444.

Mander, J. (1978). *Four arguments for the elimination of television.* New York: William Morrow.

Mandler, J., & Johnson, N. (1977). Remembrance of things parsed: Story structure and recall. *Cognitive Psychology, 9,* 111–151.

Mares, M. L. (1996). *Positive effects of television on social behavior: A meta-analysis* (Report Series No. 3). Philadelphia, PA: Annenberg School of Communication, University of Pennsylvania.

Mares, M. L., & Woodard, E. H. (2001). Prosocial effects on children's social interactions. In D. G. Singer & J. L. Singer (Eds.), *Handbook of children and the media* (pp. 183–205). Thousand Oaks, CA: Sage.

Mares, M. L., & Woodard, E. H. (in press). Positive effects of television on children's social interactions: A meta-analysis. In R. Carveth & J. Bryant (Eds.), *Meta-analyses of media effects.* Mahwah, NJ: Lawrence Erlbaum Associates.

Mays, L., Henderson, E. H., Seidman, S. K., & Steiner, V. J. (1975). *On meeting real people: An evaluation report on* Vegetable Soup. Albany, NY: New York State Education Department.

McCall, R. B., Parke, R. D., & Kavanaugh, R. D. (1977). Imitation of live and televised models by children one to three years of age. *Monographs of the Society for Research in Child Development, 42*, 5.

Meadowcroft, J. M., & Reeves, B. (1989). Influence of story schema development on children's attention to television. *Communication Research, 16*, 352–374.

Medin, D. L., & Ortony, A. (1989). Psychological essentialism. In S. Vosniadou & A. Ortony (Eds.), *Similarity and analogical reasoning* (pp. 179–195). Cambridge: Cambridge University Press.

Medved, M., & Medved, D. (1998). *Saving childhood: Protecting our children from the national assault on innocence.* New York: Harper Collins.

Meltzoff, A. N. (1985). Immediate and deferred imitation in fourteen- and twenty-four month-old infants. *Child Development, 56*, 62–72.

Meltzoff, A. N. (1988). Imitation of televised models by infants. *Child Development, 59*, 1221–1229.

Mickel, N. (1998). *Usability testing report for children's testing:* Sesame Street *interactive-TV demo.* Unpublished research report. Palo Alto, CA: WebTV.

Mielke, K. W. (1988). Making informal contact. In M. Druger (Ed.), *Science for the fun of it: A guide to informal science education* (pp. 45–50). Washington, DC: National Science Teachers Association.

Mielke, K. W. (1990). Research and development at the Children's Television Workshop. *Educational Technology Research and Development, 38*(4), 7–16.

Mielke, K. W. (2001). A review of research on the educational and social impact of *Sesame Street*. In S.M. Fisch & R. T. Truglio (Eds.), *"G" is for "growing": Thirty years of research on children and* Sesame Street (pp. 83–95). Mahwah, NJ: Lawrence Erlbaum Associates.

Mielke, K. W., & Chen, M. (1983). Formative research for *3-2-1 Contact*: Methods and insights. In M. J. A. Howe (Ed.), *Learning from television: Psychological and educational research* (pp. 31–55). London: Academic Press.

Mindel, C. H., & Dangel, R. F. (1990). *The* Sesame Street *PEP project: Final research report.* Arlington, TX: The University of Texas at Arlington.

Miron, D., Bryant, J., & Zillmann, D. (2001). Creating vigilance for better learning from television. In D. G. Singer & J. L. Singer (Eds.), *Handbook of children and the media* (pp. 153–181). Thousand Oaks, CA: Sage.

Mulliken, L., & Bryant, J. A. (1999, May). *Effects of curriculum-based television programming on behavioral assessments of flexible thinking and structured and unstructured prosocial play behaviors.* Poster presented at the 49th annual conference of the International Communication Association, San Francisco, C A.

Mundorf, N., & Laird, K. R. (2002). Social and psychological effects of information technologies and other interactive media. In J. Bryant & D. Zillmann (Eds.), *Media effects: Advances in theory and research* (2nd ed, pp. 583–602). Mahwah, NJ: Lawrence Erlbaum Associates.

Naigles, L. R., & Mayeux, L. (2001). Television as incidental language teacher. In D. G. Singer & J. L. Singer (Eds.), *Handbook of children and the media* (pp. 135–152). Thousand Oaks, CA: Sage.

Naigles, L., Singer, D., Singer, J., Jean-Louis, B., Sells, D., & Rosen, C. (1995). *Watching "Barney" affects preschoolers' use of mental state verbs.* Paper presented at the annual meeting of the American Psychological Association, New York, NY.

National Assessment of Educational Progress. (1986). *The reading report card.* Princeton, NJ: Educational Testing Service.

National Assessment of Educational Progress. (1991). *Trends in academic progress: Achievement of U.S. students in science, 1969–1970 to 1990; mathematics, 1973–1990; reading, 1971–1990; and writing, 1984–1990.* Washington, DC: U.S. Department of Education.

National Association for the Education of Young Children. (1990). NAEYC position statement on school readiness. *Young Children, 1,* 21–23.

National Center for Educational Statistics. (1998). *Issue brief: Internet access in public schools.* Washington, DC: U.S. Department of Education.

National Center for Educational Statistics. (1999). *The NAEP 2001 civics report card.* Washington, DC: U.S. Department of Education.

National Center for Educational Statistics. (2002a). *The NAEP 2001 geography report card.* Washington, DC: U.S. Department of Education.

National Center for Educational Statistics. (2002b). *The NAEP 2001 U.S. history report card.* Washington, DC: U.S. Department of Education.

National Commission on Excellence in Education. (1983). *A nation at risk: The imperative for educational reform.* Washington, DC: U.S. Department of Education.

National Council for the Social Studies. (1993). A vision of powerful teaching and learning in the social studies: Building social understanding and civic efficacy. *Social Education, 57,* 213–223.

National Council for the Social Studies. (1994). *Expectations of excellence: Curriculum standards for social studies.* Silver Spring, MD: Author.

National Council of Teachers of Mathematics. (1989). *Curriculum and evaluation standards for school mathematics.* Reston, VA: Author.

National Education Goals Panel. (1997). *The National Education Goals report summary, 1997: Mathematics and science achievement for the 21st century.* Washington, DC: Author.

National Education Research Policy and Priorities Board. (1997). *Building knowledge for a nation of learners: A framework for education research, 1997.* Washington, DC: U.S. Department of Education.

National Research Council. (1989). *Everybody counts: A report to the nation on the future of mathematics education.* Washington, DC: National Academy Press.

National Research Council. (1990). *Reshaping school mathematics: A philosophy and framework for change.* Washington, DC: National Academy Press.

National Research Council. (1995). *National science education standards: Observe, interact, change, learn.* Washington, DC: National Academy Press.

National Research Council. (1998). *Preventing reading difficulties in young children.* Washington, DC: National Academy Press.

Nelson, K. (1996). *Language in cognitive development.* Cambridge, England: Cambridge University Press.

Neuman, S. B. (1988). The displacement effect: Assessing the relationship between television viewing and reading performance. *Reading Research Quarterly, 23,* 414–440.

Neuman, S. B. (1991). *Literacy in the television age: The myth of the TV effect.* Norwood, NJ: Ablex.

Newburger, E. C. (2001). *Home computers and Internet use in the United States: August 2000.* Washington, DC: U.S. Department of Commerce, U.S. Census Bureau.

Newcomb, A. F., & Collins, W. A. (1979). Children's comprehension of family role portrayals in televised dramas: Effects of socioeconomic status, ethnicity, and age. *Developmental Psychology, 15,* 417–423.

NFO Research, Inc. (1990). Reading Rainbow *study: Final report.* (ERIC Document Reproduction Service No. ED 331 027)

Nielsen New Media Services. (1993). Ghostwriter *study, wave II: May, 1993.* Dunedin, FL: Author.

Noble, G. (1983). Social learning from everyday television. In M. J. A. Howe (Ed.), *Learning from television: Psychological and educational research* (pp. 101–124). London: Academic Press.

Noble, G., & Creighton, V. M. (1981). Australia Naturally—*Children's reactions.* Armidale, Australia: Author.

Noble, G., & Noble, E. (1979). A study of teenagers' uses and gratifications of the *Happy Days* show. *Media Information Australia, 11,* 17–23.

Norman, D. A., & Bobrow, D. G. (1976). On the role of active memory processes in perception and cognition. In C. N. Cofer (Ed.), *The structure of human memory* (pp. 114–132). San Francisco: W. H. Freeman.

Novick, L. R. (1988). Analogical transfer, problem similarity, and expertise. *Journal of Experimental Psychology: Learning, Memory, and Cognition, 14*(3), 510–520.

Omanson, R. C., Warren, W. H., & Trabasso, T. (1978). Goals, themes, inferences, and memory: A developmental study. *Discourse Processing, 1,* 337–354.

Overton, W. F. (Ed.). (1983). *The relationship between social and cognitive development.* Hillsdale, NJ: Lawrence Erlbaum Associates.

Pace, A. J. (1980). *The ability of young children to correct comprehension errors: An aspect of comprehension monitoring.* Paper presented at the annual meeting of the American Educational Research Association, Boston, MA.

Pace, A. J. (1981). *Comprehension monitoring by elementary students: When does it occur?* Paper presented at the annual meeting of the American Educational Research Association, Los Angeles, CA.

Paik, H., & Comstock, G. (1994). The effects of television violence on antisocial behavior: A meta-analysis. *Communication Research, 21,* 516–546.

Paivio, A. (1971). *Imagery and verbal processes.* New York: Holt.

Palmer, E. L. (1993). *Toward a literate world: Television in literacy education—lessons from the Arab region.* Boulder, CO: Westview Press.

Palmer, E. L., & Fisch, S. M. (2001). The beginnings of *Sesame Street* research. In S. M. Fisch & R. T. Truglio (Eds.), *"G" is for "growing": Thirty years of research on children and* Sesame Street (pp. 3–23). Mahwah, NJ: Lawrence Erlbaum Associates.

Palmer, E. L., & MacNeil, M. (1991). Children's comprehension processes: From Piaget to public policy. In J. Bryant & D. Zillmann (Eds.), *Responding to the screen: Reception and reaction processes* (pp. 27–44). Hillsdale, NJ: Lawrence Erlbaum Associates.

Papert, S. (1998, June). Does easy do it?: Children, games, and learning. *Game Developer,* 88.

Paulson, F. L. (1974). Teaching cooperation on television: An evaluation of *Sesame Street* social goals programs. *AV Communication Review, 22,* 229–246.

Pearl, D., Bouthilet, L., & Lazar, J. (Eds.) (1982). *Television and behavior: Ten years of scientific progress and implications for the eighties: Vol. 1. Summary report.* Washington, DC: U.S. Government Printing Office.

Peel, T., Rockwell, A., Esty, E., & Gonzer, K. (1987). Square One Television: *The comprehension and problem solving study*. New York: Children's Television Workshop.

Perkins, D. N., & Salomon, G. (1994). Transfer of learning. In T. Husén & T. N. Postlethwaite (Eds.), *The international encyclopedia of education* (2nd ed., pp. 6452–6457). Oxford: Pergamon.

Pezdek, K., & Hartman, E. F. (1983). Children's television viewing: Attention and comprehension of auditory and visual information. *Child Development, 54*, 1015–1023.

Pezdek, K., Simon, S., Stoeckert, J., & Kiely, J. (1987). Individual differences in television comprehension. *Memory and Cognition, 15*, 428–435.

Pezdek, K., & Stevens, E. (1984). Children's memory for auditory and visual information on television. *Developmental Psychology, 20*, 212–218.

Plaza Sésamo IV Department of Research and Content (1993). Summary of *Plaza Sésamo* IV formative research to develop health and safety messages characters (English trans. of Spanish). Unpublished research report.

Polsky, R. M. (1977). *Getting to* Sesame Street*: Origins of the Children's Television Workshop*. New York: Praeger.

Postlethwaite, T. N., & Wiley, D. E. (1992). *The IEA study of science II: Science achievement in twenty-three countries*. Oxford: Pergamon Press.

Postman, N. (1985). *Amusing ourselves to death*. New York: Penguin.

Potter, W. J. (1987). Does television viewing hinder academic achievement among adolescents? *Human Communication Research, 14*, 27–46.

Program Research Department. (1999). *Building on Sesame Street project: Second year impact study* (unpublished research report). New York: Children's Television Workshop.

Raver, C. C. (2002). Emotions matter: Making the case for the role of young children's emotional development for early school readiness. *Social Policy Report, 16*(3), 3–18.

Rayner, K., Foorman, B. R., Perfetti, C. A., Pesetsky, D., & Seidenberg, M. S. (2001). How psychological science informs the teaching of reading. *Psychological Science in the Public Interest, 2*, 31–74.

Read, S. J., & Miller, L. C. (1995). Stories are fundamental to meaning and memory: For social creatures, could it be otherwise? In R.S. Wyer (Ed.), *Knowledge and memory: The real story* (pp. 139–152). Hillsdale, NJ: Lawrence Erlbaum Associates.

Reed, S. K. (1993). A schema-based theory of transfer. In D. K. Detterman & R. J. Sternberg (Eds.), *Transfer on trial: Intelligence, cognition, and instruction* (pp. 39–67). Norwood, NJ: Ablex.

Reeves, B., & Greenberg, B. (1977). Children's perceptions of television characters. *Human Communication Research, 3*, 113–117.

Reeves, B., & Nass, C. (1996). *The media equation: How people treat computers, television, and new media like real people and places*. Cambridge, UK: Cambridge University Press.

Reeves, B., Newhagen, J., Mailbach, E., Basil, M., & Kurtz, K. (1991). Negative and positive television messages: Effect of message type and message context on attention and memory. *American Behavioral Scientist, 34*, 679–694.

Reiser, R. A., Tessmer, M. A., & Phelps, P. C. (1984). Adult–child interaction in children's learning from *Sesame Street*. *Educational Communication and Technology Journal, 32*, 217–223.

Reiser, R. A., Williamson, N., & Suzuki, K. (1988). Using *Sesame Street* to facilitate children's recognition of letters and numbers. *Educational Communication and Technology Journal, 36,* 15–21.

Renninger, K. A. (1998). Interest, task difficulty, and gender. In L. Hoffman, A. Krapp, & K. A. Renninger (Eds.), *Interest and learning: Proceedings of the Seeon conference on interest and gender* (pp. 228–238). Kiel, Germany: IPN.

Research Communications Ltd. (1987). *Research findings for audience evaluation of "How About" science reports.* Dedham, MA: Author.

Research Communications Ltd. (1992). *The impact of using the FUTURES series on junior high school students.* Dedham, MA: Author.

Revelle, G. L., & Medoff, L. (2002). Interface design and research process for studying the usability of interactive home-entertainment systems by young children. *Early Education and Development, 13,* 423–434.

Revelle, G. L., Strommen, E. F., & Medoff, L. (2001). Interactive technologies research at the Children's Television Workshop. In S. M. Fisch & R. T. Truglio (Eds.), *"G" is for growing: Thirty years of research on* Sesame Street (pp. 215–230). Mahwah, NJ: Lawrence Erlbaum Associates.

Reynolds, R. E., & Anderson, R. C. (1982). Influence of questions on the allocation of attention during reading. *Journal of Educational Psychology, 74,* 623–632.

Rice, M. L. (1984). The words of children's television. *Journal of Broadcasting, 28,* 445–461.

Rice, M. L., & Haight, P. L. (1986). "Motherese" of Mr. Rogers: A description of the dialogue of educational television programs. *Journal of Speech and Hearing Disorders, 51,* 282–287.

Rice, M. L., Huston, A. C., Truglio, R., & Wright, J. C. (1990). Words from *Sesame Street*: Learning vocabulary while viewing. *Developmental Psychology, 26,* 421–428.

Rice, M. L., & Sell, M. A. (1990). *Executive summary: Exploration of the uses and effectiveness of* Sesame Street *home videocassettes.* Lawrence, KS: Center for Research on the Influences of Television on Children.

Rice, M. L., & Woodsmall, L. (1988). Lessons from television: Children's word learning when viewing. *Child Development, 59,* 420–429.

Richards, J. I., Wartella, E. A., Morton, C., & Thompson, L. (1998). The growing commercialization of schools: Issues and practices. *Annals of the American Academy of Political and Social Science, 557,* 148–163.

RMC Research Corporation. (1993). *Pilot summative report:* Sesame Street *Preschool Educational Project Initiative.* Portland, OR: Author.

Roberts, D. F., Foehr, U. G., Rideout, V. J., & Brodie, M. (1999). *Kids & media @ the new millennium.* Menlo Park, CA: The Henry J. Kaiser Family Foundation.

Roberts, D., Hearold, C., Hornby, M., King, S., Sterne, D., Whitely, L., & Silverman, T. (1974). *Earth's a Big Blue Marble: A report of the impact of a children's television series on children's opinions.* Stanford, CA: Institute for Communication Research, Stanford University.

Roche, J. W. (1993). Blackstone's mathmagic. *The Mathematics Teacher, 86,* 733–734.

Rockman Et Al. (1996). *Evaluation of* Bill Nye the Science Guy: *Television series and outreach.* San Francisco, CA: Author.

Rockman Et Al. (2002). *Evaluation of* Cyberchase *phase one pilot study: Vol. 1. Executive summary.* San Francisco, CA: Author.

Rogoff, B. (1990). *Apprenticeship in thinking: Cognitive development in social context.* New York: Oxford University Press.

Rolandelli, D. R. (1989). Children and television: The visual superiority hypothesis reconsidered. *Journal of Broadcasting and Electronic Media, 33*(1), 69–81.

Rolandelli, D. R., Wright, J. C., Huston, A. C., & Eakins, D. (1991). Children's auditory and visual processing of narrated and non-narrated television programming. *Journal of Experimental Child Psychology, 51,* 90–122.

Rosen, C., & Sroka, I. (1992). *Research summary: Formative research in support of the development and production of* What Kids Want to Know About Sex and Growing Up. New York: KRC Research & Children's Television Workshop.

Rumelhart, D. E. (1975). Notes on a schema for stories. In D. G. Bobrow & A. M. Collins (Eds.), *Representation and understanding: Studies in cognitive science* (pp. 211–236). New York: Academic Press.

Rushton, J. P. (1982). Television and prosocial behavior. In National Institute of Mental Health (Ed.), *Television and behavior: Ten years of scientific progress and implications for the eighties: Vol. 2. Technical reviews* (pp. 248–321). Washington, DC: U.S. Department of Health and Human Services.

Rust, L. W. (2001). *Summative evaluation of* Dragon Tales: *Final report.* Briarcliff Manor, NY: Langbourne Rust Research, Inc.

Rutherford, F. J., & Algren, A. (1990). *Science for all Americans.* New York: Oxford University Press.

Sahin, N. (1990, September). *Preliminary report on the summative evaluation of the Turkish co-production of* Sesame Street. Paper presented at the International Conference on Adaptations of *Sesame Street,* Amsterdam, The Netherlands.

St. Peters, M., Fitch, M., Huston, A. C., Wright, J. C., & Eakins, D. (1991). Television and families: What do young children watch with their parents? *Child Development, 62,* 1409–1423.

Salomon, G. (1977). Effects of encouraging Israeli mothers to co-observe *Sesame Street* with their five-year-olds. *Child Development, 48,* 1146–1151.

Salomon, G. (1983). Television watching and mental effort: A social psychological view. In J. Bryant & D. R. Anderson (Eds.), *Children's understanding of television: Research on attention and comprehension* (pp. 181–198). New York: Academic Press.

Salomon, G. (1984). Television is "easy" and print is "tough": The differential investment of mental effort in learning as a function of perceptions and attributions. *Journal of Educational Psychology, 76,* 647–658.

Salomon, G. (1991). Transcending the qualitative–quantitative debate: The analytic and systemic approaches to educational research. *Educational Researcher, 20*(6), 10–18.

Salomon, G., & Leigh, T. (1984). Predispositions about learning from television and print. *Journal of Communication, 34,* 119–135.

Salomon, G., & Perkins, D. N. (1989). Rocky roads to transfer: Rethinking mechanisms of a neglected phenomenon. *Educational Psychologist, 24*(2), 113–142.

Salomon, G., Perkins, D. N., & Globerson, T. (1991). Partners in cognition: Extending human intelligence with intelligent technologies. *Educational Researcher, 20*(3), 2–9.

Sanders, J. R., & Sonnad, S. R. (1980). *Research on the introduction, use, and impact of* Thinkabout: *Executive summary.* Bloomington, IN: Agency for Instructional Television.

Schank, R. C., & Abelson, R. P. (1995). Knowledge and memory: The real story. In R. S. Wyer (Ed.), *Knowledge and memory: The real story* (pp. 1–85). Hillsdale, NJ: Lawrence Erlbaum Associates.

Schauble, L., & Peel. B. (1986). *The "Mathnet" format on* Square One: *Children's informal problem solving, understanding of mathematical concepts, and ideas and attitudes about mathematics.* New York: Children's Television Workshop.

Schiefele, U. (1998). Individual interest and learning—what we know and what we don't know. In L. Hoffman, A. Krapp, & K. A. Renninger (Eds.), *Interest and learning: Proceedings of the Seeon conference on interest and gender* (pp. 91–104). Kiel, Germany: IPN.

Schmitt, K. (1999). *The three-hour rule: Is it living up to expectations?* (Rep. No. 30). Philadelphia, PA: Annenberg Public Policy Center, University of Pennsylvania.

Schmitt, K. (2001). Infants, toddlers, and television: The ecology of the home. *Zero to Three, 22*(2), 17–23.

Schmitt, K., & Anderson, D. R. (2002). Television and reality: Toddlers' use of information from video to guide behavior. *Media Psychology, 4,* 51–76.

Schoenfeld, A. H. (1988). Problem solving in context(s). In R. I. Charles & E. A. Silver (Eds.), *Research agenda for mathematics education: Vol. 3. The teaching and assessing of mathematical problem solving* (pp. 82–92). Hillsdale, NJ: Lawrence Erlbaum Associates and Reston, VA: National Council of Teachers of Mathematics.

Schramm, W. (1977). *Big media, little media.* Beverly Hills, CA: Sage.

Schramm, W., Lyle, J., & Parker, E. B. (1961). *Television in the lives of our children.* Stanford, CA: Stanford University Press.

Sell, M. A., Ray, G. E., & Lovelace, L. (1995). Preschool children's comprehension of a *Sesame Street* video tape: The effects of repeated viewing and previewing instructions. *Educational Technology Research and Development, 43*(3), 49–60.

Sesame Street Research. (1991). *Visiting Ieshia.* Unpublished research report. New York: Children's Television Workshop.

Sesame Street Research. (1993). *Play date: Two boys play and eat.* Unpublished research report. New York: Children's Television Workshop.

Shantz, C. U. (1975). The development of social cognition. In E. M. Hetherington (Ed.), *Review of child development research* (Vol. 5, pp. 257–323). Chicago, IL: University of Chicago Press.

Shiffrin, R. M., & Schneider, W. (1977). Controlled and automatic human information processing: II. Perceptual learning, automatic attending, and a general theory. *Psychological Review, 84,* 127–190.

Siegler, R. S. (1989). Mechanisms of cognitive development. *American Review of Psychology, 40,* 353–379.

Signorelli, N. (1993). Television, the portrayal of women, and children's attitudes. In G. L. Berry & J. K. Asamen (Eds.), *Children and television: Images in a changing sociocultural world* (pp. 229–242). Newbury Park, CA: Sage.

Silverman, L. T., & Sprafkin, J. N. (1980). The effects of *Sesame Street*'s prosocial spots on cooperative play between young children. *Journal of Broadcasting, 24,* 135–147.

Simpson, R. D., & Oliver, J. S. (1990). A summary of major influences on attitude toward and achievement in science among adolescent students. *Science Education, 174,* 1–18.

Singer, D. G. (1982). The research connection. *Television and Children, 5,* 25–35.

Singer, D. G., & Singer, J. L. (1994a). Barney and Friends *as education and entertainment: Phase 1, study 2—Content analysis of series "200."* New Haven, CT: Yale University Family Television Research and Consultation Center.

Singer, D. G., & Singer, J. L. (1994b). Evaluating the classroom viewing of a television series: "Degrassi Junior High." In D. Zillmann, J. Bryant, & A. C. Huston (Eds.), *Media, children and the family: Social scientific, psychodynamic, and clinical perspectives* (pp. 97–115). Hillsdale, NJ: Lawrence Erlbaum Associates.

Singer, D. G., Singer, J. L., Miller, R. H., & Sells, D. J. (1994). Barney and Friends *as education and entertainment: Phase 2: Kindergarten sample—Can children learn through kindergarten exposure to* Barney and Friends? New Haven, CT: Yale University Family Television Research and Consultation Center.

Singer, J. L., & Singer, D. G. (1976). Family television viewing habits and the spontaneous play of preschool children. *American Journal of Orthopsychiatry, 46,* 496–502.

Singer, J. L., & Singer, D. G. (1981). *Television, imagination, and aggression: A study of preschoolers.* Hillsdale, NJ: Lawrence Erlbaum Associates.

Singer, J. L., & Singer, D. G. (1993). *Series "100":* Barney & Friends *as education and entertainment.* New Haven, CT: Yale University Family Television Research and Consultation Center.

Singer, J. L., & Singer, D. G. (1994). Barney and Friends *as education and entertainment: Phase 2—Can children learn through preschool exposure to* Barney and Friends? New Haven, CT: Yale University Family Television Research and Consultation Center.

Singer, J. L., & Singer, D. G. (1995). Barney and Friends *as education and entertainment: Phase 3—A national study: Can children learn through preschool exposure to* Barney and Friends? New Haven, CT: Yale University Family Television Research and Consultation Center.

Singer, J. L., & Singer, D. G. (1998). *Barney & Friends* as entertainment and education: Evaluating the quality and effectiveness of a television series for preschool children. In J. K. Asamen & G. L. Berry (Eds.), *Research paradigms, television, and social behavior* (pp. 305–367). Thousand Oaks, CA: Sage.

Singer, J. L., & Singer, D. G. (2000). Barney and Friends *as education and entertainment: Series "600."* New Haven, CT: Yale University Family Television Research and Consultation Center.

Singhal, A., & Rogers, E. M. (1999). *Entertainment-education: A communication strategy for social change.* Mahwah, NJ: Lawrence Erlbaum Associates.

Singley, M. K., & Anderson, J. R. (1989). *The transfer of cognitive skill.* Cambridge, MA: Harvard University Press.

Smith, R., Anderson, D. R., & Fischer, C. R. (1985). Young children's comprehension of montage. *Child Development, 56,* 962–971.

Smith, S. L., & Wilson, B. J. (2002). Children's comprehension of and fear reactions to television news. *Media Psychology, 4,* 1–26.

Spilich, G. J., Vesonder, G. T., Chiesi, H. L., & Voss, J. F. (1979). Text processing of domain-related information for individuals with high and low domain knowledge. *Journal of Verbal Learning and Verbal Behavior, 18,* 275–290.

Sprafkin, J. M., Liebert, R. M., & Poulos, R. W. (1975). Effects of a prosocial example on children's helping. *Journal of Experimental Child Psychology, 20,* 119–126.

Square One TV Research. (1988). *Season II appeal/Season III formative study.* Unpublished research report. New York: Children's Television Workshop.

Stein, S. B. (1979). *Learn at home the* Sesame Street *way.* New York: Simon & Schuster.

Sternberg, R. J., & Frensch, P.A. (1993). Mechanisms of transfer. In D. K. Detterman & R. J. Sternberg (Eds.), *Transfer on trial: Intelligence, cognition, and instruction* (pp. 25–38). Norwood, NJ: Ablex.

Steyer, J. P. (2002). *The other parent: The inside story of the media's effect on our children.* New York: Atria Books.

Stipp, H. (1995, May). *Children's exposure to TV news and reality-based programming.* Paper presented at the annual meeting of the International Communication Association, Albuquerque, NM.

Stipp, H. (1998, July). Should TV marry PC? *American Demographics, 20,* 16–21.

Tannenbaum, P. H. (1980). Entertainment as vicarious emotional experience. In P. H. Tannenbaum (Ed.), *The entertainment functions of television* (pp. 107–131). Hillsdale, NJ: Lawrence Erlbaum Associates.

Tarpley, T. (2001). Children, the Internet, and other new technologies. In D. G. Singer & J. L. Singer (Eds.), *Handbook of children and the media* (pp. 547–556). Thousand Oaks, CA: Sage.

Thomas, R. M. (1992). *Comparing theories of child development.* Belmont, CA: Wadsworth Publishing Company.

Thorndike, E. L. (1913). *Educational psychology* (Vol. 2). New York: Columbia University Press.

Thorndike, E. L., & Woodworth, R. S. (1901). The influence of improvement in one mental function upon the efficiency of other functions. *Psychological Review, 8,* 247–261.

Thorndyke, P. W. (1977). Cognitive structures in comprehension and memory of narrative discourse. *Cognitive Psychology, 9,* 77–110.

Thorson, E., Reeves, B., & Schleuder, J. (1985). Message complexity and attention to television. *Communication Research, 12,* 427–454.

Thorson, E., & Friestad, M. (1989). The effects of emotion on episodic memory for television commercials. In P. Cafferata & A. Tybout (Eds.), *Cognitive and affective responses to advertising* (pp. 305–325). Lexington, MA: D.C. Heath.

Trabasso, T., Secco, T., & van den Broek, P. (1984). Causal cohesion and story coherence. In H. Mandl, N. L. Stein, & T. Trabasso (Eds.), *Learning and comprehension of text* (pp. 83–111). Hillsdale, NJ: Lawrence Erlbaum Associates.

Tressel, G. (1988). A rationale. In M. Druger (Ed.), *Science for the fun of it: A guide to informal science education* (pp. 20–23). Washington, DC: National Science Teachers Association.

Troseth, G., & DeLoache, J. (1998). The medium can obscure the message: Understanding the relation between video and reality. *Child Development, 69,* 950–965.

Trotta, L. (1998). *Building blocks: A guide for creating children's educational television.* Studio City, CA: Mediascope Press.

Truglio, R. T., Lovelace, V. O., Seguí, I., & Scheiner, S. (2001). The varied role of formative research: Case studies from 30 years. In S. M. Fisch & R. T. Truglio (Eds.), *"G" is for "growing": Thirty years of research on children and* Sesame Street (pp. 61–79). Mahwah, NJ: Lawrence Erlbaum Associates.

Ulitsa Sezam Department of Research and Content. (1996). Research on the studio characters and sets based on the segments "Zeliboba's big family," "Things can be reused," and "Sharing apples" (English trans. of Russian). Unpublished research report.

Ulitsa Sezam Department of Research and Content. (1998, November). *Preliminary report of summative findings.* Report presented to the Children's Television Workshop.

UNICEF. (1996). *Executive summary: Summary assessment of* Plaza Sésamo *IV—Mexico* (English trans. of Spanish). Unpublished research report. Mexico City, Mexico: Author.

U.S. Department of Education, National Center for Educational Statistics. (1982). *Digest of education statistics: 1982.* Washington, DC: U.S. Government Printing Office.

U.S. Department of Education. (1997). *A call to action for American education in the 21st century.* Washington, DC: U.S. Government Printing Office.

Vorderer, P. (2000). Interactive entertainment and beyond. In D. Zillmann, & P. Vorderer (Eds.), *Media entertainment: The psychology of its appeal* (pp. 21–36). Mahwah, NJ: Lawrence Erlbaum Associates.

Vorderer, P., Knobloch, S., & Schramm, H. (2001). Does entertainment suffer from interactivity?: The impact of watching an interactive TV movie on viewers' experience of entertainment. *Media Psychology, 3,* 343–363.

Vygotsky, L. S. (1978). *Mind in society: The development of higher psychological processes.* Cambridge, MA: Harvard University Press.

Wagner, S. (1985). *Comprehensive evaluation of the fourth season of* 3-2-1 Contact. New York: Children's Television Workshop.

Walker, J. R., & Bellamy, R. V. (2001). Remote control devices and family viewing. In J. Bryant & J. A. Bryant (Eds.), *Television and the American family* (2nd ed., pp. 75–89). Mahwah, NJ: Lawrence Erlbaum Associates.

Walma van der Molen, J., & van der Voort, T. (1997). Children's recall of television and print news: A media comparison study. *Journal of Educational Psychology, 89,* 82–91.

Walma van der Molen, J., & van der Voort, T. (1998). Children's recall of the news: TV news stories compared with three print versions. *Educational Technology Research and Development, 46,* 39–52.

Walma van der Molen, J., & van der Voort, T. (2000). The impact of television, print, and audio on children's recall of the news: A study of three alternative explanations for the dual-coding hypothesis. *Human Communications Research, 26,* 3–26.

Wartella, E. (1995). Media and problem behaviours in young people. In M. Rutter & D. Smith (Eds.), *Psychosocial disorders in young people: Time trends and their origins.* Chichester, England: Wiley.

Wartella, E., & Jennings, N. (2001). Hazards and possibilities of commercial TV in the schools. In D. G. Singer & J. L. Singer (Eds.), *Handbook of children and the media* (pp. 557–570). Thousand Oaks, CA: Sage.

Watkins, B. A., Calvert, S. L., Huston-Stein, A., & Wright, J. C. (1980). Children's recall of television material: Effects of presentation mode and adult labeling. *Developmental Psychology, 16,* 672–674.

Wenglinsky, H. (1999). *Does it compute?: The relationship between educational technology and student achievement in mathematics.* Princeton, NJ: Education Testing Service. Available: *www.ets.org/research/pic/dic/preack.html.*

Wickens, C. D. (1974). Temporal limits of human information processing: A developmental study. *Psychological Bulletin, 81,* 739–755.

Williams, F., & Natalicio, D. S. (1972). Evaluating *Carrascolendas*: A television series for Mexican-American children. *Journal of Broadcasting, 16,* 299–309.

Williams, M. E., Hall, E., Cunningham, H., Albright, M., Schiro, K., & Fisch, S. (1997). Ghostwriter *research history and bibliography.* New York: Children's Television Workshop.

Williams, P. A., Haertel, E. H., Walberg, H. J., & Haertel, G. D. (1982). The impact of leisure-time television on school learning: A research synthesis. *American Educational Research Journal, 19,* 19–50.

Williams, T. M. (Ed.). (1986). *The impact of television: A natural experiment in three communities.* Orlando, FL: Academic Press.

Wilson, B. J., Kunkel, D., Linz, D., Potter, J., Donnerstein, E., Smith, S. L., Blumenthal, E., & Gray, T. (1997). *National television violence study* (Vol. 1). Thousand Oaks, CA: Sage.

Wilson, B. J., Linz, D., Federman, J., Smith, S. L., Paul, B., Nathanson, A., Donnerstein, E., & Lingsweiler, R. (1999). *The choices and consequences evaluation: A study of Court TV's anti-violence curriculum.* Santa Barbara, CA: Center for Communication and Social Policy, University of California, Santa Barbara.

Wilson, B. J., & Smith, S. L. (1998). Children's responses to emotional portrayals on television. In P. A. Anderson & L. K. Guerrero (Eds.), *Handbook of communication and emotion: Research, theory, applications, and contexts* (pp. 533–569). San Diego, CA: Academic Press.

Wilson, C. E. (1974). The effect of medium on loss of information. *Journalism Quarterly, 51,* 111–115.

Winn, M. (1977). *The plug-in drug.* New York: Penguin.

Winsten, J. A. (1994). Promoting designated drivers: The Harvard Alcohol Project. *American Journal of Preventive Medicine, 10,* 3, 11–14.

Witt, E., & Johnston, B. (1988). *A study of the effects of* It Figures *with and without support materials* (Research Report No. 104). Bloomington, IN: Agency for Instructional Television.

Wood, D. J., & Middleton, D. (1975). A study of assisted problem solving. *British Journal of Psychology, 66,* 181–191.

Wood, J. M., & Duke, N. K. (1997). Inside "Reading Rainbow": A spectrum of strategies for promoting literacy. *Language Arts, 74,* 95–106.

Woodard, E. H. (2000). *Media in the home, 2000: The fifth annual survey of parents and children* (Rep. No. 7). Philadelphia, PA: Annenberg Public Policy Center, University of Pennsylvania.

Wright, J. C., Huston, A. C., Murphy, K. C., St. Peters, M., Piñon, M., Scantlin, R., & Kotler, J. (2001). The relations of early television viewing to school readiness and vocabulary of children from low-income families: The Early Window project. *Child Development, 72,* 1347–1366.

Wright, J. C., Huston, A. C., Scantlin, R., & Kotler, J. (2001). The Early Window project: *Sesame Street* prepares children for school. In S. M. Fisch & R. T. Truglio (Eds.), *"G" is for "growing": Thirty years of research on children and Sesame Street* (pp. 97–114). Mahwah, NJ: Lawrence Erlbaum Associates.

Wyer, R. S. (Ed.). (1995). *Knowledge and memory: The real story.* Hillsdale, NJ: Lawrence Erlbaum Associates.

Yotive, W. M. (1995, December). Square One Mathtalk: *Using technology to help teachers implement the NCTM standards.* Paper presented at the 27th annual conference of the National Staff Development Council, Chicago, IL.

Yotive, W. M., & Fisch, S. M. (1998). Educational television and interest in academic subjects: An overview of research at the Children's Television Workshop. In L. Hoffman, A. Krapp, & K. A. Renninger (Eds.), *Interest and learning: Proceedings of the Seeon conference on interest and gender* (pp. 197–204). Kiel, Germany: IPN.

Yotive, W., & Fisch, S. M. (2001). The role of *Sesame Street*-based materials in child care settings. In S. M. Fisch & R. T. Truglio (Eds.), *"G" is for growing: Thirty years of research on children and* Sesame Street (pp. 181–196). Mahwah, NJ: Lawrence Erlbaum Associates.

Zero to Three/National Center for Clinical Infant Programs. (1992). *Heart Start: The emotional foundations of school readiness.* Arlington, VA: Author.

Zielinska, I. E., & Chambers, B. (1995). Using group viewing of television to teach preschool children social skills. *Journal of Educational Television, 21,* 85–99.

Zill, N. (2001). Does *Sesame Street* enhance school readiness?: Evidence from a national survey of children. In S. M. Fisch & R. T. Truglio (Eds.), *"G" is for "growing": Thirty years of research on children and* Sesame Street (pp. 115–130). Mahwah, NJ: Lawrence Erlbaum Associates.

Zillmann, D., Masland, J. L., Weaver, J. B., Lacey, L. A., Jacobs, N. E., Dow, J. H., Klein, C. A., & Banker, S. R. (1984). Effects of humorous distortions on children's learning from educational television. *Journal of Educational Psychology, 76,* 802–812.

Zillmann, S., Williams, B. R., Bryant, J., Boynton, K. R., & Wolf, M. A. (1980). Acquisition of information from educational television programs as a function of differently paced humorous inserts. *Journal of Educational Psychology, 76,* 170–180.

Author Index

A

Abelson, R. P., 179, 185
Acord, K., 128
Aidman, A. J., 108
Akersman, A., 125
Albin, K., 148
Albright, M., 66
Alexander, K. L., 29
Algren, A., 84
Allport, A., 145
Anderman, E., 100
Anderson, D. R., 2, 3, 6, 20, 23, 29, 31, 32, 41, 43, 49-50, 51, 52, 53, 54, 55, 64, 75, 79, 104, 114, 141, 146, 148, 158, 165, 175, 177, 189, 192, 198
Anderson, J. R., 168, 169, 171
Anderson, R. C., 156
Appleton, H., 17, 22
Armstrong, G. B., 143
Asington, J. W., 189
Atkin, C. K., 96, 97
Austin, S., 130, 131

B

Bachen, C. M., 99
Bachman, K. M., 86, 88, 92, 177
Baddeley, A., 159
Bahrt, A., 8
Baker, L., 174
Baker, L. S., 37
Ball, S., 21, 23, 33, 59, 64, 68, 110, 114

Bandura, A., 115, 116, 180, 181, 184, 185, 187, 189
Banker, S. R., 183
Barnett, W. S., 35, 126
Barr, R., 49, 54
Barron, B., 132
Barton, P. E., 71
Basil, M., 183
Bassok, M., 168, 171, 172
Baumeister, R. F., 179
Bederson, B., 19
Beentjes, J. W. J., 143
Bellamy, R. V., 204
Benfield, C. M., 68
Bennett, D. T., 75, 76, 77, 79, 80, 81, 87, 165, 171, 175, 186
Bennett, W. J., 56, 95
Bereiter, C., 16, 168
Berkowitz, L., 116, 180, 186
Bernstein, L. J., 19, 112
Binkley, M. R., 56
Birnbaum, D. W., 103
Block, C., 130, 131
Bloom, B. S., 16
Blumenthal, E., 3, 106
Bobrow, D. G., 145, 154
Bogatz, G. A., 21, 23, 33, 59, 64, 68, 110, 114
Boltman, A., 19, 20
Bottoms, C. L., 72
Bouthilet, L., 146
Bovill, M., 2
Bower, G. H., 146, 179
Boyer, E., 36
Boynton, K. R., 183
Brand, J. E., 99, 110

Subject Index

Y

Yogi Bear, 7

Z

"Zombie viewers," 2–3, 20